LIFE's
America

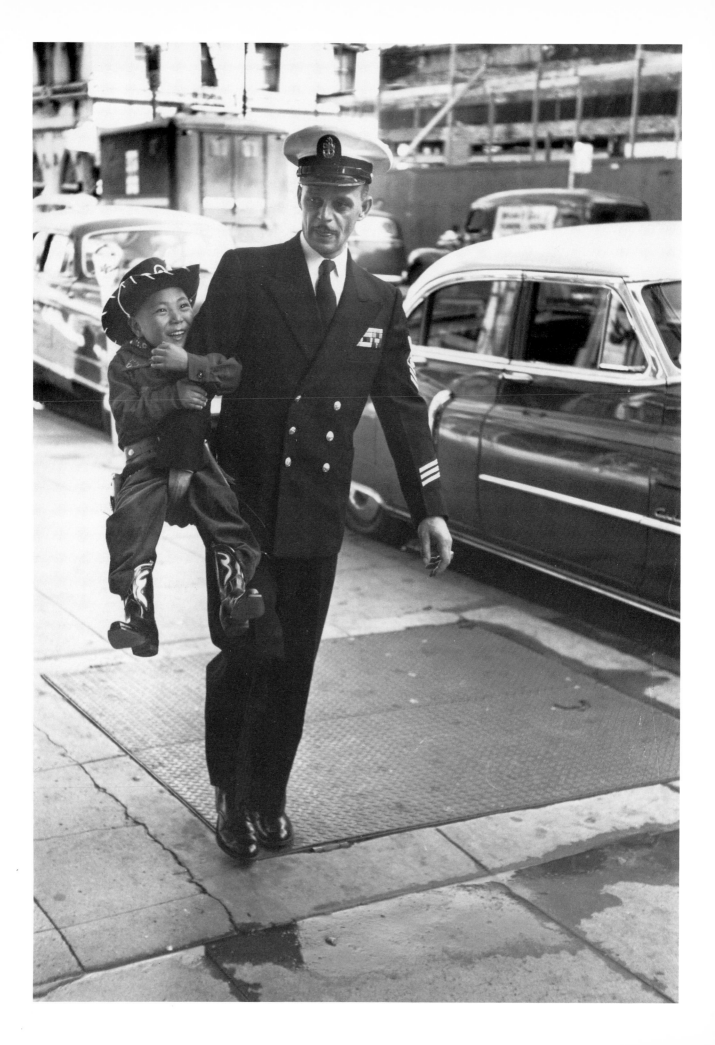

LIFE's America

America

FAMILY AND NATION IN
POSTWAR PHOTOJOURNALISM

Wendy Kozol

Temple University Press • *Philadelphia*

Temple University Press, Philadelphia 19122
Copyright © 1994 by Temple University. All rights reserved
Published 1994
Printed in the United States of America

The paper used in this publication is acid free for greater permanence.

Library of Congress Cataloging-in-Publication Data

Kozol, Wendy, 1958–
    Life's America : family and nation in postwar photojournalism / Wendy Kozol.
        p.   cm.
    Includes bibliographical references and index.
    ISBN 1-56639-152-0—ISBN 1-56639-221-7 (pbk.)
    1. Photojournalism—United States—History—20th century. 2. *Life* (New York, N.Y.) 3. United States—Social life and customs—1945–1970. 4. Family—United States—History—20th century. 5. Popular culture—United States—History—20th century.
    I. Title.
    TR820.K68   1994
    070.4′9′097309045—dc20   93-26030

PHOTO CREDITS

CONTENTS

PREFACE

The theme of "family values" has repeatedly surfaced in the media in the late 1980s and early 1990s in response to a host of complex issues, including economic upheavals, contestations over gender, racial, ethnic, and sexual identities, and the growing AIDS epidemic. As popular political discourses attempt to narrate these complex situations, some argue that "family values" will preserve and strengthen the nation against social disruptions. The intimate association between personal identities and a national ideal reveals a reliance in contemporary culture on domesticity to define political agendas about pressing social problems.

For many people, the term "family values" connotes a specific form of family—the white, nuclear family consisting of a male breadwinner and a mother who stays at home with the children. Since the end of World War II, American audiences have seen news photographs, television shows, and numerous other portraits of this family form. In the last decades of the twentieth century, however, a range of alternatives to the nuclear family ideal, including single mothers, extended families and gay parents, struggle to claim the politically charged space of domesticity as their own. Where these discussions will lead, and how such negotiations will trans-

late into legislation for domestic partners or family-leave plans, is hard to predict. At the least, these debates signal changes in private worlds, public actions, and the social transformations that negotiate the boundaries between the two.

Despite attempts to define more inclusive concepts of "family," many of which derive from two decades of feminist challenges to discrimination, the visual portrait of the white, middle-class family remains emblematic of American domestic life. Less than 15 percent of Americans conform to this pattern, yet many people still find it difficult to see that this picture is just traditional not universal. Images exert power precisely because their expressiveness shapes visual perceptions about the world. With this in mind, it is instructive to reconsider the visual artifacts that have created and promoted the nuclear family as quintessentially American at a time when people increasingly depend on the mass media for information.

This book explores the origins of the visual portrait of domesticity that has dominated American culture since World War II. Postwar mass media fashioned a cultural ideal of family through stories and pictures about a world of middle-class domesticity. The power of this domestic culture was twofold. First, pictures and stories claimed merely to reflect a shared social reality, a claim that ignored the active role of cultural representation in constructing and shaping knowledge. Second, domesticity was a powerful ideal at a time of social change and political upheaval. Domestic portraits explained often ambiguous and conflicting issues in recognizable, even comforting, terms. Nowhere did the power of domesticity appear more forcefully than in the news, which carries great cultural currency as an objective and truthful genre.

In this book, I examine news photographs published in *Life* magazine, one of the most popular American magazines in the twentieth century and the most important picture magazine of its day. At the height of its popularity in the 1940s and 1950s, *Life* published numerous portraits of families, appealing to an audience largely composed of middle-class readers. Photojournalism's ability to capture the image (if not the experience) of news events took on great immediacy, even urgency, in the 1940s and 1950s when broad social transformations altered the lives of *Life*'s middle-class readers. After the Depression and World War II, Americans had high expectations that the postwar world would bring a return to "normalcy." Contrary to many retrospective accounts and much popular memory, however, the postwar period was a time of social and political instability. Increased mobility uprooted many populations from traditional communities, and shifting work patterns and challenges

to traditional social relations destabilized the expected comforts promised with the end of the war. Americans faced disturbing issues like the Cold War, the threat of atomic annihilation, massive labor strikes in the industrial sector, and the increasingly visible protests against racism. Red baiting was perhaps the most visible sign of social fracture, but gay bashing and racial confrontations likewise cracked the veneer of social consensus. Beyond reporting on the postwar baby boom or the middle-class flight to suburbia, *Life* turned to "representative" families to visualize American responses to the compelling crises and social developments of the day.

Photojournalism was uniquely situated in the postwar period to represent the intersection of national politics and culture. Like many other media, *Life* routinely referred to the United States as "America." Although today we recognize that this usage ignores other countries in the region, it is useful to explore the historical meanings and implications of this term. Despite the magazine's inclusive claim, depictions of "America" and "Americans" were limited. The credibility of *Life*'s photographs carried great weight in conveying a specific ideal as a transparent or unmediated visual truth about society. Factual or realistic news portraits of "actual" families presented a particular image, based on dominant social norms of gender, race, class, and sexuality, as representative of national identity. This book examines the consequences of translating social and political issues into narratives about representative families. In the process of narrating the news, pictures of families promoted ideals about home and private life, public issues, social identities, and ultimately, the nation itself.

This study, then, is not a history or biography of *Life* magazine, nor do I analyze the work of individual photographers, writers, or editors or catalogue the topics featured in the magazine. Instead, I am interested in the pictures the magazine published—its product and its statement. Specifically, I examine the social language of news photo-essays about families through close readings that examine composition, lighting, framing, and subject matter of the photographs in conjunction with written texts. Analysis of the layout of photo-essays reveals the narrative drive of *Life*'s format for reporting the news and the ideological power of that narrative. Audiences did not, nor were they meant to, read isolated photo-essays; they read them along with other photo-essays and advertisements and related them to other cultural discourses. Locating these visual analyses within a discussion of the historical processes of the period, I hope to show how visual images represent the power relations that structure the social worlds depicted in *Life*. Recent analyses of popular culture have focused on the ways that American media reproduce social hierarchies of race, class, gender, and ethnicity. By studying *Life*'s representations of American families I examine the visual processes that privilege certain people and exclude others. By regarding these photographs as a collective text from the perspective of what was available for readers' consumption and scrutiny, I show how photojournalism addressed its readers' desires and expectations, as well as their insecurities and anxieties, about domesticity and the nation in the postwar period.

Much of our current knowledge of social life derives from visual imagery. *Life* was instrumental in codifying the visual aspects of the news and was influential in establishing the prevalence of the image in advertising, education, and politics. In its role as a key producer of postwar culture, it is significant that *Life* envisioned the nation in terms of the white, middle-class, heterosexual, nuclear family. By asking how family portraits function in culture to mobilize and privilege certain ideologies, I hope to illuminate the connections between the family and the state that have dominated American culture since World War II.

ACKNOWLEDGMENTS

This research was partially funded by a Stout Fellowship from the University of Minnesota. I thank the American Studies Department at the University of Maryland, Baltimore County, for a generous leave of absence that made possible the timely completion of this project. I also gratefully acknowledge the dean of Oberlin College for financial support for the reproduction costs. The photographs are reproduced with the permission of Time Inc. Paul Arbor and Maryann Kornely at *Life* Picture Sales were especially helpful.

At various stages of this work, numerous scholars have engaged in provocative debates with me about popular culture. I would like to thank Betty Bergland, John Bloom, Jane Healey, David Noble, Riv-Ellen Prell, Nancy Roberts, April Schultz, Andrea Volpe, and Julie Weiss for their generous support and insightful critiques of parts or all of this work. I would also like to thank Erica Doss, James Guimond, Karen Huck, and Glenn Willumson for sharing their work on *Life* magazine. Elaine Tyler May and Susan McClary have given me much encouragement, and their scholarship has deepened my understanding of cultural politics. Amy Farrell and Susannah Michalson provided critical readings and long telephone conversations that strengthened this study. Lynn Powell generously rescued me with a timely intervention that helped me to clarify my argument.

Christin Mamiya graciously read too many drafts with efficiency and skill that provided me with incisive criticisms and stimulating discussions. The Flaming Bitches made this a better study through careful readings of each draft and by challenging me to consider more deeply the complexities of visual representation. One of my greatest intellectual pleasures is being a member of this writing group, which includes Ann Cooper Albright, Sibelan Forrester, Wendy Hesford, Yopie Prins, and more recently Camille Guerin-Gonzalez. Pat McDermott keeps me focused with her perceptive insights, and I have learned much from her. I gratefully acknowledge the wonderful support of Janet Francendese and Mary Capouya of Temple University Press.

Friends such as Mark Bockrath, Barbara Buckley, Abby Frucht, Kerry Langan, John Machnauer, Mike Michalson, Nancy Winship, and Michael Zimmerman make this a more engaging and interesting world. I deeply appreciate Liz Burgess's enduring friendship and support for my work. The Wojtals and Frank and Mildred Kozol have been very encouraging of my work and helped in innumerable ways. I thank Paula and Lee Kozol for providing me with an intellectual environment when I was growing up that embraced social justice, feminism, and the role of culture in making sense of our worlds. My sisters, Penny and Melanie Kozol, sustain me, as always, with their friendship.

Finally, I wish to thank two people whose enthusiasm for this study encouraged me to explore new intellectual challenges. George Lipsitz's scholarship is a model of critical thinking and insightful political analysis. I am most grateful to him for teaching me that the diverse and contested terrain of culture provides us with the means, both big and small, to resist all sorts of oppression. Steven Wojtal's enthusiasm for this project generated wonderful discussions that shaped the central argument, and his editing skills made this a more readable book. His friendship enriches my life while his sense of humor and great meals provide me with daily pleasures. I dedicate this book to him.

LIFE's
America

CHAPTER 1

DOCUMENTING THE ORDINARY
Photographic Realism and <u>LIFE</u>'s Families

The people in the audience looked at the pictures, and the people in the pictures looked back at them. They recognized each other.

—EDWARD STEICHEN, from Meltzer, *Dorothea Lange*, 1978

The cover of *Life*'s January 7, 1957, issue features a color photograph of a smiling Vice President Richard Nixon embracing two young girls in white dresses (*illustration 1*). Against a darkened background, raking light focuses attention on the figures in the center of the composition. Meanwhile, a group of men standing behind them blocks off any view of the background, pushing the three figures closer to the picture plane and the viewer. The framing of the composition accentuates the informal poses of the main figures by abruptly cutting off the sides, as if this were a snapshot. The tightly cropped space, the informality of the composition, the close proximity to the viewer, and the smiling faces create a casual intimacy. In addition, the girls' costumes and props indicate a celebration: one girl wears a star on her forehead; the other holds a small wooden cradle with a doll in it.

At first glance, nothing about this picture seems out of the ordinary. The depiction of a vice president engaged in diplomatic activities with other officials crowding behind seems

commonplace. In retrospect, Nixon's joviality may seem odd to those who remember him from the late days of the Watergate scandal, but in the 1950s, audiences frequently saw pictures of Nixon cheerfully enacting vice-presidential duties on goodwill campaigns. The two girls are also not difficult to read. They wear costumes for a passion play, a Catholic ritual that makes "news" sense right after Christmas. Moreover, the girl holding a cradle in her role as the Madonna is reminiscent of other scenes of young girls playacting the promise of future motherhood.

The caption, however, introduces a discordant note: "Hungarian Refugees and Vice President." The accompanying news story explains that Nixon was photographed while visiting a relocation center for these refugees.[1] *Life*, a general magazine devoted to contemporary social and political issues, would be expected to report on the Hungarian uprising of 1956 and U.S. attempts to solve the refugee problem. What is curious is that *Life* would represent an international crisis and a pivotal moment in the Cold War through a picture of the vice president hugging two girls whose youth and affectionate intimacy remind us that he is a father of two daughters. How do we understand this photograph that moves between public and private spheres, between

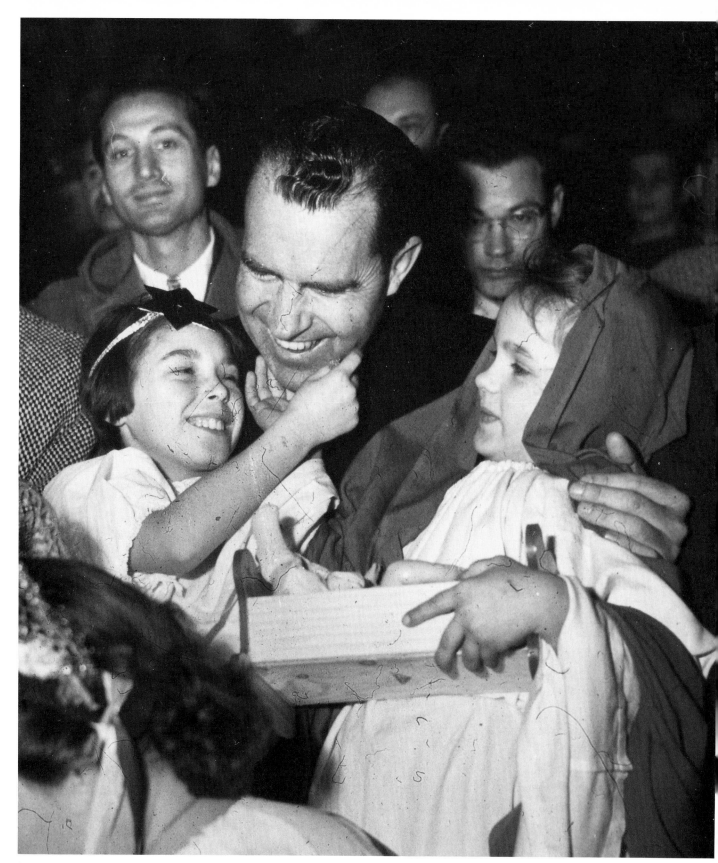

1

Nixon as the Cold Warrior and Nixon as a father himself? Does he embrace the two girls as refugees of a political conflict or because of their youthful innocence and the femininity hinted at by the allusion to maternity? The opening photograph of the news report shows a desperate scene of refugees crossing the Austrian border at night in a snowstorm. *Life* then turns rather abruptly to the United States and an immigrant Hungarian family. Here, perhaps, we see the point of Nixon's paternal embrace: the United States offers a haven for those escaping communism. In the photoessay, the writer explains the connection between the vice president and the news story by stating that Pal and Rose Csillag and their children have the opportunity "to be what Vice President Nixon called 'the kind of people who make good Americans.'"

Members of the generation or more who grew up with *Life* may remember fondly a picture magazine that displayed the world to them in pictures like these of Nixon and the Csillags. Sifting through memories of this magazine that so many people eagerly bought and read, we might ask what gave these photographs the power to frame and interpret reality for its readers? *Life* frequently claimed that photographs capture universal emotions or conditions. Yet, the didacticism of Nixon's statement about good Americans should prompt us to be skeptical of transparent readings of the images. Perhaps the photograph of refugees in the snow connotes the fear and desperation common to those who

flee oppression. But the picture on the facing page, which shows the Csillags' nine-year-old daughter in a schoolroom participating in the ritual pledge of allegiance with a group of American children, challenges simplistic assumptions (*illustration 2*). Photographer Carl Mydans frames the shot so that a flag in the foreground intrudes diagonally into the composition in front of Irene Csillag. A claim of universality tells us little about the potential readings of this photograph for Americans in 1957, but locating this image in the context of post–World War II political and social concerns offers richer understanding of how news photo-essays activated historical meanings through composition, layout, and narrative. In other words, how do the photographs define the Csillags as good Americans, and in turn envision "America"?

Another way to frame this question is to ask why *Life* uses seemingly trivial photographs of the Csillags, comfortably settled in their new home with a new television set and a washer and dryer, to report on the Hungarian refugees or U.S. diplomatic solutions? Although Americans often separate politics and culture into distinct categories, political discourses depend on cultural ideals and beliefs to frame rhetoric in recognizable terms. Two years after this photograph was published, Nixon engaged in a verbal battle with Nikita Khrushchev at the opening of the American National Exhibition in Moscow. In this exchange, now referred to as the "kitchen debates," the vice president

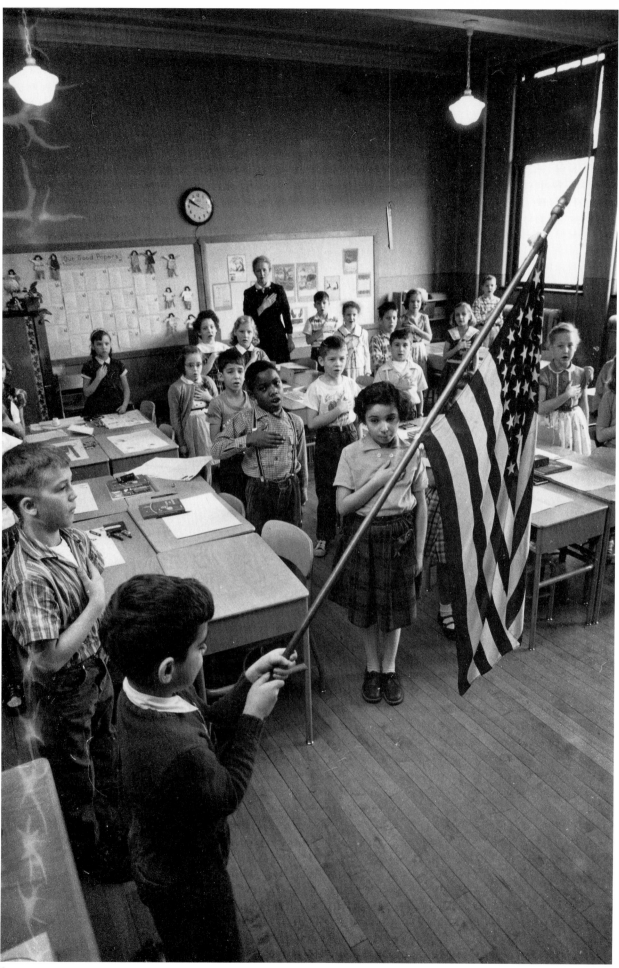

relied on cultural ideals about domesticity and the accessibility of consumer goods to draw Cold War distinctions. He pointed to suburban homes filled with appliances and cared for by full-time housewives supported by their breadwinner husbands as evidence of the superiority of American democracy over Soviet communism.[2]

Nixon's reliance on a language of domesticity points to the centrality of cultural ideals in political discourses. Indeed, cultural values are entwined with political structures and ideas as much as power relations are embedded in cultural spaces.[3] Family pictures in *Life*'s news stories reveal the historical entanglement of political and cultural modes in postwar culture. Realistic visual media like photographs are crucial vehicles for representing and legitimating the political and ideological because they seem familiar and are presumably easily read. Photographs of the family, presented as incidental information or as evidence of individual responses to crises, draw on the cultural values circulating in the society that both produces and consumes such images to transform actual events into symbolic meanings. A realistic aesthetic upholds these social norms as natural. Yet, contradictions, slippages, and instabilities in representation enable audiences to negotiate with pictures to make sense of their lives.

As the most popular general magazine of the 1940s and 1950s, with an estimated readership of twenty million,[4] *Life* played an important cultural role through its represen-

tation of the postwar world. In offering its readers the most extensive visual portrait of postwar American society, *Life* institutionalized many prominent characteristics of visual news practices. These characteristics depended on social and political ideals of the middle-class nuclear family that have, in turn, perpetuated structures of inequality in American society. Photography was an especially effective vehicle for news coverage because, through its realistic codes and mechanical apparatus, it presumed to depict the real world. *Life*'s news reporting frequently turned to "ordinary" families to represent the newsworthy concerns of postwar society. This book considers the photo-essays in *Life*'s news section, titled "The Week's Events," from 1945 to 1960.[5] I explore representative families that appear there in light of the questions provoked by Richard Nixon's hug and Irene Csillag's salute, about the relationship between public and private spheres and between nationalism and domestic ideals.

One could argue that *Life* merely reflected changes in postwar America. After more than a decade of economic crisis and war, Americans turned toward private life, and perhaps *Life*'s news reporting simply reflected the trend toward a renewed domesticity. The demographics of *Life*'s audience seem to reinforce this argument. Readers were typically white, middle class, and active consumers. To argue that the news simply reflects social reality, however, does not take into account the role of cultural discourses in constructing and mediating perspectives on that reality. Close examination of *Life* reveals that the news not only reproduces social values but privileges certain values at the expense of others. At the same time, we must also recognize that discourses are never monolithic or stable. Contradictions and ambiguities persist, as in news coverage about people who do not conform to dominant ideals. The Csillags' ethnic difference and working-class status, for example, contradict the ideal of middle-class America that the photo-essay promotes. Rather than reduce representations to singular meanings, it is far more productive to consider visual images as problematic sites open to different readings depending on historical conditions and the reader's orientation.

The powerful but contradictory messages in visual news reporting need to be understood for a number of reasons. The credibility of photojournalism derives from traditions of realism in photography and news representation. In claiming the power to represent the world, *Life* reinforced common beliefs about technology, representation, and social structures. News coverage of some of the most critical issues facing Americans in the postwar period relied on a domestic iconography that blurred the boundaries between public and private spheres and shaped national identity in the process. What is at stake in news photographs is the ability to visualize social identities, to privilege some, to ridicule others, and to deny the existence of yet others. By considering the cultural power of visual

news to shape audiences' perceptions about their worlds, this study also has implications beyond its historical parameters.

Photographic Realism and Cultural Politics

Life, which began publishing in 1936, was the first and most popular of the American picture magazines, and the only weekly publication of photojournalism. The picture magazine was influenced by newsreels, documentaries, and other media exploring the representation of contemporary events in the 1930s. *Life*'s almost immediate success spawned other picture magazines; among them was *Look*, which first appeared in 1937, a biweekly that never achieved the circulation figures of *Life*.[6] Television, the other major source of visual news, became commercially available after World War II, and in a remarkably short time most Americans had at least one television set in their homes. Broadcast news, however, had a slower start. Although the networks began broadcasting fifteen-minute news programs in 1947–1948, they did not develop their own news film staffs until the 1950s and did not make a substantial commitment to the pictorial gathering of the news until the early 1960s, at which time they rapidly became the most significant cultural sources of visual news.[7] During the immediate postwar period, then, *Life* was the primary vehicle for conveying the news visually to a mass audience.

By the early twentieth century new technologies enabled newspapers to reproduce photographs profitably, and photographs rapidly replaced engravings as the main medium of popular illustration. Confronted with an explosive array of new visual media that included amateur photography and the cinema, audiences grew increasingly familiar with visual forms of news. Rotogravure sections of newspapers and documentary photography by reformers such as Lewis Hine and the photographers of the 1930s Farm Security Administration established precedents for visual reporting. *Life*, however, was the first magazine with a national audience to devote itself to representing the political and social world primarily through photographs. World War II proved pivotal in the development of international pictorial news-gathering techniques. Each week, *Life* photojournalists sent pictures back from the war, thereby expanding the visual world for American audiences. During the war, the romantic image of the intrepid star photojournalist appeared in the figures of photographers like Margaret Bourke-White and Robert Capa, who often risked considerable danger to capture their assignments on film. From the outset, *Life*'s parent company, Time Inc., committed large sums of money to the magazine for high-quality reproductions, large photographic spreads, and, in the 1950s, expensive color images. The magazine also enhanced its cultural prestige by publishing the work of photographers like Capa, Bourke-White, W. Eugene Smith, and Alfred Eisenstaedt.

Life was a general magazine with regular sections on news, sports, Hollywood, medicine, and social life. It structured this content (what magazine publishing refers to as the editorial material) around two cornerstones: the "big news picture story" and the "big special feature." The two cornerstone photo-essays featured extensive photographic spreads that represented various topics through visual narratives. Although written texts were important, the visual dominated the magazine. Despite the ascendancy of visual images in twentieth-century news media like *Life*, journalism histories, and even some studies of television news, have focused primarily on print or speech as the carrier of meaning in the news.[8] Less attention has been paid to photojournalism except for studies of individual photographers, like Bourke-White and Smith, which contribute extensively to our knowledge of photographers' objectives and their perspectives on working for institutions like *Life*.[9] When viewed collectively, however, there is a remarkable consistency in *Life*'s pictures by a wide variety of photographers who, for the most part, shared assumptions about the ability of photography to present a truthful portrait of the real world.[10]

I examine both the work of famous photographers and the routine and mundane pictures in the news section. These photographs carried the cultural weight not only of familiarity but also of legitimacy as factual evidence. Each issue began with The Week's Events section, which covered a variety of news topics from election campaigns to economic forecasts and labor strikes. This section opened with one of the two cornerstone features, "the big news picture story." One editor described this photo-essay, which typically devoted five to seven pages to a current news item, as "the biggest news that is best recorded by the camera."[11] The imperative that the story be photogenic determined both topics and forms of coverage; in so doing, *Life* reinforced trends that now make visual images essential to most news practices.[12] *Life* also featured here the Picture of the Week, which ranged from serious and often disturbing images of world events to silly antics and trick photographs; similarly the rest of the articles in this section ranged from novelty pictures to photographs of global significance. *Life*'s importance as a conduit for the news, its cultural prestige, and its wide circulation established this section as a model for representing the news in other visual media.

In the 1936 prospectus for his new magazine, publisher Henry Luce, chair and founder of Time Inc., articulated assumptions about the camera that were essential to *Life*'s project:

> To see life; to see the world; to eyewitness great events; to watch the faces of the poor and the gestures of the proud; to see strange things . . . the women that men love and many children; to see and to take pleasure in seeing; to see and be amazed; to see and be instructed; thus to see, and to be shown, is now the will and new expectancy of half mankind.[13]

This statement reveals a belief, and also a conceit, that the camera, and therefore *Life*, has the power to reveal the world. Luce speaks of the expectancy of half of mankind to see, but, we must ask, which half is shown and which half does the looking? For instance, the reference to gender roles implies that women exist solely as the object of men's gaze. This is an especially interesting comment in light of surveys demonstrating that men and women read *Life* in almost equal numbers. Similarly, in his statement about the poor, Luce clearly identifies his audience as well as articulates the appeal of looking at the poor (who are distinct here from the proud), and the exotic. If we interrogate this notion of seeing, then we can examine how cultural assumptions about the camera affect *Life*'s photographic representations. "Seeing" becomes not a mirror but a way of framing differences and forming boundaries to define normative society.

The assumptions embedded in Luce's prospectus raise questions about how *Life* "eyewitnessed" great events and the ideological implications of photographic "instruction." News photographs in *Life* adhered strictly to a realistic aesthetic, a visual strategy with a long tradition of credibility as a truthful depiction of the social world. While important similarities exist between factual and fictional genres,[14] contemporary journalists and their audiences distinguish news discourses by their apparent or at least professed objectivity. The neutrality of discourse itself, however, is challenged in poststructuralist critiques (of language, culture, authorship, and audiences) that argue that the politics of representation is crucial to understanding any cultural text. Such challenges to neutrality have a special imperative when dealing with photographs that claim transparent or mechanical reproduction of the real world. Mechanical apparatuses did not determine that the media would rely on a realistic aesthetic; instead, realism as a representational form arose in response to structural developments in modern society. Indeed, there are important historical relationships between realism and the rise of empiricism, individualism, and bourgeois capitalism in modern Western cultures.[15] Thus, we need to understand "realism" as a historical and historically changing form of representation. Social, ideological, and institutional relationships supported beliefs that technology can quantify social experiences. In particular, the concept of the media as "empty vessels," or conduits for the truth, validated the credibility of the news.

Sight has become the dominant perceptual mode in American twentieth-century mass media, relying primarily on photographic realism, a representational strategy that shapes complex and multivocal events, issues, and social conditions in highly formulaic ways.[16] News photographs depict actual events and people, but the means of representation are cultural, not natural. Photographs in *Life* rigidly adhered to Western conventions of perspective and sharp focus, supporting the illusion of looking through a window. *Life* also codified the photo-essay as a new form of communicating the news that told a story through photographs arranged in a logical, and seemingly causal, order. The visual narrative was accompanied by a written text, the extent of which varied depending on the topic. Despite the considerable power of written texts to shape and direct readers' perceptions of the pictures, photographic realism seems especially unmediated since editorial interventions are masked by the common-sense relationships of presumably transparent images. The Csillag photo-essay, for example, reports on the complex, contradictory, and ambiguous situation of Cold War antagonisms through a conventionalized narrative that uses domesticity to impose order and meaning on the event. Photographs show the family arriving in the United States, where they board a train and then appear on the front porch of their new house. Other photos depict Rose Csillag inside the house engaged in activities of the private sphere like washing clothes. The order of the visual journey makes the domestic ideologies and gender divisions embedded in the narrative appear logical and natural.

Another powerful technique of realism, which the magazine adapted from earlier news traditions, was metonymy, the use of "ordinary" individuals to represent broader social conditions. *Life* explained abstract or complex problems, issues, or events through visual portraits of "real" people. Along with celebrities and other famous people, "ordinary" characters served an important news function because even though they were "strangers," as representatives their easily recognizable social roles made them deeply familiar.[17] *Life*'s determination of what constituted the ordinary, and how the ordinary was presented, shaped the ideological perspective of the magazine. The Csillag photo-essay, for example, naturalizes the ideology of domesticity by presenting this as a news story about an individual family that assimilated comfortably into American society.

Realism is the aesthetic means through which *Life*'s news discourse, the visual and textual codes that form its system of representation, organized the complexities of postwar American society into coherent portraits.[18] Typical of news discourses, *Life*'s orderly portraits made sense of the world in ways that reinforced a dominant world view. The logic of the Csillag story, for instance, turns on an assumption about what is desirable by implying that the goal of the Hungarian uprising was to secure a life like that achieved by Americans. Easily recognizable pictures that captured the minutiae of daily life become the convincing evidence of "ordinary" American domesticity. Ideology is thus constructed and reinforced through the camera's presumably objective gaze by mapping out a selective cultural space that privileges one way of life as representative of the nation.[19]

In saying this, however, I want to acknowledge Allan Sekula's observation that realism does not always serve the interests of the state but, as a representational strategy, can be used to undermine or subvert power relations. He insists that it is essential to evaluate realism in terms of who produces the images, in what institutional contexts, for which audiences.[20] My interest in studying the visual news goes beyond challenging the transparency of photographs. The prominence of the family in the Hungarian refugees news story raises questions about the role of the media in limiting contradictions and legitimating dominant social relations. Most important, how and to what extent do the news media produce and reproduce the dominant values of American society?

Social practices do not exist outside of or independent from representations of those practices, yet, as Stuart Hall cautions, power is not simply dispersed everywhere through discourse but is materially grounded. In this context, therefore, we need to ask how the news media regulate material relations within and between civil society and the state.[21] News organizations have legal independence from the state and in that regard are semi-autonomous institutions. However, these cultural institutions are structurally integrated in capitalist systems, and they participate in reproducing dominant culture through ideological strategies that legitimate hegemonic social and political relations.[22]

The incongruities in the Csillag photo-essay between an ideal of American domesticity and the family's ethnic and class differences reveal an interesting problematic: how can we explain contradictions embedded in news discourses while arguing that they serve to reproduce the dominant values of society? Antonio Gramsci's model of hegemony is useful for interpreting *Life* as a complex, even contradictory, discourse and yet one that clearly puts forth a dominant ideological message. Gramsci argues that as long as they maintain control of coercive power like the military and police, rulers in most modern societies find it more effective to rule by consent than by force. Dominant classes maintain hegemonic power by continually forging alliances of heterogeneous constituencies, forming what he labels "historical blocs." Hegemony is not a permanent or stable structure of power, but is always potentially vulnerable and must be continually secured. Since appeals for legitimacy take place within concrete historical circumstances, hegemony must be struggled over rather than imposed by those in power.[23] Because hegemony depends as much on consent as on force, ideology is what wins consent and secures legitimacy, what Hall calls the " 'cement' in a social formation."[24]

Ideology itself is not univocal but rather a complex fusion of various ideological elements. Moreover, no unadulterated truth stands outside texts nor can texts purely manipulate readers, because ideology is not imposed but produced through material social and cultural practices. Instead of functioning on the particular level of supporting specific government policies (although the magazine often did this also), news media like *Life* function on a broader level to support and reproduce hegemonic relations. News media rarely privilege one voice but instead typically support an ideological field that combines different positions into a common world view.[25] The objective of ideological analysis, therefore, is to understand how a particular system of representation offers us a way of knowing or experiencing the world. *Life*, for instance, presented civil rights protests by focusing on personal crises and responses. This attention to personal experiences legitimated social struggles but it did so at the expense of criticizing the structural foundations of racism in American society. The magazine focused on issues of individual merit or failure in character rather than addressing the hierarchies and power relations that structure society. Although *Life* reported on most of the national issues circulating in the dominant culture, it did so in ways that often masked, co-opted, or simplified social differences. In a changing, even bewildering, postwar world, *Life* offered a statement about the United States through family pictures that was neither transparent nor simplistic but ideologically determined and determining.

Representative Families

Life's different sections presented a wide variety of pictures ranging from voyeuristic representations of starlets, to photographic displays of the mushroom clouds accompanying nuclear tests, to essays on Regionalism that often ridiculed modern art. In its other cornerstone, the big special feature, the magazine frequently published the work of major photojournalists such as W. Eugene Smith's "Country Doctor." This section elevated the reportorial nature of photojournalism to an artistic position and added to the prestige of the journal. This study, however, focuses on representative families in The Week's Events news section. Families were not the only way that *Life* represented postwar American society, but they were a frequent and important presence. It is unwise to dismiss pictures of families as irrelevant or trivial to the "real" work of news reporting, for the entanglement of political and gender ideologies in the news section played an important cultural role in shaping readers' knowledge of postwar events.

Life was certainly not the first to turn the camera on the family. Portrait photography and amateur photography established the popularity of family portraiture by the mid-nineteenth century. In addition, there have been strong affiliations between photographic representations of the family and national identity, most prominently perhaps in pictures of presidents with their families. Further, traditions of documentary photography have focused on needy families as a means of portraying social ills. To understand what family photographs mean, however, we have to examine them within the historical context of production and reception, since the concept of family, as well as nation, changed over time. When *Life* first began publishing in the 1930s, it followed the practice of documentary photography that informed its middle-class audiences about the farm crisis and labor conflicts through pictures of impoverished families. During and after World War II,

however, *Life* increasingly depicted middle-class families themselves to promote patriotic sentiments and, later, American social life. *Life*'s contribution, then, was to focus on the representative middle-class family in news stories to signify a national cultural identity.

In its news coverage of the 1956 Hungarian uprising, for instance, the story about the assimilated immigrant family provides the metonymic signifier of what Nixon (and the United States) offers to the young girls on the cover and to all the refugees. In depicting "good Americans," the photo-essay encodes patriarchal values central to some of the most prevalent and powerful hegemonic narratives in American culture. During the postwar years, *Life* emphatically promoted an ideology of domesticity that attempted to make traditional gender roles appear natural and ahistorical. The top half of one two-page spread shows Rose Csillag shopping, using a washing machine, and watching television with the children. While the text emphasizes the novelty of these activities for the Hungarians, visual images of a woman performing gender-specific tasks define the Americanized home. Other photographs of the mother shopping and the father at work similarly visualize stereotypical American gender roles. Theorists have too often ignored the role of gender in constructing the news; they overlook the way that masculine ideals are embedded in the public world of politics, the presence of conventional feminine ideals, and challenges to these ideals. Thus, scholars who ignore gender reproduce masculinist models of the news as a public and degendered realm.[26] In contrast, media critics like John Fiske have analyzed the news as a masculinist discourse that reproduces and perpetuates social assumptions about the division of public and private spheres.[27] Yet, we need to go beyond acknowledging a privileged male discourse to explore how gender and family ideals shape cultural constructions of public spheres. We have to understand not only how the news represents ideals of femininity and masculinity but how, as Joan Scott writes, "politics constructs gender and gender constructs politics."[28] What is at stake in promoting conventional heterosexual norms for both men and women through photographs of families like the Csillags is how news reports supported an ideological alignment of a specific social form with national identity.

The association of certain families with "America," as well as the exclusion and stereotyping of others, played a significant role in *Life*'s vision of the world. The unprecedented postwar economic boom led many social critics, including Henry Luce, to claim that affluence promised a progressive future that would incorporate everyone, thereby ending economic inequalities.[29] Postwar America, however, was a society built on hierarchical class, race, gender, and sexual differences. Representations of family life, therefore, had implications beyond constructions of gender and sexuality because these images also promoted specific class and race ideals. Media

scholars have been concerned with race and class as content or subject matter in the news.[30] However, fewer analyses have considered how structural features actively construct ideals of race and class even when these are not the overt topic of the news story. When *Life* turned to representative families to signify the United States, it was always white families, as in the photographs of the "kind of people who make good Americans," which clearly show white European immigrants. Other kinds of families appear in the magazine as representatives of social issues or political problems, but never as representatives of "America." In contrast to the Csillags, other social groups, such as Latinos, are typically depicted as poor, illiterate, and violating the norms of the nuclear family. Certainly, *Life* was not the first to connect an ideal of the United States to a concept of Whiteness. In a society in which racial divisions determine privilege and oppression, all Americans are marked by race; to be white is to belong to a social category just as it is to be African American, Asian, or Latino. Throughout the nineteenth and twentieth centuries, people with otherwise antagonistic interests have coalesced around their common whiteness against people of color.[31] Yet whiteness is not a unified or stable category but one whose meanings change historically. The magazine's postwar ideological efforts to define the United States depended on pictures of white families that visually connected racial privilege to national identity.

Similarly, *Life* represented the middle

class as the norm of American society and working-class people as different and outside that norm. News stories about labor conflicts accomplished this distinction by identifying the working class as a group while leaving the middle class unidentified except as "Americans." The story about the Csillags may appear to contradict this claim since they were clearly not middle class. The final photograph, for example, shows Pal Csillag at work in a bakery. Nonetheless, the depiction of assimilated immigrants denies class positions and economic barriers. The writer quotes the Csillags' wealthy uncle on the accessibility of the American Dream through men's hard work: "I told him he has the same chance I had if he'll apply himself and work like everyone else in this country." The reference to "everyone else" reproduces deeply familiar myths about equality and democracy. *Life* addresses its audience through realistic strategies that tried to present a seamless narrative in which the Hungarians appear as a "classless" family just like other American families.

By using gender, sexuality, race, and class as frames of analysis, we can see how the structure and content of news stories combine to present a highly politicized portrait of American society.[32] As with gender, when critics and historians consider only news stories in which people of color are the topic, they run the danger of perpetuating differences by presuming the white middle class as the norm against which others are evaluated. Similarly, the absence of segments of the population, including gays and lesbians, and rare depictions of the elderly, Native Americans, and Asian Americans, reveal how the legitimacy of news discourses naturalized the white, middle-class family as the social norm. This is crucial because, through the denial or invisibility of hierarchical relations of difference, representations make the nuclear family appear natural and transhistorical. The middle-class norm, however, was an invented tradition, a return to a reality that had not previously existed for most people.[33] *Life*'s focus on this family form ignored or limited representation of different social groups as well as other relations such as community networks and extended families.

Although *Life* sought to manage conflicts through reassuring portraits of social stability, not all Americans conformed to this narrative ideal and contradictions persisted. As a journal dedicated to current events, *Life* necessarily introduced news stories that contested its own ideological unity. Complex meanings competed with each other in these texts, playing out the social tensions of postwar society. For example, in the final picture of the Csillag photo-essay, the owner of the bakery stands behind Pal Csillag while reaching around him in an awkward position to demonstrate proper baking techniques. Echoing Nixon's embrace of the young girls, the owner's arms encircle the immigrant, who lacks knowledge, showing him how to work, how to be an American. The owner's paternalism together with ethnic differences and class status creates unstable, shifting meanings that cannot be securely fixed to one reading. Pictures like this remain open to critical, even oppositional readings (as we will see in the published letters to the editor). Despite the potential for different readings, *Life* sought to win consent for a preferred reading through discursive strategies that constrained the range of options in favor of dominant positions.[34] In the Csillag photo-essay, the author elides differences by using the uncle's comment that Pal Csillag had equal opportunities if "he'll apply himself and work like everyone else in this country." This statement ignores the difficulties of language and employment discrimination while encouraging a reading of the photograph as a visual reflection of this work ethic and the American Dream.

Historical Dialogues

Claims of photographic universality misdirect our attention from the ways in which visual images mobilize particular ideological meanings in specific historical contexts. Since any discourse interacts with other discourses in the social moment in which they are produced and consumed, we can observe a dialogic relationship between historical developments in social values, economic trends, labor relations, and political conflicts and *Life*'s depictions of those conditions.

Early histories of the postwar years defined this as a period of consensus, or social and class harmony. The postwar period, of course, is best known as the era of the baby boom. Across the social spectrum, Americans were marrying younger and having larger families at an earlier age. Unprecedented prosperity also created great changes in American incomes, work habits, and consumption patterns. More recently, however, historical revisions have rejected the notion that postwar Americans shared a consensus of values and objectives, finding instead great instabilities and contestations in race relations and class antagonisms. Even within the domestic ideology of the middle class, there is evidence of discontent and unease.[35] Far from being a unified, or consensus culture, postwar America faced national conflicts and the escalation of global tensions. At home, despite the economic boom, social changes were equivocal for white women and people of color, opening up some opportunities while closing down others. Evidence of instabilities and conflicts necessitates the rejection of nostalgic reflections about an easier, safer, or more harmonious age.

The concept of consensus, however, need not be entirely rejected. Even though Americans did not achieve consensus, many cultural representations promoted a vision of unity and homogeneity. The ideology of domestic consumption, after all, strove for stability in order to generate greater buying. Similarly, Cold War rhetoric frequently contrasted communism with a homogeneous society of domestic consumers. In popular culture, a vast range of materials constructed a cultural landscape focused on domesticity, suburban homes, and heterosexual norms. Recently, scholars of postwar media have analyzed fictional forms such as television situation comedies and Hollywood films. These studies examine how images of the family eased anxieties about postwar social transformations and negotiated the conflicts between a rhetoric of family solidarity and the fragmentation intrinsic to suburbanization and consumer consciousness. Television in the 1950s relocated social and cultural anxieties, such as ethnic tensions and work identities, into the privatized concerns of the family. In comedies about working-class and ethnic families, like "The Honeymooners," as well as in middle-class domestic sitcoms like "Father Knows Best," narratives typically centered around the problems of gender relations and child rearing.[36] Films also addressed familial anxieties in domestic melodramas like *The Imitation of Life* and stories about disaffected youths like *Rebel without a Cause*.[37] In popular literature, the success of advice books by experts, ranging from Dr. Benjamin Spock's advice on raising children to home-improvement manuals, suggests anxieties and needs not fulfilled by traditional family and community networks.[38]

Life's reliance on representative families to depict news topics corresponded to and reinforced cultural values about domesticity, gender, and social identities current in a wide range of cultural, social, and political arenas. Indeed, the news shares much with other mass media, relying on narrative forms to shape events and issues into dramatic stories that reproduce dominant social values. Yet, as an advertising- and subscription-driven medium with close ties to politics, *Life* imaged the ideological terrain somewhat differently from films, advice books, or television. *Life* presented itself as a popular forum about the public world of politics, economics, science, military affairs, and history. Because the magazine was committed to news and information, its use of family imagery intersected with public concerns in ways different from other popular cultural products. Earlier traditions of realistic representation influenced the forms of *Life*'s discourse and its responses to social and political transformations.

Chapter 2 of this study examines the rise of empirical and photographic discourses in the early twentieth century in order to trace the historical development of photojournalism. Changes in news photography, along with technological innovations, supported the emergence of photojournalism in the 1930s. Within a matrix of institutional, social, and cultural traditions, *Life* introduced a new form of visual communication, the photo-essay. The excitement with which audiences greeted the new picture magazine and their tacit acceptance of photographic authenticity, apparent most readily in letters to the editor, indicate the cultural significance of this news format. *Life*'s photo-essays worked as effectively as they did because of the ways in which the magazine encouraged readers to identify with what they saw. Chapter 2 also analyzes the general characteristics of the photo-essay and how it addressed its middle-class readers by using family pictures and other strategies to encourage readers to identify with an ideal of community depicted in its pages.

Chapter 3 examines both the defining characteristics of *Life*'s representative family and how the ideal of a consensus society of middle-class, white, nuclear families formed the foundations of a national identity. Rhetorical strategies articulate nationalism by constructing differences that form boundaries between "us" and "them." For example, the immigrant abandoning the other side of the boundary validates the "us" of national identity. One of the consequences of family representation, then, was the cultural regulation of private life through an emphasis on a singular domestic ideal that promoted homogeneity and uniformity and silenced differences. In this way, *Life*'s depictions of the opportunities and freedoms of capitalist society helped sustain postwar political tensions by contrasting the nation with communism, even when the stories were not overtly about the Cold War. A detailed analysis of nationalism in *Life* reveals the consequences of a domestic ideal held up to American readers as a mirror of themselves in a global world.

The presence of representative families in the news contradicts a popular conception about American social life that draws a sharp distinction between public and private spheres of activity. The concept of a distinct private world developed in conjunction with

industrial capitalism, which encouraged the privatization of domestic life separate from the world of politics, work, and public concerns. Individualism and its accompanying ideals of the private citizen and the sanctity of the home presume that the state does not or cannot enter the home. In postulating separate public and private spheres, however, we deny the political nature of private experiences and struggles. Moreover, the relationships between public and private spheres have important ramifications because what is included and excluded from political discourse profoundly affects social experiences.

The family has great cultural appeal as the locus of social and personal relations and therefore has been a logical place of intervention for politicians and others interested in social developments and political policies. In this regard, the mass media play key roles through their structuring of social worlds in terms of domesticity. Chapter 4 examines the role of the private sphere in *Life*'s news stories about public concerns in order to examine how the family as a cultural ideal legitimated national policies. Cold War rhetoric, for instance, frequently relied on family imagery to justify foreign policies. Economics also mingled with patriotism and capitalism in stories that urged families to be better consumers, claiming it was their patriotic duty to help sustain economic growth. This chapter participates in current feminist reconsiderations of the public and private by exploring the role of the news as a discourse that shapes, regulates, and negotiates knowledge about social experiences.

As the major photojournalism magazine, *Life* also discussed the postwar social tensions surrounding class, race, and gender politics. News reporting generates a critical dialogue about society when it represents social and political conflicts, as in articles about marginalized and oppositional groups. African Americans' demands for civil rights, for instance, disrupted the vision of a stable and secure society. Similarly, even as postwar culture promoted domesticity, fewer families throughout the decade were living out this dream as women continued to enter the work force in increasing numbers. *Life*'s photo-essays addressed the tensions between these cultural ideals and social realities in ways that at times challenged its own ideals. Representational strategies sought to contain contradictions and unequal relations of power by framing political challenges as familial concerns. In this regard, *Life* not only participated in the construction of a postwar middle-class culture but also shaped readers' perceptions of other social groups. Chapter 5 examines contradictions and ideological struggles in photo-essays about representative families. *Life*'s news stories often retained meanings resistant to legitimation even as textual devices and surrounding discourses attempted to limit political criticisms and social differences.

Photographs are polysemic texts, that is, they are open to different interpretations and can be read in a variety of ways. Captions and other accompanying texts attempt to close or direct interpretations, but never do so completely. Although representations are abundantly meaningful, those meanings are neither unified or stable, nor are they read the same way by all audiences.[39] Therefore, cultural practices, including forms of representation that promote dominant culture, are sites of struggle over meaning. Representational strategies such as inclusive pronouns, direct address, and visual realism encouraged identification in order to incorporate the reader into *Life*'s imaginary collective. Family, presented as if the reader shared not only the same relations but the same commitments and ideals, was one of the most powerful frames that *Life* used to direct preferred readings. By examining both *Life*'s domestic ideal and the limitations of this narrative, we can explore the cultural politics of postwar photojournalism.

CHAPTER 2

LOOKING AT LIFE
A Historical Profile of Photojournalism

LIFE takes for its field not all the news but all the news which now and hereafter can be seen; and of these seen events it proposes to be the pictorial record.

—Advertisement in *Fortune*, December 1936

Four months after the end of World War II, *Life* featured a news story entitled "U.S. Normalcy: Against the Backdrop of a Troubled World 'LIFE' Inspects an American City at Peace."[1] In this December 3, 1945, story about citizens of Indianapolis adjusting to postwar conditions, photographs depict a frightening world of international political conflicts. One picture shows V. M. Molotov and three other Soviet leaders on a reviewing stand. An ominous caption foreshadowing Cold War tensions states that Molotov claimed "Russia would have atomic energy soon." Another photograph depicts an elderly Jewish man's face bloodied in an attack by a Cairo mob next to a photograph of Hermann Göring and Rudolf Hess at the Nuremberg trials. Pictures of the unstable and war-torn world also include images of child refugees from China, Poland, Italy, and Hungary. Photographs of massive industrial strikes across the United States along with news coverage of unemployment and readjustment difficulties reveal parallel domestic turmoils facing Americans

in 1945. A picture of a walkout at a Chevrolet factory in Detroit, two photographs of picket lines, and one of an empty warehouse underscore the threat of economic instability associated with reconversion to a peacetime economy. At the same time, a picture of a divorce court session displays the personal costs to Americans.

Juxtaposed to these images of national and international conflicts, *Life* shows people in Indianapolis preoccupied with "the important problems of their own communities: good schools, good homes and good highways." The first photograph in the December 3, 1945, essay depicts a crowd standing in front of a movie theater at night. A banner hanging below the marquee announces the film *Mama Loves Papa* (*illustration 3*). Other scenes of postwar prosperity include a picture of a fashion show and a family gathered to welcome home a soldier wearing a uniform covered with medals. Full-page photographs feature the Women of the Moose in fancy attire at an initiation ceremony and students cheering at a football game. These images, *Life* reassuringly notes, demonstrate that citizens of Indianapolis had turned "their minds and energies to work, football games, automobile trips, family reunions and all the pleasant trivia of the American way of life."

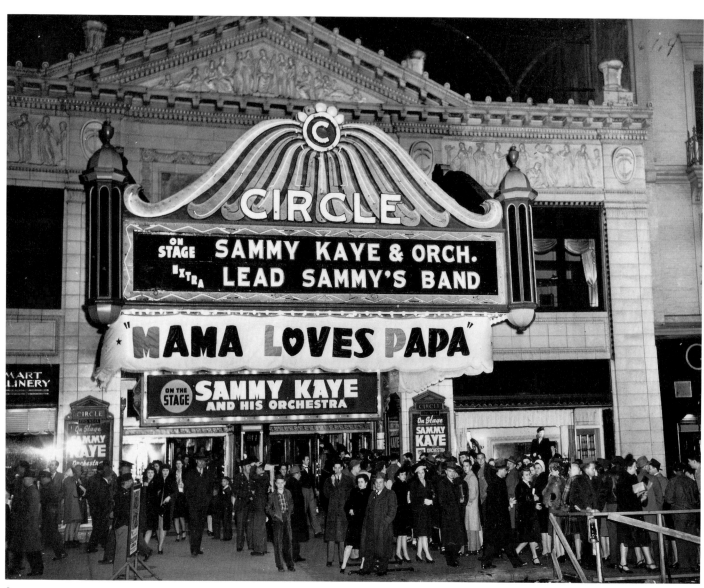

3

The "U.S. Normalcy" article presents the complexities of early postwar life through contrasting images of tumultuous public events and domestic leisure activities. Underlying this depiction is the presumption that photographs are able to show transparently the processes and effects of readjustment. Claims of photographic authenticity include the introductory explanation that *Life*'s pictures "record this return to normalcy" because they show "what the people are doing there and what they are concerned with." If, however, we accept the arguments made in recent years by cultural theorists that all information is culturally determined in specific historical contexts, then, as Allan Sekula notes, "We can no longer ascribe an intrinsic or universal meaning to the photographic image."[2] Despite *Life*'s claim that photographs mimetically "record" reality, the photograph is a complex system in which multiple factors such as lighting, composition, subject matter, captions, and accompanying texts combine to construct meanings. Furthermore, historical conditions determine the production and reception of photographic meaning. The first picture in this article, for example, does more than simply depict a crowd attending a movie. Despite the crises around the world, these well-dressed white citizens of Indianapolis have the money and time to go to the movies. Thus, the photograph carries connotations about Americans' leisure time and economic resources in the aftermath of World War II. Moreover, the title *Mama Loves Papa* sug-

gests that the film belongs to the genre of family comedies or domestic melodramas in which misunderstandings drive the narrative through heterosexual conflicts toward marital resolution. The opening photograph thus associates the mass media and consumer culture with family values.

This photograph also has status as "news" since the photo-essay was the first story in The Week's Events section. The large headline "U.S. Normalcy" reinforces the photograph's, and ultimately the essay's, association of national stability with leisure time, commercial culture, and domesticity. The author explains that the phrase "return to normalcy" was coined by President Warren Harding after World War I, thereby alluding to the affluence and national stability as well as American isolationism of the 1920s. The verb "to return" connotes both the physical return of soldiers and an idyllic past, as if it were possible for the "ordinary" people portrayed in this photo-essay to "return" to a previous state of being.

The photograph of a fashion show also reinforces the theme of returning for it signals the lifting of wartime restrictions on fabric. *Life* ties consumption to signs of postwar recovery by envisioning ways to spend the money Americans saved during the war. In this case, the picture uses gender codes that had become standardized in twentieth-century advertising and fashion photography. Seated amid crowded tables, a white man stares at a white woman standing directly in front of him in a bathing suit. Like wartime pinups of female movie stars, the model poses in three-quarter profile in the center of the composition. She is available both for the man's gaze and for the viewer's. After four years in which over ten million men were absent from the home front, this picture hails the return of hetero-sexual relations. But, lest we read this as an uncomplicated return to "patriarchy," we need to understand the historically shifting gender relations of the 1940s. During the war, Americans negotiated gender expecta-tions when men went away to fight and women joined the paid labor force, many in tradi-tionally male-segregated jobs. Although these work conditions broke down certain stereo-types about women, as Maureen Honey points out, wartime propaganda, movies, and pin-ups also reasserted conventional femininity.[3] The picture of the fashion show ignores the tensions produced in the complex terrain of relations between men and women that oc-curred at the end of the war in both social and work arenas. Far from being merely a "window on to the world," photography encodes social norms and privileges certain perspectives on a historical moment.

This photo-essay, then, is not a transpar-ent reflection of one medium-sized city in postwar America. Instead, *Life* constructs a specific vision of postwar society by focusing on an exemplary site. The essay even hints at the symbolic level of its representation when the text quotes the State Publicity Bureau's definition of Indianapolis as the "most Ameri-can of cities in the most American of states." Praised for its quintessential Americanness, this city becomes representative of national concerns and objectives. In this way, the news story does not reflect or record reality so much as selectively construct a narrative about these issues. Stuart Hall explains that the news relies on "the set of on-going beliefs and constructions about the world which most of its readers share."[4] Generalizations about the "American way of life" go undefended be-cause they depend for their comprehension on common attitudes and beliefs circulating among *Life*'s middle-class audience. In par-ticular, images of consumption and domes-ticity offer a vision of the United States that its readers could share. Of course, this photo-essay speaks less to those caught up in social conflicts, like the striking workers, than it does to a middle-class audience reading about these problems. In the picture of the Detroit strikers, a crowd of African American and white men in work clothes directly faces the camera in the middle distance. Yelling and waving their arms, the men rush menacingly into the foreground toward the camera. This representation of hostility indicates that, at least here, the camera does not serve the interests of the working class. Instead, *Life*'s narrative places its readers behind the lens, and urges them to envision themselves as part of a society coping with the problems of others.

As the 1936 advertisement for *Life* in this chapter's epigraph claims, this news article on reconversion appears unmediated in making a pictorial record of all the news that can be seen. Roland Barthes suggests that dominant forms of popular culture construct ideology through myths that make history appear natural.[5] By stepping back from photography's mimetic appeal, we can not only begin to question the transparency of images but, more important, to consider the historical developments that led to readers' general acceptance of the news value of photojournalism. A tradition of accepting photographs as credible evidence lies behind the magazine's claim of depicting "real" Americans. Photojournalism did not appear fully formed but came out of a historical matrix of ideas, institutions, and social conditions that established conventions for news reporting based on concepts of objectivity and authenticity.[6] The historical conditions that gave rise to these conventions include not only the specific postwar context but also longer traditions in photography and news representation. In the late nineteenth and early twentieth centuries, news organizations, government agencies, and social reformers first established photographs as evidence when they adopted the medium for purposes of documentation. After obtaining legal and cultural status as evidence, photography in turn helped to legitimize the news as a credible medium of information.

Early in the medium's history, photographers also recognized the camera's ability to address emotional desires and needs. Photographs in *Life* like that of the army soldier with his family drew on a long tradition of presenting immediately recognizable subject matter for its readers. The affective meanings contained in visual images, however, are complex, not monolithic. Striking workers on the picket line can represent a threat to social stability, but they can also represent frustration and anger that may elicit readers' sympathy and understanding in light of the problems associated with readjustment. In this way, photographs rarely secure fixed meanings.

Life successfully acquired a mass audience by its extensive use of visual evidence that appealed both because of its presumed factual news values and because of the immediacy of its emotional address. The magazine's success occupies a specific historical juncture when a wide audience found those appeals compelling. It is necessary, then, to trace the historical and social expectations that grant photographs the power to represent the world. Why, in other words, did a generation that had just lived through experiences it would have liked to believe were anything but normal find *Life*'s representation of "normalcy" acceptable, even credible?

Traditions of Objectivity and Emotion in Photography

The debate over photography's veracity is as old as the medium itself. Since 1839 when the daguerreotype became commercially available, photographers and critics have debated whether photography is an art form or a mechanical record of reality.[7] Never resolved, this debate continues as people appropriate the technology for different purposes. Thus, although viewers sometimes recognize the camera's manipulative abilities, they frequently accept certain photographic practices as objective. Photojournalism developed in part from institutions and social practices that secured photography's status as documentation.

Since its introduction, observers have praised photography's technical capacities and mimetic qualities. By the late nineteenth century, a variety of institutions relied on photographs as empirical evidence. During this period, many in the middle class blamed the increasing chaos of urban environments on immigrants and working-class people who were struggling to survive in the severe conditions of early industrialization. To help control these conditions, local government institutions used photography for surveillance and record keeping. In rationalizing its bureaucracies, the state relied on photography to organize, classify, and define criminals, deviants, the insane, the poor, and the needy. Police departments adopted the "mug shot" to keep track of criminals; psychiatrists and other medical practitioners used photographs to classify diseases they assumed to be apparent in their patients' physiognomy. Photography's apparent empiricism gained support from scientific positivism that claimed one could both know and represent reality. Positivism in turn helped establish the medium's legal status.[8] Only certain institutional discourses,

of course, such as police photographs, have the legitimacy to claim this status for photography, yet such validation made similar claims by newspapers and magazines seem more plausible.

Reform movements also recognized the capacity of the camera to document social conditions. In the 1890s, newspaper reporter Jacob Riis turned to photography in his efforts to expose the social problems in New York's immigrant ghettos. Riis was one of the first American photographers to establish a solid link between photography and social reform by using pictures to illustrate his book *How the Other Half Lives* (1890), a detailed account of the horrific conditions in these slums. As Peter Hales points out, Riis's pictures firmly established photography as "the preeminent mode of proof in the rhetoric of social and urban reform for the next ninety years."[9] The camera's ability to capture details and the pictures' unposed and unplanned appearances gave Riis's images an unmediated look. Hales demonstrates, however, that Riis carefully planned his compositions to accentuate the squalor and make the immigrants look degraded and pitiful. In this way, Riis visually replicated social relations by turning the camera's gaze toward powerless subjects. Photography has the ability to establish a terrain of the Other by turning the subject into an object captured by the film and put on display as a spectacle. The spectator's gaze can be a form of domination, especially when the image records differences—Riis's pictures of mothers, for instance, showed pitiful women barely able to care for their children. Maren Stange rejects arguments that his photographs were simply humanitarian. Instead she demonstrates that social reform photography functioned as a tool of surveillance that reproduced dominant class relations. Riis's depictions of families reinforced class differences by invoking Victorian cultural expectations about domesticity and maternal care that distanced the viewer from the subject of the image. In combining realism and voyeuristic sensationalism, Riis introduced several of the major components of reform photography.[10]

By the twentieth century, photography had clearly established its status as legal evidence. Social worker Lewis Hine's photographs of immigrant children laboring in factories, for instance, supplied visual evidence instrumental to the passage of protectionist legislation in the 1910s. Unlike Riis's photographs, which often made immigrants appear either pitiful or offensive, Hine's photographs show children as strong and full of spirit—seemingly at odds with their surroundings. Moreover, in contrast to Riis's pictures of mothers in abject poverty, Hine's series of tenement mothers with small children emphasizes tenderness and maternal care.[11] This Progressive reformer relied on new sociological methods of documentation such as detailed captions to offer empirical evidence about his subjects. His photographs appeared in social work journals like *Survey*, exhibitions, and public relations brochures addressed to middle-class audiences and reformers. These contexts further reinforced social acceptance of the camera as a recording device. As Stange points out, however, embedded in Hine's representations, as in reformist ideologies, was a "pro-corporate orientation of progress."[12] For instance, his famous Ellis Island photographs use close-up and low-angle shots to dignify subjects overcoming their circumstances. These "objective" images reinforced early twentieth-century bourgeois attitudes about family life, charity, and social responsibility. Sympathetic portraits of mothers presumably appealed to reform-minded audiences as much for their statements about domesticity as for a faith in the camera's recording of poverty.

Seemingly neutral documents that encoded complex forms of emotional and objective address also developed in the popular press. News publishers were among the first to recognize the appeal of illustrations. As early as the 1840s, the penny presses published engravings copied from daguerreotypes. Dan Schiller argues that newspapers struggling to distinguish themselves from the partisan press adopted realistic writing styles as well as the use of engravings to bolster their claims for journalistic standards of accuracy and truth.[13] After the Civil War, newspapers increasingly published illustrations. Magazines such as *Frank Leslie's Illustrated Magazine* appeared by mid-century as another outlet for visual representation. News media, however, did not adopt photography until after 1880, when new technologies made halftone reproductions viable. Despite some initial resistance by editors and engravers' unions, photographs increasingly replaced earlier forms of illustration, and between 1900 and 1914, many newspapers adopted the new technologies of photographic illustration. During this period, news photographers such as Jimmy Hare and John Hemnent provided magazines and newspapers with photographs of political conflicts like the Spanish-American War.[14]

Newspapers increasingly turned to photography as one of several novelties designed to boost circulation. Rising literacy among growing urban populations intensified competition among newspapers. They responded by introducing a variety of attractive features in addition to photography such as contests, comics, and sports pages. In so doing, the papers increased their cultural importance as both sources of information and as lucrative commodities in the urban centers of industrializing America. Immigrants and Americans from rural areas who were new to the cities faced a changing or unfamiliar world. The mass media provided these new urban dwellers with information about society and addressed emotional needs previously fulfilled through traditional community culture. Walter Benjamin argues that in the age of mechanical reproduction, societies lose their cultural heritages through the break up of space and time, thereby isolating individuals from community and tradition. He notes that "by focusing on hidden details of familiar objects, by exploring commonplace milieus under the ingenious guidance of the camera, the film . . . extends our comprehension of the necessities which rule our lives."[15] In other words, Benjamin argues that photography, like other forms of mechanical reproduction, alienates viewers from traditional culture even as it serves to reintegrate them in a "world" that serves to compensate for this alienation. Although news media claim to be informational, communications scholars demonstrate that the news functions like other forms of mass media to construct social knowledge in its broadest sense.[16] Social knowledge, including concepts of family, community, and nation, offers compensation or emotional reassurance in a world where these have often become inaccessible or abstract concepts. In this regard, photography's ideological power lies in the immediacy and accessibility of its visualization of the world.

The tabloids of the 1920s profoundly influenced news photography because they both popularized the use of photographs and developed representational strategies based on an emotional address. The first successful American tabloid, the *New York Daily News*, began publishing in 1919. Within a few years, the *Daily News* reached a circulation of one million readers. In 1924, two other tabloids, the *New York Evening Graphic* and the *New York Daily Mirror*, began to compete with the *Daily News* for this lucrative market. Tabloids were characterized by an increased use of photographs and an emphasis on crime, sex scandals, and human-interest stories. They combined photographs of personalities with descriptions of events written in a style that depended on inclusive personal pronouns. Rather than using the abstract rational mode of address common to traditional newspapers, tabloids emphasized intimacy and community, thereby easing the isolation and alienation created by urban environments.[17] Tabloid journalists, for example, shaped celebrated court trials of crime and divorce into a narrative genre that frequently blurred fact and fiction to maintain the suspense. Despite claims that each scandal was unique, the tabloids relied on a generic format of stereotypical plots, stock characters, and formulaic descriptions. Popular crime scandals focused on ordinary people like Ruth Snyder and her lover, Judd Gray, who were executed by the State of New York for the murder of Snyder's husband in 1927. Their love story was anything but extraordinary, and yet it captured New York's attention. The case sensationalized adultery by dramatically punishing deviance and reasserting the primacy of the marital relationship. Sensational narratives like this one became rituals shared by the community of tabloid readers, rituals that reaffirmed social boundaries.[18]

Although many features of the popular press had been introduced by the turn of the century, a distinguishing contribution of 1920s journalism was the tremendous increase in the number of photographs. Between 1920 and 1930, the volume of pictures per newspaper per week increased by 205 percent.[19] During this decade, however, the majority of pictures were head shots, posed portraits, and location shots because cameras were bulky and slow. Therefore, sensational photographs proved to be invaluable scoops. The *Daily News* sold one million additional copies of the issue carrying a hidden-camera photograph of the electric-chair execution of Ruth Snyder on the front page. Impressive circulation increases accompanying photographic coups encouraged photographers and editors to produce ever more sensational imagery. In their search for novel pictures, the tabloids focused on criminals and the underclass, who were more vulnerable to press intrusions than powerful elites and government officials. Nevertheless, by the 1920s, even celebrities and politicians were no longer able or willing to protect their privacy from the curious gaze of the tabloid camera.[20] Photographs' easily recognizable subject matter elicited emotions ranging from a feeling of intimacy with a favorite film star to the voyeuristic pleasure of identifying the criminal personality in the prisoner's face.

Tabloids also routinely used touched-up and altered photographs. The *Evening Graphic* went furthest in fabricating imagery with composographs that used models to re-enact events for combination or faked pictures. Serving a different representational strategy from empirical evidence, composographs and altered photographs derived from a tradition of newspaper illustration not dependent on photographic rules of realism. In small print, the newspaper did identify these images as composographs. Nonetheless, these pictures probably also benefited from the "prestige of denotation" associated with photographic realism.[21] Composographs demonstrate the ambiguities surrounding the use of this new medium in the 1920s as editors and photographers struggled to define the characteristics of news photography. The remarkable circulation success of tabloids such as the *Daily News* eventually forced traditional newspapers to adopt many of their techniques. By the 1930s, newspapers covered not only sensational events and celebrities but also incorporated other features first popularized by the tabloids: sports news, the woman's page, and most significantly, photographs.

In the late nineteenth and early twentieth centuries, rising literacy, better transportation systems, and national advertisers also supported the emergence of mass circulation, general interest magazines like *Cosmopolitan* and *McClure's*. They increasingly depended on a variety of visual representations, including halftone photographic reproductions. As a national outlet for advertisers, magazines became showcases for visual displays of consumer goods, including a greater use of photographs to create a more visually oriented medium.[22] Increasingly, editors experimented with ad placement to facilitate the flow of reading between editorial material and advertisements. Sally Stein argues persuasively that the *Ladies' Home Journal*, the leading woman's magazine in the early twentieth century, established the visual precedents for picture magazines through editorial transformations that turned the *Journal* into "a predominantly visual experience, constructing an audience of spectators and, by extension, consumers."[23] The visual conventions established in the *Journal* and other mass-circulation magazines familiarized audiences with pictorial realism. This familiarity in turn enhanced claims of the camera's ability to record reality later made by *Life*.

The growing dominance of the visual in magazines and newspapers paralleled the growth of other mass media such as film and the continued popularity of amateur photography. These factors all supported the emergence of photojournalism. Technological innovations and experiments with aesthetic forms during the 1920s and 1930s coincided with the American mass media's consolidation into a national commercial culture. Transportation and communication advances enabled greater coverage and transmission of national news events.[24] It was during this growth of a national commercial culture that publisher Henry Luce decided to issue a picture magazine of news and entertainment.

Life Begins

During the late 1920s, wire services and photo-agencies began to supply photographs to newspapers and magazines. New flash units and small-format cameras widened the range of conditions under which photographs could be taken, and photographic imagery expanded beyond the head shots and formal poses that had dominated news photography. In the late 1920s and the 1930s, photographers began to explore a variety of styles, including candid shots and action pictures. European photographers such as Felix Mann and Erich Solomon excited audiences with novel and often intimate views of famous politicians and events that appeared to open up the world to new visual perceptions. In Germany during the 1920s, such weeklies as the *Münchner Illustrierte Presse*, edited by Stefan Lorant, and the *Berliner Illustrirte Zeitung* with editor Kurt Korff experimented with the content and size of images, coherent layouts, and picture series to tell a news story. With the rise of National Socialism in the early 1930s, many of these photographers and editors immigrated to the United States and Britain. Some had a direct influence on *Life*: Korff advised *Life* in the late 1930s and early 1940s, and Alfred Eisenstaedt, who came to the United States in 1936, immediately began a career-long association with the magazine.[25]

Luce's recognition of the popularity of new photographic technologies led him to explore the commercial viability of a picture magazine. In 1933, Time Inc. began to test the market potential for the new magazine through experiments with visual reporting in the *March of Time* (MOT) as well as photographic layouts in *Time* and *Fortune*. MOT, which started in 1931 as a weekly radio dramatization of the news, changed in 1935 to a monthly newsreel. In this period, MOT staged events since incidents often did not occur in front of a camera. With estimated audiences of over twelve million viewers by 1936, these staged newsreels accustomed viewers to seeing the news in pictures.[26] Audiences' willingness to accept reenactments suggests that the desire for imaging reality outweighed the need for veracity.

Time, which started publishing in 1923, had made only limited use of photographs, primarily head shots of famous people. In the 1930s, however, layouts increasingly used multiple pictures of events in news stories. On February 25, 1935, for example, *Time* published three pages of photographs of Franklin D. Roosevelt by Thomas McAvoy, the first candid shots of an American president. Unlike formal portraits, candid photographs of the president laughing and smoking appeared to offer an intimate view of his personality. Even more than *Time*, *Fortune* explored the possibilities of photography, often with extensive photographic layouts. An expensive magazine targeted to businessmen, *Fortune* reproduced sheet-fed gravure photographs on high-quality paper. The magazine's commitment to superior photographic reproductions was unprecedented in American magazines, except for Alfred Stieglitz's art photography magazine, *Camera Work*.[27]

To acquire a national audience for *Life*, Luce felt that it was imperative to produce high-quality photographic reproductions so as to distinguish the pictures in the new magazine from the poor-quality reproductions in newspapers. At the same time, he recognized the need to keep the magazine affordable for its targeted middle-class audience. These decisions delayed the initial publication of *Life*. Rotogravure processes had limited mass reproduction of photographs to grainy pictures on pulp newspaper stock, but by 1936, *Life*'s printers had developed cheaper forms of coated stock that kept prices down while ensuring a clarity that made the images seem more realistic. They also invented heat presses and faster drying inks to mass produce fine-quality prints. In addition, Time Inc.'s distribution networks facilitated *Life*'s ability to reach a national audience.[28]

Life first appeared on November 23, 1936, with Margaret Bourke-White's cover photograph of the Works Progress Administration's (WPA) Fort Peck Dam project. Like so many of Bourke-White's modernist photographs of American technology from the 1930s, the low-angle shot shows a monumental structure looming over two small figures in the foreground.[29] The inside cover also showcased technology with a full-page photograph of a doctor in an operating room holding a newborn male infant upside down at the moment of his birth. The headline underneath the photograph reads "*Life* Begins." As they would do repeatedly throughout its history, the editors use the photograph to make a pun on the magazine's title. The caption underneath the photograph explains that "the camera records the most vital moment in any life: its beginning." Despite the universal claim of "any life," this photograph depicts not a private experience but rather the public world of American professional medicine. Doctors and nurses dressed in surgical outfits work in a modern operating room. The surgical masks and dim lighting obscure the adults' faces, turning them into representatives of their profession. Similarly, the caption emphasizes the child's metaphoric status by avoiding any references to his name. Significantly, the framing of the photograph excludes the mother from the scene. Together, the cover photograph and the first image in the new photojournalism magazine equate American technology with a vision of reproduction that ignores social, class, and cultural differences.

Life's use of a visual pun to personify the magazine is part of its aggrandized claim to "show" the world to its readers. Throughout the magazine's history, *Life* frequently used the visual trope of birth to signify "universal" values. *Life* faced a monumental task in finding a visual language to make connections between its readers and national and international affairs. In turning the project itself into a metaphor, "Life Begins," the paternalistic claims of the editors locate the magazine within a family sphere. This same paternal voice connecting birth to a geopolitical field appeared in a wide range of stories from a 1938 "Birth of a Baby" photo-essay, which mixed scientific reporting with voyeuristic curiosity, to a feature story on a pregnant woman having her first child, connecting gender ideals to national identity, in a 1956 special issue "The American Woman."[30]

American news media have conventionally focused on the richest and the poorest, whose difference from a presumed audience makes them newsworthy. *Life* also displayed a consistent fascination with the private lives of celebrities, politicians, monarchs, and other public figures. The magazine frequently depicted famous people as ordinary individuals, publishing pictures of them with their families at weddings, holding newborn babies, and in posed portraits. Reporting on the actions of the wealthy and other elites treated them as if they were intrinsically newsworthy. During the prewar years, *Life* also focused attention on the neediest members of society. When reporting on those in trouble, in crisis, or impoverished, it typically turned to representative families. The magazine's attention to these families was strongly influenced by documentary photographers, especially those working for government agencies, who used photography to depict Americans' experiences of the Depression. During the first years of publication, *Life* was an important outlet for New Deal agencies' photographs of droughts, floods, and other economic crises. The magazine garnered respectability by publishing prestigious government-sponsored publicity photographs, but the practice was mutually beneficial since pictures magazines like *Life* also gave government projects access to national audiences.[31] Among the most influential of

these projects was the Farm Security Administration (FSA) photography file, mandated to record the plight of the rural poor.

As part of New Deal reform ideology, the FSA photography file appealed to viewers' sense of responsibility and charity by "exposing" the sufferings and problems of the poorest agricultural workers. The FSA photography project developed from traditions of social-reform photography and continued to represent the poor in terms of dominant American values and beliefs about domestic life and work responsibilities—values that would have been intelligible and acceptable to viewers who were themselves observing, rather than sharing, these experiences.[32]

Despite an insistence on darkroom purity, documentary photography did not disavow emotional address but instead merged verisimilitude with affective appeal.[33] For instance, FSA photographs of mothers with small children were pivotal to the government's construction of a cultural message of liberal reform. These women signified familial stability and traditional gender roles, ideals that helped mobilize congressional and public support for reform programs.[34] Photographers' historical reliance on family pictures demonstrates the ways in which the aesthetics of realism connects domesticity to other cultural concerns. Moreover, the popularity of photography, particularly among amateurs, has supported this cultural focus on the family. Since the 1880s, when Kodak introduced the portable box camera, amateur photographers have enthusiastically photographed their families and social worlds. Indeed, the variety of domestic images, from snapshots and formal portraits to Hine's tenement mothers, reveals most significantly the adaptability of the family as a cultural image in expressing ideological positions.

Prior to the 1940s, Life followed the tradition of representing social problems through domestic imagery. Accompanying the other economic instabilities of the Depression, labor conflicts characterized the 1930s, as unions escalated their activities in the face of rising unemployment. Life's representations of these events frequently turned to working-class families to exemplify both problems and solutions. In a January 18, 1937, article, "U.S. Labor Uses a Potent New Tactic—The Sit-Down Strike," a two-page spread features Bud Simons, a union president, and his family.[35] Photographs reveal his wife in her home at night when, as Life explains "she must be both mother and father to her three children because Bud Simons spends most nights at the plant." Four scenes depict the mother helping the three children prepare for bed including one photograph of her with the youngest child on her lap wrapped in a bath towel (illustration 4). As with FSA photographs, here visual strategies represent the family engaged in daily activities. Close-up and medium-distance shots using sharp focus and strong lighting not only reveal the impoverished conditions of their lives but, equally important, create an emotional inti-

macy that brings the viewer closer to these individuals struggling against external odds. Significantly, the visual strategy emphasizes the separation of the father and his family: Bud Simons does not appear in any of the domestic scenes. Instead, pictures show him presiding over a union meeting and talking with other strikers. The headline, "Bud Simons Spends the Night away from Wife and Children,"and the visual absence of the father from the family represent the threat to the social order. The written narrative further articulates the magazine's editorial perspective by condemning the union activities of men like Simons. Negative depictions of strikers contrast with praise of the automobile industry because "the thing they made has rolled forth to change the character of every civilized country." Such comments and images supported the magazine's pro-business editorial policy, which opposed New Deal legislation on trade unions. Descriptions of industrial magnates routinely praised them as great leaders or visionaries. In addition, editorials often condemned strikes and decried work stoppages as anarchic and un-American. Although it frequently published photographs of the Depression and government relief programs, Life was not sympathetic to President Roosevelt and the New Deal. Luce was a staunch Republican, and Life, like other Time Inc. magazines, routinely criticized the administration.[36]

Although Life's conservative editorial position addressed the divisions among classes, the photographs' reliance on individual fami-

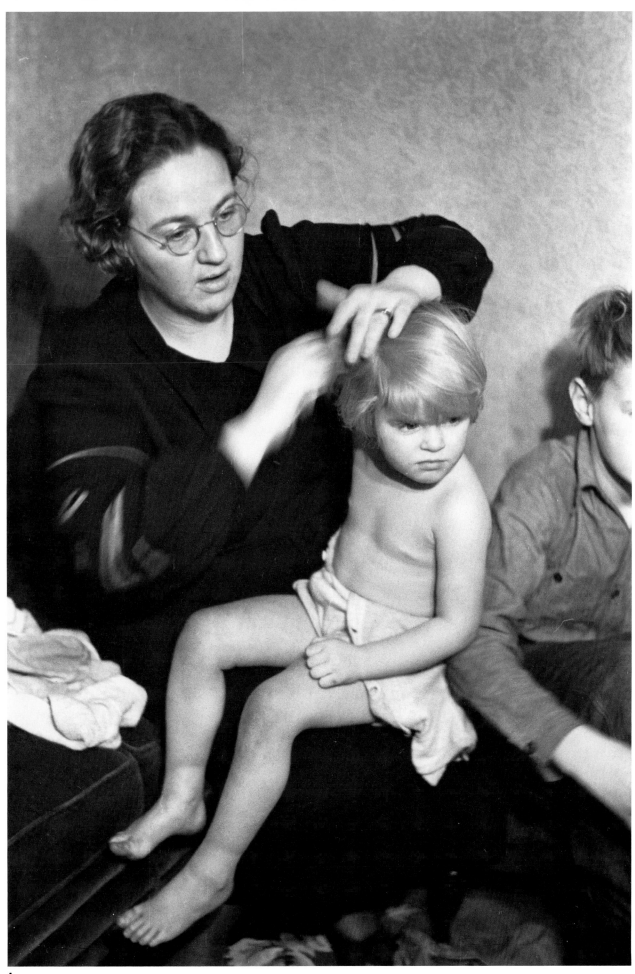

lies as metonyms for social problems often resulted in ambiguous or contradictory messages. In the 1930s, photographs portrayed families in trouble (specifically working-class families and poor families on relief) as a means of visualizing social problems foreign to its middle-class readers. Cultural clichés shaped representations of poor families into ideologically charged messages about social and political issues. Sometimes these portraits fostered empathy by aligning the representative families with values familiar to middle-class readers; other times, as in the case of the Simons, the intimacy of the photographs competes with the text that marks the father's absence. Whether sympathetic or critical, *Life* used family images to represent class, although not racial, differences. Here, as elsewhere in the 1930s, *Life* focused primarily on European immigrants as laborers in a discourse notable for the absence of pictures of Native American, Latino, Asian American, or African American workers. In prewar photographs that turned to the family to represent social conditions, *Life* typically used the camera as a class tool enabling middle-class audiences to gaze at the family in crisis. During the war, however, *Life* increasingly turned its cameras toward the middle-class, making it the subject of the camera's gaze. Chapter 3 explores the shift toward portraits of bourgeois life and its consequences for postwar domestic and national ideologies.

When *Life* began publishing, photography's legal status and mimetic appeal endowed the magazine's photographic claims of veracity with an important degree of credibility. In this way, documentary and social-reform photography as well as news media significantly influenced photojournalism. Equally important, photography's affective appeal, which these earlier traditions also explored, became an integral part of photojournalism. *Life* took the photographic language of documentary and refined it into a more commercial language of photojournalism, in which advertising and editorial content complemented each other. As a result, photohistorians have often dismissed photojournalism as a commercial, and, therefore, debased version of documentary.[37] To distinguish between *Life* and documentary photography on the basis of commercial considerations, however, underestimates the similarities in these two projects' ideological orientations. Consider, for example, the FSA photography file. The FSA's best known images are of migrant workers and sharecroppers living in destitute conditions. Equally important, however, were idealized portraits of small-town America. FSA photographer Russell Lee's series "Pie Town" included images of pioneer farmers and community sings that reinforced ideals of small-town America. Evoking cultural myths about the United States, such photographs legitimated New Deal projects by visualizing a traditional society. In fact, *Life* photographers learned a great deal about visually representing cultural values from documentary photography. When Lee's colleague Arthur Rothstein set out to depict small-town America in "Saturday Night, Main Street, Iowa Falls, Iowa," he showed groups of families and friends standing outside a movie theater.[38] Whether or not Frank Scherschel, the photographer for the "U.S. Normalcy" photo-essay, knew Rothstein's picture, the similarities in content and composition with his photograph of the movie theater indicate the prevalence of this iconography to signify leisure, entertainment, social stability, and, ultimately, normality. Despite overt political differences between the more conservative magazine and social-reform practices, photographers influenced by broad cultural currents employed similar strategies to record their social worlds.

Life's photojournalism, however, can be distinguished from documentary and other traditions by the representational strategies the magazine developed amid changing social and political conditions. These strategies include the narrative form of the photo-essay, the integration of photo-essays and advertisements into a commodity package, and finally, the specific focus on middle-class culture. A definition of photojournalism, then, begins with an analysis of institutional frameworks, social conditions, and consumption patterns of American society at mid-century.

Photojournalism in an Advertising-Driven Medium

The first issue of *Life* was an immediate success. All 250,000 newsstand copies sold out

the first day, and within three months the magazine was selling a million copies weekly. But the really dramatic circulation statistics came in the postwar years. Circulation rose steadily from 1946 to 1956 when it reached its peak with 5.8 million subscribers.[39] The combination of the economic boom and better educated consumers who had more leisure time resulted in substantial growth for magazines after the war, as evidenced by the near doubling of their advertising revenues between 1946 and 1955.[40] Although *Life*'s circulation statistics were impressive, production costs were high, and subscription and newsstand sales did not entirely cover costs, much less contribute to profits. *Life* did benefit from being part of a multimagazine group that arranged advantageous paper purchases and printing contracts for all its publications as well as providing greater leverage with national distributors. In addition, Time Inc. often concentrated subscription activities and even at times combined editorial and research activities.[41] Throughout its existence, *Life*'s publishers struggled between high production costs and the desire to keep subscription and newsstand prices low. Since subscriptions paid only for the cost of paper and printing, the magazine relied heavily on advertising revenues for profits. *Life*'s dependence on advertisers followed a trend begun in the nineteenth century when national advertisers first found an outlet for selling new consumer products in the national magazines.[42]

In 1936, Luce wrote a proposal for advertisers in which he stated that "pictures are faster than words . . . in advertising, pictures hurry where text creeps. Pictures invite a look, where long texts repel. Pictures dramatize where text narrates and describes. Pictures sell."[43] This type of sales pitch proved successful, and *Life* acquired more than three hundred advertisers before the publication of the first issue, selling over $1 million worth of space.[44] Throughout the postwar decades, *Life* obtained a major share of magazine advertising dollars, reaching its peak in 1956. In that year, the magazine carried 4,655 pages of ads yielding $137.5 million revenue on an average of 91 advertising pages per issue.[45]

Life was popular with advertisers for several reasons. First and foremost, as the most successful general magazine in the country, *Life* commanded a readership in the 1940s and 1950s of more than five million readers; this was consistently higher than its nearest competitors, *Saturday Evening Post*, *Colliers*, and *Look*. In addition, *Life*'s page size was slightly larger (10½ by 14 inches) than both the *Saturday Evening Post*'s and *Vogue*'s so that it could accommodate advertising plates used in these magazines.[46] Moreover, many advertisements used photographs that were hard to distinguish from editorial content. For instance, in the news section in which the "U.S. Normalcy" article appeared, a testimonial ad for Ponds cream uses a photo-essay layout. Below a large headline, a photograph shows a close-up of a woman's face. Alongside the photograph, the ad copy identifies

Christina Muir Newberry II, who is engaged to be married. Below the headline and the picture of Newberry, other photographs develop the narrative about her "real life" by showing the engagement ring, Newberry doing volunteer work, and a jar of Ponds. Needless to say, advertisers liked the strategy of emulating photo-essays and competing for audiences' attention by creating designs that blurred the line between editorial content and ads, turning the product into a type of news that gained legitimacy by visual association.

In the postwar period, the consumer products industry depended on the mass media to publicize products and, more important, to promote consumption ideologies that encouraged audiences to abandon ideals of thrift and spend more on consumer goods. Indeed, the advertisements figure in the presentation of photojournalism since reading is not a discrete act but involves interaction with the entire magazine. Although *Life* moved other sections (e.g., the table of contents) during its history, from ten to twenty pages of ads always preceded the first news story, requiring readers to search past them to find the articles. Placement and content of ads and stories, therefore, reinforced consumption and domestic ideologies. John Fiske cautions, however, that the relationship between ads and text is not causal or logical. Instead, the connections "are devolved to the viewer where their associative nature will allow them to be made subconsciously."[47] In other words, editors did not plan layouts that matched specific ads with particular photo-essays, but the proximity of advertisements nonetheless influenced the reception of editorial material.

Ads in *Life* created an image of a middle-class world of affluence and domesticity in which conflicts center around choices among consumer products. In the first section of the December 3, 1945 issue, an ad for the National Life Insurance Company promotes a new policy by which consumers could use equity like refrigerators to secure loans when buying a house. The drawing depicts a suburban street with a picket fence in front of a refrigerator instead of a house. The refrigerator's door stands open to reveal goods inside, visually tying consumer products to the ideal of the home. This ad assumes an affluent audience for it speaks exclusively to readers who have the resources to secure loans to buy suburban homes. Advertisers also took advantage of patriotic sentiments still high in December 1945. An ad for Pacific Worsteds Woolens shows a man in a military uniform stretched out in an armchair next to a Christmas tree. A woman, presumably his wife, kneels beside the tree. Rather than promote a specific product, the ad copy welcomes returning servicemen home, thereby reinforcing assumptions that home for them means a wife and Christmas tree. These ads demonstrate some of the ways in which the language of advertising in *Life* prepared readers for the ideological significance of news stories whose narrative solutions often advocated consumption.

News stories in turn facilitated a favorable reception of the advertisements.[48] In *Life*'s 1945 story of postwar readjustment, for instance, the picture of a soldier returning home surrounded by friends and family echoes the composition of several ads that depict soldiers with their families, like the one for Pacific Worsteds Woolens. Equally important, the photo-essay presents a view of the world supportive of consumption ideology. Under a headline entitled "American Way of Life: The People of Indianapolis Are Absorbed in Pleasant Trivia," the text provides statistics on increased consumer activities as evidence of Americans' return to "normalcy." At the same time, photographs of buyers at a fashion show and people going to the movies provide "evidence" of this prosperity.

The "U.S. Normalcy" photo-essay also documents consumption through representative individuals whose success and ownership of products signify American economic prosperity. In a two-page spread on businessman Wallace O. Lee, a quarter-page photograph shows Lee seated behind a desk, wearing a suit and talking on the telephone. Piles of papers stacked on his desk indicate he is a busy man, while pictures of his family on a table behind him call attention to his domestic values. *Life* further visualizes Lee's success in a series of small pictures that depicts him driving from his "elaborate" home past buildings that he owns to his office. These photographs and the accompanying text display a busy, successful man "absorbed in his family, his job and his community." A photograph of Lee driving his daughter to school, like a preceding advertisement for Mercury automobiles of a family in a car, displays class status and paternal relations in association with consumer goods. The layout unites leisure, consumption, and economic success in this vision of postwar prosperity. Photoessays like this one support advertisements by presenting the United States as a nation of affluent middle-class Americans with shared social values.

The forms of address in both advertising and news reports in *Life* reveal assumptions about the nature of its audience, assumptions based on the results of demographic and marketing surveys *Life* sponsored to determine the composition and consumption habits of its readership. A study done in 1957 described *Life*'s readers as having high education and income levels, coming primarily from professional and managerial occupations, and being evenly distributed between men and women. Of all households reached by six average issues of *Life*, 61 percent accounted for the purchase of 69 percent of all goods and services in that year, clearly demonstrating the readers' economic power.[49] Not only was *Life* responding to its perceived audience, it was also courting specific demographic groups.

Throughout the period *Life* sponsored numerous demographic studies to attract advertisers. Obviously, class is a crucial category in these marketing surveys because advertisers wanted to know the economic status of their audience. Other questions reveal assumptions about race and gender that indicate ideological biases common to media presumptions about the public during this period. The 1957 study, for instance, assumes that readers maintain conventional gender roles by directing questions about washing machines and refrigerators to women while asking men about car purchases. This survey does not include race as a category, probably because marketing researchers and advertisers did not consider Latinos and other ethnic groups part of the consumer market. Through the asked and unasked questions, this study imagines *Life*'s readers as white, middle-class people who conform to dominant gender roles.

Middle-class Americans interested in visual news media turned in great numbers to *Life* after the war, in part because the magazine had developed a reputation for aggressive reporting techniques. The magazine had a substantial budget for news gathering and a large well-paid staff. In the 1950s, *Life*'s managing editor had an editorial budget of about $10 million a year, double that of the *Saturday Evening Post* and quadruple that of *Look*.[50] Famous photographers worked for *Life* because it provided them with economic resources as well as access to an enormous audience. The magazine's reputation often enabled photographers to obtain exclusive stories, which in turn enhanced its prestige. *Life* went after the fast-breaking news around the world, frequently at enormous expense from copy deadline extensions, staff overtime, and printing and distribution cost overruns.

The magazine's commitment to "pocketbook journalism" also included the purchase of exclusives like Winston Churchill's memoirs and a 1959 article on the Mercury astronauts.[51]

In the 1930s, Luce was a force in establishing the editorial direction of the magazine. His control over hiring the senior editorial staff, and his participation in editorial decisions, gave him considerable power. With the expansion and success of Time Inc. in the postwar years, however, Luce was less involved in the daily running of the magazine. Nonetheless, he monitored the product and kept abreast of staff and editorial changes, personally editing an issue of each of Time Inc.'s publications every year.[52]

Luce promoted attitudes and desires that clearly appealed to the middle-class audience of his highly successful magazine. In 1948, he wrote in a memorandum to *Life*'s editorial staff:

> Life as it is lived in America today is a strange and wonderful tension between the particular problems of little people (all of us and our families) and the surge of great "historic forces." . . . If we can bring together in one magazine a feeling for all the little "human" problems and all the little episodes of human life together with an awareness and intelligent disclosure of the "great historic" forces—that surely will be a very great achievement.[53]

Luce's description of the little people as "all of us and our families" demonstrates the importance of domesticity in his conception of *Life*'s audience. The publisher spoke most directly to *Life*'s readers through the editorials he occasionally wrote for the magazine. In the twentieth-anniversary issue, the editors quoted Luce as saying, "We hope to cover every important subject—science and medicine, war and peace, business and politics. But our biggest assignment is to cover the human family and especially the American people."[54] As with the internal memo quoted above, Luce positions the family squarely at the center of *Life*'s project. Here, he assumes the family to be unified and representable in unproblematic terms.

Like Luce, *Life*'s staff self-consciously thought and wrote about the magazine in frequent memos evaluating the product. The editors conceived of *Life* as a magazine directed at midwestern, middle-class, white Americans who held conventional ideas about domestic roles and had political expectations about the United States' hegemonic power in the postwar world.[55] Edward Thompson, *Life*'s managing editor during the peak years of success, for instance, described the magazine itself in the language of domesticity when he wrote "*Life*, to me, is a friendly neighbor, almost one of the family."[56]

Editors often provided photographers on assignment with detailed shooting scripts based on extensive research. These scripts included editors' objectives for the story and requests for certain types of shots.[57] Such planning and preparation raise the question of the level of conscious intent on the part of *Life* personnel to create a particular vision of American society. How, and to what extent, did a self-conscious articulation of *Life*'s purpose translate into the photo-essays? *Life* photographers typically overshot on assignment, enabling editors to choose the proper pictorial expression or theme. Editors on average chose approximately ten thousand photographs from the five hundred thousand pictures they looked at each year.[58] Even in the absence of shooting scripts, photographers did not shoot randomly. Deadlines and editors' expectations, as well as competition among photographers to get published, influenced the types of pictures taken. Staff photographers came to know which photographs pleased editors. Tight deadlines meant also that photographers typically shot film in regularized ways so editors could depend on certain kinds of images.[59] In addition, photographers had little to do with the writing and layout of the photo-essays. Tensions periodically arose when photographers became frustrated by this exclusion or by the struggle to obtain bylines.[60]

Despite specific direction, however, the vision of Luce and his editors did not necessarily translate into ideological instructions to photographers. Objectivity was a powerful ideology that operated equally on photographers and editors, many of whom believed in the capacity of photographs to reproduce facts transparently. Staff photographer Carl Mydans, for instance, wrote that "we had an insatiable drive to search out every fact of American life, photograph it and hold it up proudly, like a mirror, to a pleased and astonished readership."[61] Given the popularity and success of *Life*, editors' and photographers' unconscious participation in their culture clearly worked in conjunction with a more conscious recognition of their audiences' interests and concerns. Photographers and editors knew how to manipulate lighting, camera angles, and layouts to create a sympathetic or unpleasant portrait. Yet, it is not always clear whether photographers like Nina Leen or Mydans acknowledged the association, for instance, between their pictures of mothers holding babies and the Western cultural tradition of the Madonna and child. Probably some did and some did not. What is interesting is how cultural traditions are used, and reused, and how they become ideologically significant at a given moment. In addition, in *Life*, as in other mass media, an institutional structure meant that authorship was a multifaceted rather than individual endeavor. *Life* was a vast organization with as many as six issues in production at the same time and with people working at differentiated tasks. Although *Life* touted the artistry of individual photographers like Eisenstaedt and Bourke-White, other photographers did not have bylines or input on layouts. Likewise, writers were not always credited. Some might say the editors were the authors since they had final control, but they did not take the pictures or interview the families. Moreover, the published texts did not identify specific editors with particular photo-essays. Few would credit the

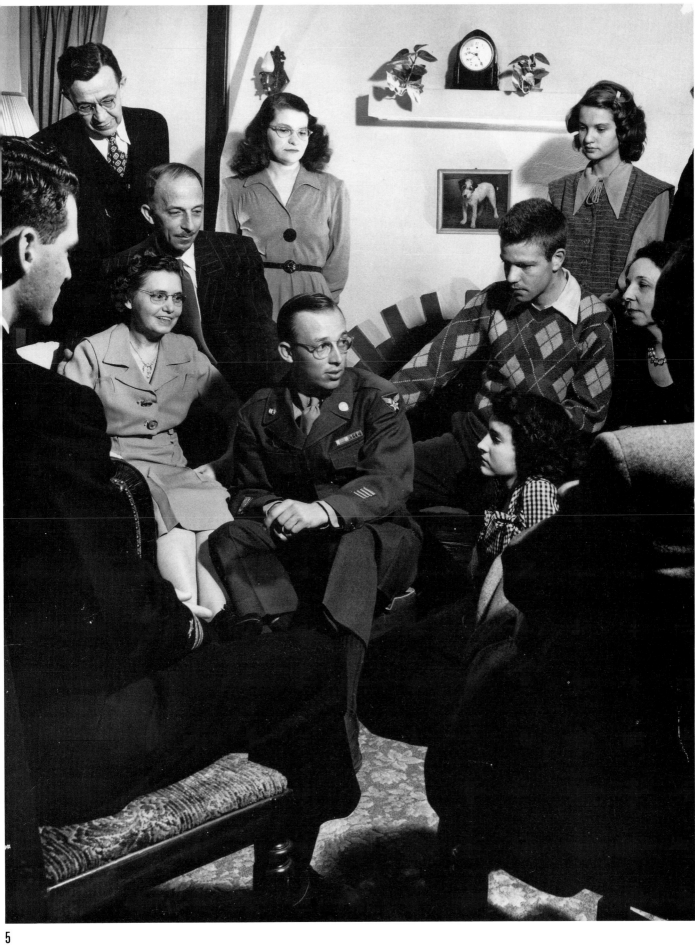

tions deny the complexities of the unemployment problems associated with reconversion. The description of the woman's job aspirations, for instance, obscures the complexities of women's postwar employment history.[72] Although photographs facilitate recognition of social problems by showing "real" people's experiences, the text ignores analyses of the broader structural issues underlying these conditions.

The example above demonstrates that although the photographs themselves construct the narrative, the captions and texts anchor specific readings of photographs even as they offer seemingly natural confirmation of the photographs' veracity. A picture of a closed Curtiss-Wright plant visualizes the problems of unemployment. The text, however, explains that as "a city of diversified industries, Indianapolis should be able to reconvert very successfully." Elsewhere, the essay repeats this assertion about reconversion, thereby directing the meaning of the photograph toward an optimistic reading of the future. Although pictures are the central focus of the essays, text and layout play a crucial role in anchoring the narrative message.[73]

Consider, for instance, the article's references to the labor disputes that produced the largest strike wave in United States history.[74] The small pictures of unemployed persons are located above the photograph of the soldier's reunion with his family. Although the placement could be read as a warning about veterans' employment prospects, the larger image of the soldier and family visually insists on an implied national stability. Moreover, by presenting Indianapolis as quintessentially American, and threats of instability as "things happening in the world outside Indianapolis," the narrative suggests that other cities like Detroit and Cleveland with strikers, blacks, and immigrants are outside or "un-American." The only people of color depicted in the essay are in the small pictures of the Detroit strikers and Asian refugees. The essay further limits the threat of instability by characterizing the unemployed as prosperous individuals who choose to wait for a "good" job. Although the photo-essay discusses social conflicts, textual strategies work to contain the threat of dissent within the wider framework of a stable society.

As a story, however, the photo-essay really offers only fragments of a narrative. This fragmentation can be compared to the cinematic narrative that is predicated not on long, unified scenes but on short takes that jump from shot to shot. The concept of suture explains how the viewer negotiates this fragmentation. Seamless editing and point of view are suturing devices that encourage the viewer to accept the transparency of the film. These devices, as Kaja Silverman explains, persuade viewers to recognize the filmic world as a familiar one in order to encourage identification with the representation.[75] Although discussed primarily in cinema studies where theoreticians have long been interested in how the viewer identifies with the classic narrative film, suture can be usefully applied to *Life*'s photo-essays. Photojournalism similarly denies the constructed nature of the medium and facilitates identification with its ideological orientation. The realism of the photographs overpowers obvious editorial mediations. Pictures of businessmen at work and teenagers cheering at a football game appear as verifications of the text's statements about Americans returning to "normal" activities. Moreover, relying on the viewer's anticipation, the narrative contrasts conflict and domestic stability throughout the essay to move the action forward. Through suturing devices such as realistic photographs and textual connections among topics, the narrative directs the viewer's attention and desire beyond the limits of individual photographs to produce a unified statement.

Narrative works through suture to position the viewer in the same discursive space as the content. This gives the reader the illusion of a stable and continuous identity within the ideal world of "normalcy" represented by the photo-essay. The comfort of narrative is the comfort of this stable identity. The prevalent use of the third-person plural pronoun further promotes a shared social world. "They were becoming absorbed again in familiar scenes, familiar objects, familiar emotions." Such inclusive language presumes a collective society that lacks diversity. Realistic photographs further facilitate an emotional connection whereby readers can recognize themselves in that familiar world. A 1945 *Life* reader of the Indianapolis essay could identify with the photograph of the welcome-home party for the World War II veteran because the domestic iconography appears deeply familiar. As one editor noted, "In the hands of a perceptive photographer, the camera brings you close to people in the news and makes you feel you really know them."[76] Easily recognizable images of home life reassure the reader that despite the tumultuous outside world, Americans at home are safe and happy. The soldier's glance to his left, as if he were unaware of the camera while he talks to someone, makes the photograph appear spontaneous. *Life* frequently used this device, in which subjects seem to ignore the intrusive cameras and hot lights in their homes, to capture on film realistic scenes of individuals engaged in daily activities. Another strategy at work here represents a departure from the often intrusive gaze of earlier documentary photographers like Riis. In this picture, the photographer occupies a position within the family circle immediately to the right of a guest who appears in half-profile with his back to the camera. In effect, *Life* has arranged this domestic celebration and then accepted an invitation to mingle with the family.

Letters to the editors further supported the narrative construction of community. In general, the letters create an impression of an audience of like-minded people. Frequently, the writers, identified by name and city of residence, explain how they felt emotionally after reading an article, or how they identified with the subject of the essay because of similar experiences. For instance, in response to the "U.S. Normalcy" article, one reader comments, "It took my mind off war and strife for a little while at least!" Such responses, because they accept the accuracy of the depiction, validate claims of realism as well as the representative status of the ordinary people in the news article. *Life* also routinely published letters that criticized the magazine's stories. These letters ensured an illusion of objectivity by demonstrating the magazine's fair-minded presentation of "all sides."

We need to be cautious, however, about drawing conclusions about audiences from the letters because of the editors' power of selection. These letters were undoubtedly written by actual readers, but *Life*'s closed-door policy prohibits access to their archives and prevented me from determining how representative the published letters were. They do indicate, however, a range of reading practices. Letter writers agreed or disagreed with the content of articles, paying most attention to factual errors or, less often, the appropriateness of certain coverage. Rarely, however, did they critique the magazine's representational strategies; instead, they repeatedly credited photographs with the power to capture reality. For instance, *Life* published four letters responding to the article on Indianapolis. Two praised the article's depiction of Americans and their kindness; the other two praised it for presenting Indianapolis as a "stuffy, stodgy and uninteresting" city. Fundamentally disagreeing about whether midwestern cities

are likable, the two camps congratulated the magazine on its accurate reporting. An editorial note explains that the *Indianapolis News* reproved *Life* for its depiction of the city as parochial and uninvolved with the outside world. Reprinted in the service of fairness, the comment seems overly defensive in contrast to the letter writers, who thus appear to validate *Life*'s representation.[77]

Life's strategies for presenting the news constitute a vocabulary of visual and textual conventions that attempted to package social tensions within an ideal portrait of American society. Devices such as narrative, choice of pronouns, and photographic realism encouraged readers to identify with this reassuring portrait. Pictures spoke to *Life*'s readers by appealing to their emotional needs, desires, or interests. In the process, however, these images privileged specific social attitudes and ideological beliefs. Through this examination of *Life*'s photojournalistic vocabulary, it becomes clear that the essay's definition of "normalcy" was limited.

The "U.S. Normalcy" essay showcases middle-class families involved in their communities, active in school affairs, and happy in their domestic settings. Throughout the postwar period, *Life* photo-essays presented the family as an apolitical terrain, relying on domestic imagery to promote a selective portrait of the public world of postwar America. Instead of suggesting that Americans were turning away from their problems by focusing on trivial matters, these photo-essays presented the seemingly trivial or private sphere of consumption and the home as sites in which to solve these problems. By repeating images of domesticity and consumption in numerous news articles, *Life* presented a stream of images so deeply familiar that they appear natural. Myth, to refer to Barthes once again, gives historical relations like the nuclear family a natural justification by making them appear universal. In the "U.S. Normalcy" article, large photographs present families as images of social accord that visually and thus ideologically overwhelm the pictures of strikes and international upheaval. Hence, the format of the photo-essay itself legitimated economic and political objectives of readjustment through pictures of middle-class families.

If *Life*'s objective was to legitimate consumer capitalism by representing a healthy and successful nation, then why did it show the problems of postwar society at all? This 1945 essay, so typical of *Life*'s postwar photojournalism, raises questions about the function of the news media and their relationship to the state. Dependent on realism, *Life* aimed to represent the whole of society, including its contradictions. It generated a critical dialogue whose consequence was to expose and articulate social tensions. To represent society, news narratives introduced problems like divorce and unemployment that revealed social instabilities seemingly at odds with *Life*'s portrait of America. The photograph of the closed industrial plant, for instance, surely provoked complex responses from readers who had so recently experienced the Depression. Indeed, this picture must have resonated with many Americans' fears in 1945 of a recession following the war. Similarly, the picture of workers threatening the camera complicates Luce's aim to turn the poor into a spectacle. Although *Life* tried to direct positive readings through captions promising a brighter future, its meanings are not predictable. *Life* was not a monolithic ideological entity but instead a complex, frequently contradictory project in which competing messages coexisted.

Despite *Life*'s dominant narrative about a postwar world capable of coping with social problems, dialogic forces both within the texts and in context with other discourses always countered this drive toward a single voice. Connotation, the meanings produced by cultural codes, originates in a wide variety of textual practices that extend beyond the specific photograph or text. Moreover, as Mikhail Bakhtin insists, these dialogic interactions are always historically determined because it is only in the act of reading that texts become meaningful.[78] Thus, *Life*'s domestic portraits must be read in the context of a postwar world struggling with international conflicts, atomic power, and challenges to dominant social, racial, and gender roles. The following chapters examine how ideology does its work through representation. What were the cultural and social codes circulating in postwar America that *Life* used to represent this world?

And what were the breaks, silences, and fis-
sures that revealed social conflicts or opened
up alternative spaces? Representation is a
political terrain of struggle because the stakes
in popular culture are the stakes of cultural
legitimation. In politically significant ways,
then, many Americans in the postwar period
developed perceptions of themselves and their
worlds through their encounters with *Life*.

CHAPTER 3

"THE KIND OF PEOPLE WHO MAKE GOOD AMERICANS"
Nationalism and <u>LIFE</u>'s Family Ideal

In fact, within the very narrow range of family products, more than gardening or cake-making . . . photography affirms the continuity and integration of the domestic group, and reaffirms it by giving it expression.

— PIERRE BOURDIEU, *Photography: A Middle-Brow Art*, 1990

Nation-ness is assimilated to skin-colour, gender, parentage and birth-era—all those things one can not help. And in those "natural ties" one senses what one might call "the beauty of the gemeinschaft." To put it another way, precisely because such ties are not chosen, they have about them a halo of disinterestedness.

— BENEDICT ANDERSON, *Imagined Communities*, 1991

*L*ife's January 5, 1953, cover photograph (*illustration 6*) depicts a woman kneeling with her arms around two blond girls who are leaning on a window sill. Behind them, a man in a business suit holds a toddler seated on the crosspiece of the window frame. Looking out of a large window, this neatly groomed white family smiles at the camera. The frame connotes a domestic setting, yet the building is clearly unfinished without any glass in the frame. By itself, this picture does not provide information about the specific type of house, but read along-side *Life*'s numerous photographs of suburbia in stories about news events, architectural designs, and the Modern Living section of the magazine, the frame easily suggests a middle-class domicile. Underneath the window frame, the caption states: "Family Buys 'Best $15,000 House.'" The cost of the house confirms a reading of the family as middle class, and the unfinished building suggests progress, a future that appears bright for this family. On a yellow banner cutting diagonally across the page, the headline connects this vision of familial intimacy to the newsworthy concerns of postwar America as it announces the topic of this special issue: "The American and His Economy."

Domesticity lies at the heart of photographer Nina Leen's portrait of middle-class suburban living, and in that sense it serves as a representative artifact of its time. In the postwar years, middle-class Americans increasingly turned toward the privatized world of home and children. Direct federal spending on highway construction and innovative home loan and taxation policies supported business efforts to create unprecedented opportunities for these Americans to inhabit single-family, detached suburban houses. At the same time, an ascendant ideology of domesticity based on strictly divided gender roles pervaded Ameri-

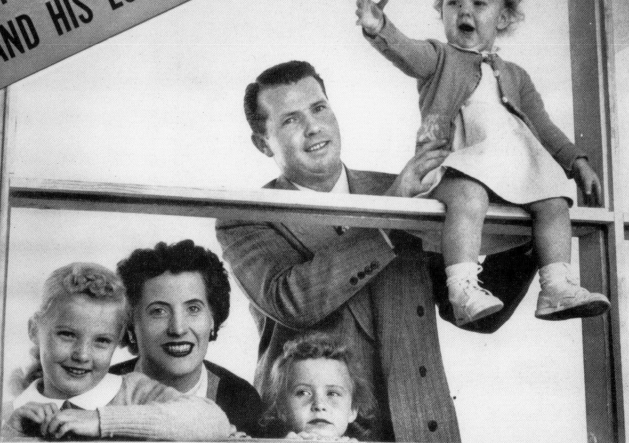

LIFE

SPECIAL ISSUE

U.S. HOME BUILDERS' BEST BUY—
CHEMICAL AGE—FARM REVOLUTION—
WHAT'S AHEAD IN BUSINESS, JOBS

THE AMERICAN AND HIS ECONOMY

FAMILY BUYS 'BEST $15,000 HOUSE'

20 CENTS

JANUARY 5, 1953

REG. U. S. PAT. OFF.

6

can life, involving such areas as hiring decisions in industry and child-rearing practices. These policies and ideals reshaped the contours of domestic life, encouraging a privatism isolated from broader community activities. Appropriately enough, the cover photograph for "The American and His Economy" underscores that turn to privatization with a visual representation containing no references to the outside world. Moreover, the composition repeats the gender divisions basic to postwar domestic ideology through the man standing above his kneeling wife and children. *Life* makes these connections between middle-class status and patriarchy explicit in the title that labels the economy "his"; her role apparently is only one of support. News images like the one of this family privileged heterosexist ideals of domesticity through photographic realism, visually inscribing culturally assigned gender roles. The woman's supportive embrace encodes her maternal responsibilities; the man's looming protectiveness identifies him as the patriarchal breadwinner. In turning the camera's gaze to the family to represent the American economy, *Life* visualizes postwar prosperity as a white, middle-class familial experience.

This celebratory cover photograph, so reminiscent of advertisements, creates a visual mystery through the unfinished building that encourages the reader to turn to the interior essay to solve. The photograph introduces a story titled "$15,000 'Trade Secrets' House," about a collaborative project in which the building industry pooled its resources to produce a design for a "good looking, skillfully engineered $15,000 house." The article shows color plates of model homes, design plans, and the various stages of building this suburban three-bedroom house. Although they represented an ideal, labeled as such by the generic "The American," the people who posed for this picture were not actors. *Life* presents Dale and Gladys Welling, the "real" family who recently bought one of these dream houses, as evidence of actual families living the American Dream. In this way, the magazine legitimizes its association of the American economy with a particular social group by individualizing the representation.

Despite the economic prosperity celebrated in this portrait, the 1940s and 1950s were a time of instability and unease. A severe housing shortage, labor unrest, McCarthyism, and the Korean War confronted postwar Americans. In addition, major technological developments in transportation and communications systems altered Americans' perceptions of themselves and their worlds. People were on the move, migrating from east to west, south to north, rural to urban, and urban to suburban. Locating "The American" in a suburban home visually narrates a pattern of migration out of urban centers experienced by many white Americans after the war. During the 1950s, 64 percent of the nation's population growth occurred in the suburbs. As

Steven Mintz and Susan Kellogg write, "Suburbanization reinforced the family orientation of postwar society."[1]

Migration, of course, took on different meanings for people of color moving from rural poverty into urban slums than for the seven million white Americans moving from inner cities to the outlying suburbs. Between 1950 and 1970, five million African Americans, largely from the South, moved into central cities.[2] In addition, millions of immigrants facing poverty and unemployment at home came to the United States during this period, often through recruitment programs designed to supply cheap labor for agriculture and other industries. For instance, more than four million Mexican workers immigrated through the *Braceros* program. New arrivals to urban areas frequently confronted racial discrimination, low wages, a lack of health care, and other social dislocations.[3] The extremely varied consequences of mobility during the postwar years created upheavals in people's economic, political, and social lives, further contributing to the anxieties and tensions of the period. The special issue addresses white mobility but ignores this other story of migration. By visually excluding people of color who were physically barred from moving into the suburbs, the issue reproduces a discourse of racism. Moreover, when *Life* depicted the city, it was portrayed either as a place of danger and crime, or as a boomtown that exemplified economic prosperity. Rarely did the magazine show families living in cities, except if they were impoverished or in crisis. In the special issue, the only pictures of cities depict urban skylines without people.

In pictures like "The American and His Economy," *Life*'s figuration of the family, including the absences, reinforced racial, class, and gender differences that in turn had profound consequences for the magazine's representation of the nation. David Halberstam argues that *Time* was the most political magazine of the Luce publishing empire. "*Life* was different, less political, more open; it was more dependent upon pictures and thus more tied to events themselves rather than to interpretation of events. . . . *Life*, by its dependence upon photography, made itself closer to the human heartbeat."[4] Halberstam narrowly conceptualizes political representation in terms that retain a faith in photographs' ability to represent events transparently, events that he conceives as sharing a single heartbeat. But photographs are mediated signs that contain politically significant messages. This is especially true because politics involves more than battles to control the government; it is also the exercise of power in symbolic and practical activities of everyday life. As John Hartley and Martin Montgomery note, "The news is active in the *politics* of sense-making, even when the stories concern matters not usually understood as political."[5] In structuring ways of understanding the world, *Life*'s family portraits played an important political role in establishing, promoting, and reproducing hegemonic social relations.

In the postwar years, *Life* solidified a photo-journalistic formula that relied on images of the middle-class family to represent a national culture. Nationalism, a powerful but contradictory cultural force that shapes social identities, can construct a popular or democratic arena of shared interests and objectives. The concept of nation, however, typically relies on historically determined geographical, cultural, and conceptual distinctions. These distinctions too often are based on exclusionary assumptions of ethnic or racial superiority.[6] In the service of the nation-state, nationalism can offer "a privileged narrative perspective on the nation ('the people') and thus justifies its own capacity to narrate its story."[7] This does not mean that nationalism is a form of false consciousness. Instead, as Benedict Anderson argues, "Communities are to be distinguished, not by their falsity/genuineness, but by the style in which they are imagined." Anderson further argues that the nation is imagined because "members of even the smallest nation will never know most of their fellow-members, meet them, or even hear them, yet in the minds of each lives the image of their communion." National ideals may be arbitrary, but their power lies in their appeal to human needs for identity, order, and immortality. In this regard, people imagine the nation as a *community* "because, regardless of the actual inequality and exploitation that may prevail in each, the nation is always conceived as a deep, horizontal comradeship."[8] Moreover, Anderson observes that the nation appears, like the family, as "the domain of disinterested love and solidarity."[9]

I find Anderson's formulation that communities are defined by "the style in which they are imagined" useful for interpreting the power of media like *Life* to envision nationhood. His term "style" refers to representation and, more particularly, to the politics of representations that construct national identity. Examining the origins of nationalism, Anderson argues that the advent of print capitalism, especially the novel and the newspaper, "provided the technical means for 're-presenting' the *kind* of imagined community that is the nation."[10] Through reading, people could "imagine" shared experiences with thousands of other readers they would never meet. Print literacy may have supported the emergence of the concept of nation, but visual mass media have even greater capacities to visualize social norms and differences that form national identities. The mass media have the power to break down geographical and cultural barriers to connect viewers to other individuals who appear to share their concerns. In so doing, as Eric Hobsbawm points out, the mass media have the ability to make "national symbols part of the life of every individual, and thus to break down the divisions between the private and local spheres in which most citizens normally lived, and the public and national one."[11]

Life, for instance, claims a transcendent nationhood by presenting Dale Welling as "The American" who loves his family. Yet, there is nothing disinterested or neutral in this portrait. Closer inspection reveals how racial, class, gender, and sexual differences encoded in photo-essays forge the boundaries of national identity. The concept of imagined communities provides a way of understanding how photojournalism encodes the multiple consciousnesses that coexist and contradict each other, for even as they depend on and reinforce traditions and conventions, photo-essays reveal the tensions and struggles to define the nation. As Stuart Hall points out, the nation is always at stake when culture is invoked because nationalism is one of the identities advanced or displaced in any cultural utterance.[12] In the hegemonic struggle to define and assert a national identity in the postwar years, *Life* vigorously promoted a vision of the American nation through pictures of nuclear families surrounded by consumer products in suburban homes. The association between family and nation formed the justification not only for the Cold War but for social relations in both intimate personal and national public arenas. *Life*'s nonfictional news status, especially its photographs, enhanced the cultural legitimacy of this narrative. In the midst of many social changes in American society, *Life*'s special gift was to make change seem traditional by locating the tensions of an unfamiliar world within the seemingly familiar and nonthreatening orbit of the "happy" nuclear family.

War and Domesticity

Prior to World War II, *Life* relied primarily on representative families in crisis or in need to articulate problems in society, elicit sympathy for state policies, or warn of dangers to the state. In response to the historical imperatives of World War II, *Life*'s news coverage expanded its iconographic reliance on representative families. Similar to the shift in media coverage that occurred during World War I, *Life*'s wartime reporting began to associate the middle-class family with ideals of patriotism and moral obligation.[13] The magazine continued throughout the postwar period to depict social problems through representative families, but beginning in the 1940s, the editors increasingly relied on images of the white, middle-class family to signify national ideals.

Although *Life* began publishing during the economic upheavals of the 1930s, the magazine acquired its impressive national audience during World War II, in large part because of the high-quality and extensive visual record offered to its readers. Many of the great war photographers, including Robert Capa, Carl Mydans, and W. Eugene Smith, published their photographs in the news section. The magazine ran an average of two to three in-depth war stories a week, making itself indispensable with the amount of information, pictures, and diagrams provided to its readers. Although occasionally critical of war production shortages, *Life* supported the Roosevelt administration's war efforts and willingly cooperated with government censorship and propaganda restrictions. Henry Luce wrote President Roosevelt ten days after Pearl Harbor offering *Life*'s services "in the days to come—far beyond strict compliance with whatever rules may be laid down for us by the necessities of war—we can think of no greater happiness than to be of service to any branch of our government and to its armed forces. For the dearest wish of all of us is to tell the story of absolute victory under your leadership."[14] The magazine played an important role in wartime appeals for family sacrifice, patriotism, and support for a variety of federal programs such as rationing, bond sales, and scrap drives.

News stories about military personnel also contributed to the war effort by showing courageous, yet ordinary, men fighting to preserve American values. A November 1942 war report contains a page of photographs of the Allied forces fighting in Africa.[15] On the opposite page, under pictures of men wounded at Guadalcanal, captions identify the soldiers by their home towns, and by the number of Japanese they had killed. The accompanying text states that "in any man's army, they were heroes. . . . Ordinary Americans all, they found all they needed of courage and killing instinct when they needed it most." In turning back to the blurry photographs of the African battles, one could read into them the same masculine courage and military prowess *Life* encourages the reader to perceive in the close-

up shots of the wounded. The Office of War Information (OWI) prohibited the publication of any pictures of American dead until 1943, which reinforced the magazine's visual representation of American military power and masculine strength.[16]

Wartime reporting associated men not only with masculinity but also with domesticity. In this November 1942 story, *Life* printed a letter that the unit commander in action at Guadalcanal wrote to his son before he was killed. The writer combines an explanation of patriotic duty and honor with a longing for his family, expressing his desire through references to such masculine activities as hunting and fishing with his son. Similarly, *Life* often visualized men's military participation through pictures of farewells and reunions between soldiers and their families. The Picture of the Week for November 25, 1940, shows a soldier hugging a small boy in a sailor suit. The father kneels to hug the crying child but holds on to his rifle which stands straight up at his side, framing the left side of the picture. The rifle, a signifier of the military reasons for his departure, acts as visual reassurance that the father is not abandoning his son but leaving to protect him. The child's uniform also envisions male military obligation as an intergenerational commitment to service and patriotic sacrifice. Thus, the picture visualizes the disruption of family life for national duty as understood and accepted by all members of the family. At the same time, the rifle, a crucial element upholding this narrative, also ruptures it by signifying violence. This rupture indicates the shifting terrain of national ideals; even patriotic imagery of the soldier going off to war to defend his family cannot easily secure national ideals.

Anderson states that for most people the nation appears "interestless," which justifies calls for sacrifices, especially in times of war.[17] Discursive strategies, however, based their war appeals as much on domestic concerns as on abstract ideals of democracy or freedom. In a study of World War II pinups, Robert Westbrook argues that government propaganda urged Americans to participate in the war effort for private moral reasons.[18] Because liberalism conceives of the function of the state as protecting citizens from interference from other individuals or states, war signals a failure of the state. Lacking compelling political imperatives for war, the state must turn to private interests in urging men to enlist and risk death. Westbrook argues that pinups encouraged men to participate in order to fulfill private (gendered) obligations to their sisters, wives, or sweethearts. Pinups of Betty Grable and other Hollywood stars both represented women as the bounty for male soldiers and connoted gender expectations of men as moral protectors. These images functioned as surrogate objects of heterosexual desire but also as symbols of the reasons American men were fighting.

Government propaganda and the mass media also turned to the private obligation of domesticity to encourage Americans' partici-pation in the war effort. News stories about weddings and the rising birth rate, along with lonely wives waiting for news of their absent husbands, appeared throughout the war. Representative families functioned to remind readers of their obligations to protect "the American way of life." The July 6, 1942, Independence Day celebration issue, for instance, combines family portraits with more conventional nationalistic symbols in its coverage of the American war effort. A color cover photograph features an American flag and a caption that reads: "United We Stand." The big news story for the week reports on the town of Harrodsburg, Kentucky, which was waiting to hear news about sixty-six soldiers of Company D missing in action on Bataan.[19] The text quotes the national anthem and patriotic slogans to urge Americans to "fight through every hardship to preserve our freedom," while photographs visualize the United States as a small town, not as an urban industrialized society. Pictures of the July 4 celebrations include a parade with home guardsmen, the Harrodsburg belles, and a church service in which parishioners pray for the soldiers. This portrait of a patriotic Southern community and the four pages of pictures of soldiers with their parents or wives feature only white people. In general, the magazine's war coverage included no news stories on soldiers or their families from other social groups. *Life* depicts community and family as signifiers of patriotic values through signs that combine dominant race and gender ideals. In the Harrodsburg article, the text quotes from several soldiers' letters addressed to their mothers telling them not to worry. Mothers carry the emotional weight of concern while masculinity is associated with protection of the family and the nation. In addition, cultural ideals also position mothers as the ones responsible for instructing their sons in moral obligations. The concluding full-page photograph reinforces the varied meanings of family as the moral obligation for war seen throughout the July 6, 1942, photo-essay. A close-up photograph shows a smiling three-year-old white girl holding a child's watering can and standing in a light-dappled garden (*illustration 7*). This picture of the daughter of the commander of Harrodsburg's Company D enhances the sentimentality of the story by focusing on the innocence of childhood to represent the moral obligation that sent her father and all the other fathers to war.

Throughout the war, advertisements reiterated the private obligation of domesticity seen in the news stories.[20] A 1943 ad for Oneida Community Silverware shows a man in uniform marrying a blond bride. The ad's vision of femininity encodes racial and heterosexual ideals in the stereotypical depiction of a beautiful white woman dressed in a conventional wedding gown. The headline emphasizes the white woman's role as object of desire, literally the prize for participation in war, by noting, "These are the things we are fighting for . . . the right to love and marry and rear children in security and peace."[21] This patriotic address

uses the first person plural, "we," to connote a community of both fighters and readers based on imagined collective goals and aspirations. These goals link domesticity to consumption, ignoring other reasons for engagement in war. Ads like this one connected women's roles, as both objects of desire and consumers, to patriotism, thus linking the female body to national objectives.

Like representations of families that provided the reasons for men to go to war, depictions of the home front similarly relied on domestic ideals. On September 25, 1944, *Life* published a special issue titled "A Letter from Home," which provided soldiers overseas with a portrait of the nation. Extra copies were sent free of charge to the troops. Of the six published letters to the editor, all praising the issue, four were clearly from military personnel. Their comments lend credibility to the magazine's authority through comments such as: "You really told us about home and the good old U.S.A." or "You have given 11,600,000 of us 'our America' past, present and future in this issue. It leaves no doubt that we certainly have something worth our sacrifices."[22] The special issue's depiction of "our America" includes expensive color photographs of pastoral harvests, cows grazing, and three boys in overalls walking down a country lane. Merging cultural signs, a color photograph of a tree-lined suburban street that looks like the country-lane picture associates suburbia with the rural idyll portrayed in the color photograph. At the same time, black-

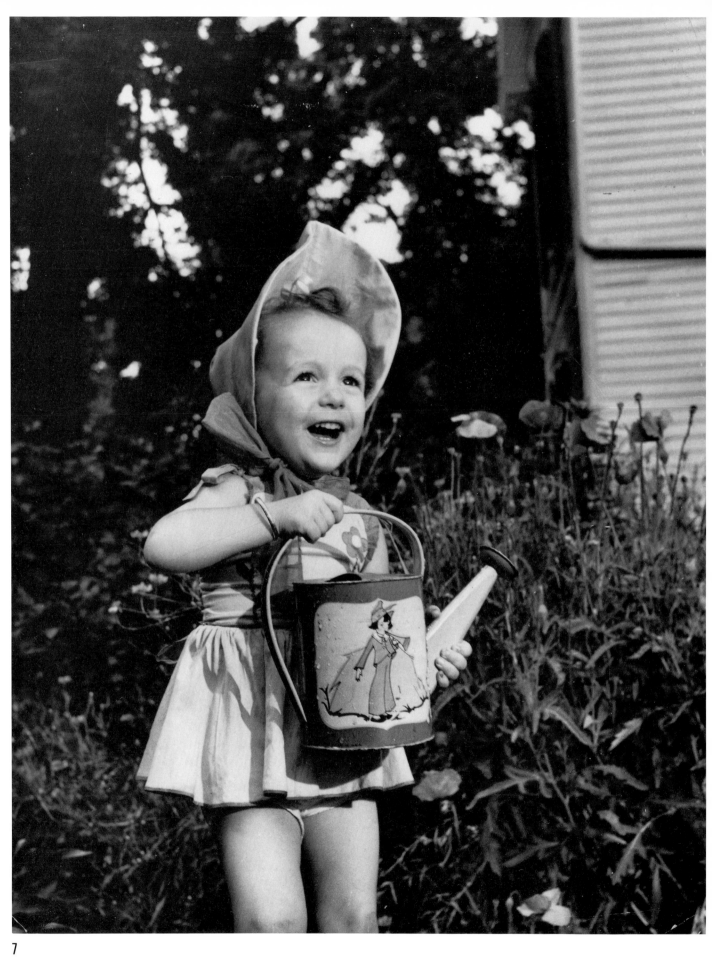

types and discrimination. The magazine industry developed a close relationship with the OWI's Magazine Bureau, which recommended story lines as well as ads and cover copy.[30] Magazines like *Life* urged women to leave their homes to participate in the defense industry, often in jobs traditionally assigned to men, such as riveting and welding.

Equally important in the mobilization effort, however, was the continuity of social values and the maintenance of traditional gender roles. Maureen Honey's study of wartime images of women examines how advertising, news stories, and employment campaigns consistently emphasized femininity. She notes that "the intertwining of decorative femininity with militarism arose from the identification of women as domestic freedom fighters and, it simultaneously reflected their continued sexual objectification."[31] *Life*'s news photographs as well as advertisements typically showed war workers with brightly painted fingernails, make-up, and well-coiffured hair. Tensions and contradictions surfaced as the campaigns tried to limit or regulate suggestions of female independence in the face of war work that challenged definitions of femininity.

Undermining threats to gender conventions posed by war work, *Life* represented working mothers and wives as part of the moral obligations on the home front. In a June 1942 photograph, a woman wearing safety glasses and head scarf drills rivet holes into a plane.[32] She does not look at the camera, suggesting that the photographer caught her in the middle of her work. In contrast to the seemingly radical depiction of a woman in overalls working as a riveter, the text emphasizes traditional gender roles. "A Pearl Harbor widow, Mrs. Evelyn J. W. Casola, takes her small but effective revenge on the enemy who killed her husband on December 7." The caption reminds us not of her financial needs or her independence but rather of her sacrifice, as a widow, for the nation. Attention to her marital status exhorts women to believe that war work was compatible with conventional femininity.

Although recruitment campaigns used patriotic rhetoric, there were few discussions about the purposes or goals of the war. The media instead told middle-class women that civilian defense work would hasten the war's end and return their loved ones. The slogan that repeatedly captured this theme was that women were "working for the duration."[33] *Life* often pictured women as temporary workers eager to return to domesticity. A September 1942 news story reports on a soldier's wife who took over her husband's business until his return.[34] A caption describes a photograph of Emily Harrison putting on a hat in sexist language that trivializes her efforts by claiming that she wore her prettiest hat to "wow" war contractors. Another picture shows her in a dress, typing, with a photograph of a man in uniform on the desk next to her. This composition connects her to male authority in a manner similar to the photograph of the war wife in the home-front issue. Other photographs, however, reveal a more ambiguous message because they depict her in a position of authority. In one large picture of the manufacturing plant, Harrison writes on a pad while talking to a man in work clothes at a machine. The caption explains that she is checking the speed and quality of each man's production. The text goes on to say that after wowing the local War Production Board with her pretty hat, she "impressed them even more with her determination and her smart business sense." Assertions of Harrison's femininity compete with acknowledgments of her business acumen, which enabled her to expand production and hire more workers. News accounts like these offered a factual counterpart to war films like *Since You Went Away* (1944), in which the absent husband also functions as a reminder of heterosexual desire alongside images of women's self-sufficiency and independence. Messages about women's capabilities competed with demands for conventional femininity and a nationalistic rhetoric that urged women to work for patriotic reasons.

Despite strategies that emphasized women's impermanent commitment to work, surveys taken in 1944 revealed that between 75 and 80 percent of the women interviewed wanted to keep their jobs after the war.[35] The government, however, viewed them only as a temporary reserve force and instituted few legislative, social, or political changes to help women keep their jobs. The lack of commitment is evident in the dearth of such support services as child care or accessible transportation.[36] At the end of the war, the media and the government worked in conjunction with business efforts to provide returning veterans with jobs by removing women war workers from heavy industry. In 1945, women experienced layoffs at a rate 75 percent higher than men. The largest involuntary reduction for women came in durable heavy goods industries, traditionally dominated by men, where one out of four women lost factory jobs.[37]

The media in 1945 often reasserted traditional gender ideals through cultural representations of acceptable female behavior.[38] Rhetoric frequently reminded women that it was their patriotic duty to give their jobs to veterans. Slogans emphasizing temporary work and domestic obligations addressed audiences in terms of the future. From the outset of World War II, the media, politicians, and social critics discussed the postwar world and frequently used visions of the future to justify military participation. As early as 1941, Luce's famous "American Century" editorial predicted American hegemony in a postwar global political economy. In support of intervention, Luce argues that "we must undertake now to be the Good Samaritan of the entire world. It is the manifest duty of this country to undertake to feed all the people of the world who as a result of this worldwide collapse of civilization are hungry and destitute." After connecting American principles with freedom of trade around the world, Luce specifically articulates reasons for an interventionist policy in Asia. "We think of Asia as being worth only a few hundred millions a year to us. Actually, in the decades to come Asia will be worth to us exactly zero—or else it will be worth to us four, five, ten billions of dollars a year."[39]

Luce was not alone in equating the United States' military objectives with its role in postwar society, nor in trying to assess how the United States would control that world. During the 1940s, internationalist positions gained popularity as intellectuals, government officials, and social critics argued that the United States would have to assume major responsibility for shaping the postwar world. Roosevelt coined the rallying cry of internationalists in his Fireside Chat immediately after Pearl Harbor: "We are going to win the war and we are going to win the peace that follows."[40] Central to these arguments was a radical shift in concepts of democracy and capitalism. David Noble argues that, until the 1940s, both progressive and republican traditions advocated isolationism to protect the United States from the corruption of international capitalist systems. Intellectuals including consensus historians like Richard Hofstadter and theologians like Reinhold Niebuhr rejected this position as they adjusted to the dramatic challenges wrought by global war. They replaced this argument with a world view that saw capitalism as the key to the survival of democracy against totalitarian regimes.[41] Similarly, in "American Century," Luce argues that capitalism was the means to ensure democracy at home and around the world. Advertisements and photo-essays in *Life* aligned democratic rhetoric with capitalist objectives, frequently

through families who were exhorted to consume as a patriotic duty. The magazine thus demonstrates one mechanism through which a historical bloc advanced its hegemony in the 1940s.

Advertisements began to envision a postwar world long before V-J Day. Unable to produce many consumer products during the war, advertisers worked hard to keep consumers interested through promises of the goods that would be available after the war.[42] These ads relied heavily on clichés of the American middle-class dream in which white women appear amid the consumer splendors of domestic life. Ads frequently showed soldiers returning home to young women and children eagerly greeting them in front of single-family houses. Such images turned an abstract concept of democracy that justified war into a visual consumer ideal. A lengthy ad campaign for Kelvinator refrigerators used the testimonial format in which women envisioned their happy lives when their husbands returned from the war. One ad titled "We'll Live in a Kingdom All Our Own" depicts a privatized vision of a nuclear family in a home with a picket fence and lovely kitchen.[43] A General Electric ad copied *Life*'s photojournalistic format to give the postwar dream increased visual credibility.[44] A before-and-after layout features the Chisholm family of White Plains, New York. Next to a picture of the patriotic Chisholms all in uniform, a small picture labeled "Before" depicts their current old-fashioned kitchen. In contrast, the largest picture, in the center of the layout, "After," visualizes postwar abundance as a modern kitchen with all new appliances. Advertisements like these repeatedly promoted postwar society as a middle-class ideal located variously in small towns or suburbs. The GE ad depicts White Plains with icons of small-town America, such as picket fences, tree-lined streets, and single-family houses. Advertisements during and after the war frequently recycled small-town iconography for suburban settings. These icons appear as well in photo-essays like the Harrodsburg article and the home front issue. Similarly, suburban developers adopted the iconography of the small town, gave streets names like Cherry Lane, and designed houses in colonial or Cape Cod styles.[45] The collapse of distinctions between suburbs and small towns served to validate the newer residential form.

News reporting during the war, however, could not so easily construct a vision of the future as advertisements since reportorial conventions necessitated a focus on current conditions in which delays in demobilization, housing shortages, employment crises, and the slow reconversion of factories intensified rather than alleviated home front problems. Nonetheless, *Life*'s reports on readjustments during 1945 promised prosperity after the war. For instance, a news story from September 1945, "Peace Brings Temporary Unemployment," shows photographs of a CIO picket, a family migrating in search of a job, and a long line of applicants outside of a U.S. Employment Service office.[46] Despite visual depictions of social instabilities, the caption underneath the picture of the employment line states that there were plenty of jobs available "but not always the kind workers happened to want." As in the Indianapolis photo-essay discussed in Chapter 2, here too the text contrasts negative conditions in the present with the promise of a stable future. The text blames the workers for their unemployment, aligning nationalistic rhetoric with class by shifting between statements crediting high employment for American prosperity and representations of discontented workers as outsiders disrupting the nation.

The layout on the following page visually tried to secure the textual claims that social problems were only "temporary." A headline announces "Most Peacetime Goods Are on Their Way Back," even though many of the products discussed were actually not available for several years. Photographs show a woman putting on stockings, another placing dishes in an automatic washer, a garbage disposal unit, and a rotary ironer. The later photographs in the story offer consumption as the solution to economic instability. The Depression had hurt the political and cultural status of capitalism, and fears of debts and doubts about materialism persisted into the 1940s. Thus, advertisers during and after the war had to displace popular suspicions about buying goods, just as the media and intellectuals challenged an earlier republican view of capitalism as the enemy of democracy. Similarly, news photographs of products for women to use in the home united traditional gender roles, domestic ideals, and consumption to construct a prophetic vision of postwar America. Class was also essential to this vision since these costly products promised to give women more leisure time and greater domestic competence. Visual claims that consumer goods offered women freedom of choice and happiness at home linked gender to nationalism by associating their consumer practices with economic recovery.

Despite cultural practices that envisioned postwar domesticity, women continued to work after the war. They were shunted out of lucrative positions but remained in the work force. Women moved from defense industries to clerical, service, and sales jobs with a concomitant reduction of income and loss of union protection. Nine out of ten women suffered a decrease in earnings as average weekly salaries dropped from fifty dollars to thirty-five.[47] *Life* ignored these statistics in stories that associated the ideal family with national trends, conditions, and objectives. Articles about veterans coping, women welcoming them home, and employers offering soldiers jobs dominated the magazine. News stories did not report on women's changed labor status or desires to remain employed. Instead, *Life* focused on reconversion in terms of male employment, economic stability, and domestic happiness when soldiers returned. In so doing, *Life* clearly expanded the representative family beyond images of neediness

to images that relied on gender, class, and racial codes to envision a social ideal rooted in suburbanization, consumption ideology, and conventional gender roles.

Family Portraits

In the early postwar years, news reports like "U.S. Normalcy" about Indianapolis, discussed in Chapter 2, and "Peace Brings Temporary Unemployment" reassured readers that instabilities resulting from reconversion were temporary. Supporting these claims, stories about boomtowns and successful businessmen visualized the "reality" of prosperity. In so doing, these reports also established the characteristics of *Life*'s family ideal. For instance, "U.S. Success Story 1938–1946," from the September 23, 1946, issue, examines the economic boom in the automobile industry by focusing on one successful auto dealer, Romy Hammes from Kankakee, Illinois.[48]

Life sent its staff photographer Bernard Hoffman back to Kankakee to do a follow-up to an article published in 1938 on economic conditions in the auto industry. In contrast to 1938, when Hammes was only moderately well off, in 1946 he was an extremely successful businessman who owned dealerships in two cities and had expanded into real estate. Hoffman depicts the dealer selling cars, looking over architectural plans, and selling real estate. The accompanying text underscores his representative status, explaining that "Romy was no isolated example. In other Kankakees were other Romys. The man who used to work a gasoline pump now ran the filling station. His boss now had three stations and was dickering for a fourth. In America the dream was still there for those who believed it strongly enough to roll up their sleeves." This statement discounts the social benefits or disadvantages of education, class, and ethnic status as it praises the self-made Hammes, and all the men like him, who climb the mythic ladder of success. In this way, *Life* represents the United States as a classless society of opportunity. Hammes's representative status makes his, and thus the United States', prosperity common. In addition, the choice of an auto dealer to illustrate American economic conditions aligns corporate capitalism, in this case the automobile industry, with the nation. In the postwar period, the magazine repeatedly credited modern corporations with bringing affluence to the nation.[49]

This portrait of corporate America depends on masculine ideals by representing men as the ones rolling up their sleeves for success. In contrast, photographs confine women exclusively to the home. Hoffman's photographs depict separate worlds of work, occupied solely by men, and home, occupied by the nuclear family. The final two-page spread begins with a headline "Romy the Man Loves His Family and His Community." The text describes community involvement in domestic terms, commenting that Hammes "has a simple, homey ideal of service both to his customers and his

community. . . . These same homey ideals permeate Romy's family life." Despite textual assertions of Hammes's community involvement, the photo-essay includes no pictures of the community, only photographs of his family. *Life* represents a privatized vision of the United States in which community has no visual place.

Visualizing "homey ideals" as a private space moves ambivalently between discourses on community and discourses on individualism. Individualism was a central theme in the postwar rhetoric of politicians and social critics, who claimed it demonstrated the existence of democracy and freedom in contrast to its suppression under communism. In this regard, Hammes exemplifies the independent, upwardly mobile businessman of corporate America. At the same time, the idea of community clearly still resonated in postwar culture, evidenced by the textual insistence on Hammes's social activities. Lynn Spigel observes these same contradictions in 1950s television, which attempted to resolve the isolation of home viewing by providing an illusion of participation in a broader community. "Facsimile" communities of neighbors and families sharing the same experiences created an imaginary unity with "absent others."[50] In a similar way, *Life* encouraged the reader to recognize in its representative families people with common activities and values.

Life's attempt to represent the "average" American by locating Hammes within a community tradition, however, narrowed dramatically to focus on the isolated family. Rather than represent community, *Life* visualizes the breadwinner ethic by measuring the success of the businessman in familial terms. The breadwinner ethos was articulated in a variety of postwar discourses, including psychoanalytic arguments about male and female roles and sociological treatises by David Riesman, William Whyte, and others.[51] This ethos carried with it the expectation "that required men to grow up, marry and support their wives."[52] Hoffman represents Hammes's success as a breadwinner through photographs of domestic possessions, such as his home and vacation cottage. One picture shows Hammes with his family seated in their boat on a lake (*illustration 9*). The photograph displays the family as evidence, like the boat, of the businessman's prosperity.[53] Patriarchy and affluence are mutually reinforced through the image of the Father as caretaker of his family and possessions.

Hoffman's photographs of Romy Hammes and his family are characteristic of the magazine's attention to individual personalities, or what Luce referred to as "the little people." Realistic photographs construct an apparently seamless narrative about the "normal life" of representative families. A humorous essay on the Beat poets at the end of the fifties uses distinctive contrasts to identify the boundaries of this normative culture. "Squaresville U.S.A. vs. Beatsville," from September 1959, upholds middle-class ideals as it ridicules social differences.[54] *Life* describes Hutchin-son, Kansas, as "the personification of traditionally accepted American virtues—a stable, prosperous community, given to conservatism but full of get-up-and-go." In contrast, the text characterizes Venice, California, as throbbing "with the rebellion of the beatnik, who ridicules U.S. society as 'square.'" Comparing suburbs, aligned with American virtues, to the decadence of Venice foregrounds the physical association of the family ideal with a specific location.

The top half of a two-page spread, with the headline "A Happy Home in Kansas," shows a family looking at a photo album and watching television in a comfortable suburban home. The photographs visually elevate consumer habits to a standard of virtue, the happy home. In contrast, underneath a headline announcing "Hip Family's Cool Pad," the photograph depicts a bearded man lying on a mattress on the floor with another man seated on a box. A barefoot woman stands in the center of the room holding a baby. In contrast to industrious men like Dale Welling and Romy Hammes, who stand and display their families and possessions, the Beat men lie on the floor, not working and not wearing suits, while the mother stands above them. Through humor and ridicule, *Life* visually privileges middle-class suburban values defined in terms of place, dress, language, and social relations.

The ordinariness of *Life*'s representative, middle-class families celebrated a single cultural standard for domestic life. Articles on politicians, celebrities, and other famous

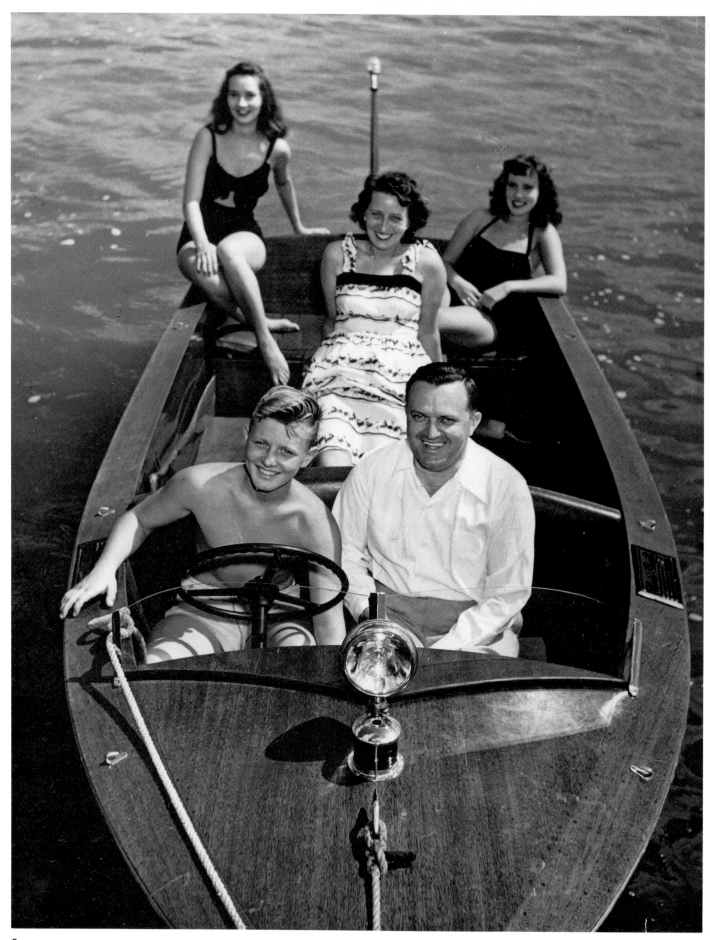

people similarly focused on family life to demonstrate their ordinary status. The magazine's coverage of male politicians included ubiquitous photographs of homes, wives, and children which connote values such as stability and responsibility, important characteristics associated with the right to rule.[55] Pictures of adoring wives and children provided an aura of moral legitimacy for male politicians by presenting the imperatives of politics and statecraft as logical and natural extensions of domestic roles.

No one exemplified *Life*'s consensus America more than Dwight D. Eisenhower. Throughout the postwar period, the magazine praised this leader first as the war hero and later as the president. Eisenhower represented stability and order as the patriarch who led the Allies to victory in World War II and concluded a peace in Korea. Calling him a patriarch is appropriate, for *Life* exploited this grandfatherly image in numerous pictures of him with his young grandchildren. Moreover, photographs of him with his wife in family settings frequently underscored the connections between his political and domestic roles. The February 2, 1953, issue on Eisenhower's inauguration relied on domesticity to depict one of the most significant moments in American politics—the transfer of power from one administration to the next.[56] A full-page photograph shows President and Mrs. Eisenhower waving to the camera as they enter "their new home" at the White House. On the facing page, Mr. and Mrs. Truman

similarly wave to the camera as they enter their "old home" in Independence, Missouri. Depicting a change of political parties and philosophies as a change of houses exemplifies the ways in which patriarchal and consumer narratives displace political differences. The photo-essay collapses affairs of state into personal concerns so that the home becomes the metaphor for the nation. Pictures like this one suggest a natural correspondence between the general's domestic authority and his fitness for political leadership.[57] Once again, *Life* visualizes nationalism as a private and isolated world. These photo-essays focus on individual men and their families rather than community, as claimed in the Hammes portrait, or promised in the pictures of the presidential leader of the national community. Such imagery ignores social structures through which people build coalitions; instead it insulates people in ways that negate their potential power as a group. Narrowing the image of nation to that of the nuclear family also foregrounds conservative gender identities.

Throughout the decade, the magazine featured politicians' wives as models of domesticity. *Life*'s July 1952 coverage of the Republican national convention includes a photograph of Mamie Eisenhower holding a baby granddaughter with a grandson next to her.[58] Such commonplace, seemingly natural pictures immediately identify Mrs. Eisenhower's primary social role as a domestic one. The text employs codes of femininity to describe Mrs. Eisenhower as a "poised, pleasant and bright-eyed woman who appeared younger than she was (55)." *Life* also foregrounds Mamie Eisenhower's status as a mother. When asked if she "as a 'soldier's wife' would worry when her soldier son went to Korea, she answered, 'That's a strange question to ask a mother. Soldier's wife or not, I'm still very much a mother.'" Patriotism and maternity mingle here to displace the politics of the United States' involvement in Korea onto a mother's private and depoliticized concerns. Such characterizations also reinforce Eisenhower's status as a credible leader through association with the values of his family.

In general, portraits of politicians and their families conformed to ideals of middle-class domesticity. Politicians were especially important in *Life* because they represented social and political authority through which they conferred legitimacy onto "everyday values." For instance, a February 13, 1950, news story about Truman's vice president, Alben Barkley, and his new bride reports on the lifestyle of this recently married couple who were popular among Washington's social elite.[59] Although the Barkleys' associations and celebrity status clearly show them not to be members of the middle class, *Life* champions the ideals of middle-class domesticity in photographs of the couple. Scenes depicting "everyday life" include a picture of Mrs. Barkley, still in her nightclothes, at the door saying goodbye to her husband

who carries a briefcase as he "leaves for the Senate."

Photographer Hank Walker's concluding picture of the Barkleys in their kitchen visually constructs the gender divisions essential to *Life*'s ideology of domesticity (*illustration 10*). Mrs. Barkley, wearing an apron, washes dishes while her husband leans against the sink next to her. Walker emphasizes domesticity by placing a chair with a dish towel draped over it at the picture plane, making it the first thing the viewer sees. There is a sense of informality in this seemingly unposed portrait, especially in the figures whose faces appear in profile, apparently oblivious to the camera, deep in conversation. Walker tightly crops the sides to focus attention on the couple in the middle ground while the kitchen wall cuts off depth in the background. The photograph's realism encourages a reading of this as an intimate scene of a couple cleaning up after dinner. Visualizing these famous people through traditional gender roles makes the roles themselves seem natural, normal, and inevitable. Moreover, the headline, "On the Maid's Night Out, Veep Presides over Dishwashing," conflates political and domestic languages, which reinforces the mutuality of political and patriarchal authority. The text anchors these conventional gender ideals by explaining that the vice president urges his wife to let the dishes dry in the rack, "but like any bride proud of her new things, she sees the chore through and carefully puts them away."

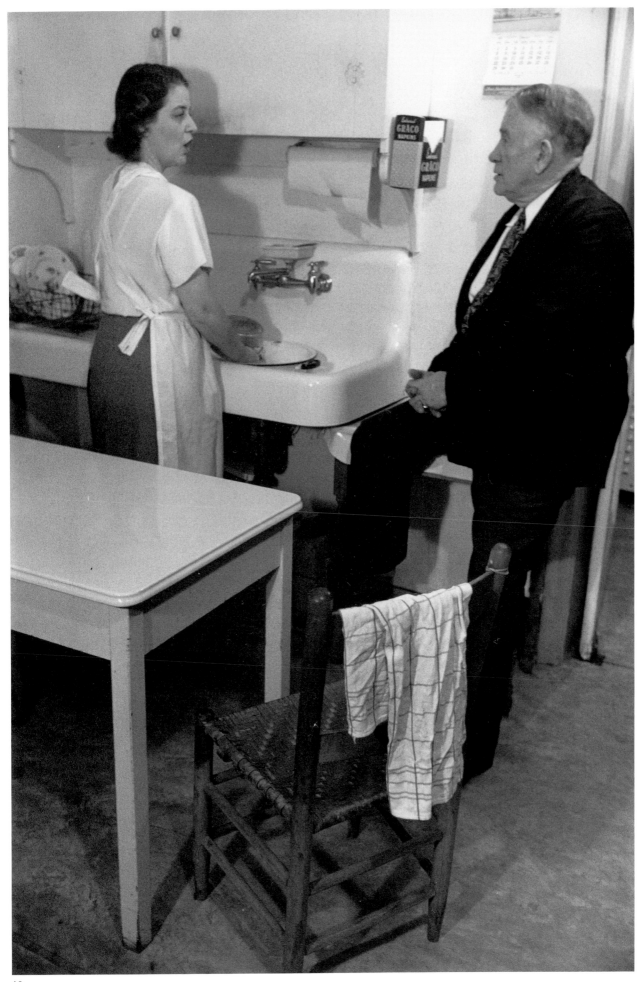

The statement "like any bride" not only associates her with stereotypes of the housewife but implies that there is an automatic connection leading from female gender to bride to housewife. In stories like this one, *Life* envisioned American politicians as breadwinners with wives who care for the home. Two women who wrote letters to the editor underscore the Barkleys' typicality by commenting on the old-fashioned sink. One of them writes that "I view my old sink with new respect. It's just like the Veep's." Such comments imply a community of readers who share the same social space as politicians. The one male letter calls attention to conventional gender divisions in which women presumably rule in the home. He comments that "Mrs. Barkley has laid the drying cloth out on a chair right in front of the Veep. Yet he sits there and 'presides.' I couldn't get away with that in my home!"[60] The published letters assume, like the article, the naturalness of historically specific gender relations in part by ignoring the active role of the camera.

Idealized pictures of women in domestic settings during the postwar period were particularly important in light of changing paid-work opportunities for women. Although women's participation in the paid labor force continued to rise, segregation in low-paying, gender-specific jobs reversed many of the gains made by women during World War II. Employers, unions, and government officials alike endorsed the downgrading of job skills for female workers. "Family wage" arguments that presented men exclusively as breadwinners and women as wives first and workers second justified a variety of discriminatory labor policies, including mass firings of women workers with seniority at the end of the war to make room for returning veterans. Other forms of assistance for male workers at women's expense included skilled apprenticeship and job training programs reserved exclusively for men and indirect government and business subsidies to male workers through home-loan and education programs tied to military service.[61] *Life* supported these trends by promoting a domestic ideology that ignored the diversity of circumstances facing working women. It also precluded options and alternative social roles for those women who did their primary work at home. Although advertisements presented this ideology relentlessly, news stories like the feature on the Barkleys provided seemingly factual evidence justifying these ideals.

Life vociferously promoted patriarchal gender divisions in such articles as a December 1956 essay by Robert Coughlan that blamed divorce on the breakdown of these divisions.[62] The writer relies on the authority of psychoanalytic and scientific discourses to characterize the sexual act in terms of aggressive masculine actions and passive female ones. Divorce results from a breakdown in these natural relations. Coughlan singles out working women for blame because when they leave the domestic sphere they become more aggressive while men become more passive and lose their natural masculine drives. This argument is similar to the theories espoused by sociologist Talcott Parsons, who promoted the nuclear family as a transhistorical ideal, associating this family form with evolutionary processes of modernization and claiming that patriarchal gender roles are universal and progressive.[63] *Life* promoted a similar ideology in its editorials and articles as well as in pictures like the one of the vice president's wife washing dishes. Photographic realism, moreover, has the visual power to circumscribe women's social roles within a domestic world.

Domesticity governed media portraits of men's responsibilities as much as it shaped depictions of women. During this period, men's role as breadwinners expanded beyond expectations that they be providers; social critics, psychologists, and others in the popular media urged fathers to participate more actively in family life. Fatherhood became a defining characteristic of masculinity and maturity. Television viewers, for instance, rarely saw sitcom fathers working, as these characters traded in public identities for participation in domestic life.[64] Similarly, a 1958 news story on Vice President Richard Nixon and his family used expensive color photographs to depict Nixon as the involved father playing with his children.[65] Hank Walker poses Nixon sitting with his family in the backyard, and playing with his daughters in a tree house. Walker creates an informality similar to that in his portrait of the Barkleys. He has the Nixons ignore the camera, which implies that this is an every-

day scene upon which the photographer has stumbled. In one photograph, the vice president sits at his desk in shirtsleeves next to his daughter Julie in pajamas as they laugh at a recording she made on his dictaphone. Silly antics of childhood turn Nixon's political responsibilities into a job that supports his family. The text also emphasizes the family's desire for privacy to give "the girls a chance to grow up the way their father would like them to." Visual images display the pleasures and joys of domestic privacy with no references to the outside world.[66]

Life participated in a postwar culture that repeatedly focused on domesticity. Books and magazines gave endless advice to parents about everything from raising families to home improvements. In broadcasting as well, both advertisements and domestic sitcoms effectively integrated familial values with the values of consumer society. Comedies like "Father Knows Best," "The Donna Reed Show," and "Leave It to Beaver," showcased ideal domestic homes in which mothers cared for the home and fathers solved their children's problems. As early as 1948, television advertisers and designers directed marketing strategies toward the middle class. To encourage middle-class consumption advertisers masked class heterogeneity through an image of the nuclear family as natural and ahistorical.[67]

Moreover, throughout the period, intellectuals, popular writers, and politicians advocated domesticity in similarly nationalistic terms. The most famous photography exhibition of postwar America, "The Family of Man," first exhibited in 1955, similarly promoted family photography in what Allan Sekula terms a "celebration of the power of the mass media to represent the whole world in familiar and intimate terms." According to Edward Steichen, who was curator of the show, by 1960, over seven million people in twenty-eight countries had seen the exhibition. This traveling show promoted American democracy by presenting the bourgeois family as universal in this "globalized utopian family album." [68]

In retrospect *Life*'s attention to the family in news stories, like other forms of popular culture, appears to be powerful evidence for a national consensus about the family in postwar America. In an age of unprecedented family formation—with marriage and childbirth occurring more frequently and earlier than at any time in the preceding three decades—the centrality of family images in news stories seems natural, even obvious. But the connection between state power and family form celebrated in *Life*'s photo-essays was neither natural nor inevitable. Rather it was the product of ideological contestations brought on by changes in American social life. *Life*'s photo-essays featuring representative families engaged in dialogue with social forces, urging readers to connect a family ideal with national imperatives.

A Nation of Families

Scholars of the postwar period invariably identify radical changes in family life as a crucial development within American society. In explaining the baby boom, they frequently argue that the cohort of adults who grew up during the Depression and World War II compensated for earlier deprivations by turning to the pleasures of domesticity. [69] Elaine Tyler May demonstrates, however, that prosperity is only a partial explanation for the baby boom because the postwar period cannot simply be read as a time of affluence and complacency. She observes that in the face of Cold War anxieties and fears, many Americans turned to the private space of their families for stability and security. [70] The powerful reach and scope of the media reinforced this process through recurrent depictions of the nuclear family as a safe and ideal haven. Rather than reflecting or recording reality, *Life*'s photo-essays created an imagined community through pictorial realism that naturalized a particular social form—the middle-class nuclear family—into a transhistorical ideal that symbolized the United States. In so doing, this imagined community also functioned to regulate social forms and deny diversity at a time when anti-Communist campaigns made differences politically dangerous. Domestic ideology, however, was not monolithic or unified but a complex cultural terrain that attempted to reconcile social and political issues, like the ones May points out, through family values. Ambiguities apparent in photo-essays that visually reproduced gender, class, and racial hierarchies, as well as struggled between community and individualism, indicate the tensions embedded in narratives that aligned domesticity with nationalism.

In this context, we need to interrogate the centrality of the family to *Life*'s ideological project of national consensus. Jürgen Habermas argues that advanced capitalism destroys personal motivations for work and connection to others by turning work into a kind of status competition tied to the accumulation of goods, rather than a calling or an opportunity to contribute to society. Traditional depictions of the family present it as a voluntary site of intimacy and warmth, but it also functions as a site of consumption. At the same time capitalism lauds the work ethic and the family as spheres of morality safe from the materialism of the outside world. These contradictions produce a "legitimation crisis," by which capitalist societies become ever more dependent for legitimacy on the very sociocultural motivations that capitalism undermines. As Habermas describes this process, capitalist societies "feed parasitically on the remains of tradition," such as religion and the patriarchal family. But legitimation is always incomplete because the families praised as the location of desire and purpose are ill equipped to fulfill this role since they exist contradictorily as units of consumption.[71]

Life's almost obsessive attention to the nuclear family in stories about social issues such as housing, labor crises, and the economy demonstrates how strategies of legitimation aligned national imperatives with domestic ideals. These strategies often relied on a rhetoric of democracy. Like the World War II appeals that borrowed heavily from a small-town ideal, *Life*'s postwar pictorial record borrowed from the rhetoric of wartime emergency by linking the family to moral obligations and patriotic behavior. Specifically, narratives about postwar social, political, and economic situations tried to legitimate consumption by making it a matter of obligation to the family and the state.

Life appealed to middle-class Americans by connecting a vision of nuclear families owning their own homes and experiencing upward mobility with national ideals. As illustrated by the presidential transfer of power and the photographic representations of the Barkleys' and the Nixons' domestic bliss, the home was a prominent symbol in *Life*'s portrait of America. In its Modern Living and Design sections, *Life* featured model suburban homes as the new architectural ideal. Merging editorial and advertising material in these sections, *Life* promoted a vision of the United States as a nation of middle-class homeowners. Luce wrote in 1946 that "it is the first job of Modern Living to show how the multiplicity of goods in an industrial age can be used with relatively better rather than relatively worse taste."[72] News stories supported this consumer aesthetic by reporting on developments in suburban living. The January 5, 1953, issue

"The American and His Economy," for instance, begins with a news story on the latest developments in suburban housing design.[73] Color plates show landscaped exteriors and the interior decor of houses with three bedrooms, 1½ baths, a fireplace, and an open floor plan. Photographic realism demonstrates the popularity of suburbia through representations of young married couples with small children standing outside their new homes in Ohio, Louisiana, Colorado, Pennsylvania, Texas, and Indiana. Pictures of real families represented middle-class Americans from different regions as participants in a shared American Dream.

Housing, however, was not just a symbol of prosperity and domestic bliss in postwar America, it was also a source of tension and conflict. According to the National Housing Agency, at least 3.5 million new houses were needed in 1946 just to provide veterans with decent housing, yet there was only enough material and labor to build 460,000 units. In addition, the influx of people of color from rural areas to industrial centers resulted in a severe housing crisis in inner cities. Poor people who were most in need of government intervention in the housing crisis faced the racially discriminatory policies of both private landlords and government agencies, as well as limited job prospects and inflated rents and grocery bills.[74] Although the National Housing Act of 1949 established "the goal of a decent home and a suitable living environment for every American family," little

progress was made in alleviating this problem. By 1964, only 550,000 of the 810,000 low-cost dwelling units promised by the Act had been completed.[75]

Instead, the federal government supported suburbanization through such programs as the FHA and VA mortgage guarantees.[76] With these government guarantees, buyers could secure mortgages at low interest rates and with small down payments, making it cheaper to buy than to rent. As taxes went up, the homeowner deduction became more important, creating an added subsidy for homeownership and an added penalty for renters. In this way, the government subsidized the move into the suburbs of millions of white Americans. Starting in 1956, federal government investments in interstate highway construction projects encouraged the use of private automobiles over public transportation and furthered suburban growth. At the same time, redlining policies and the refusal to fund renovation projects on older houses in the cities precluded poor people and people of color from participating in these social developments.[77]

Throughout the postwar years, *Life*'s news coverage of housing rarely discussed apartment buildings or urban renovation as possible solutions. Photographs of Americans living in trailers and Quonset huts, and doubling up in apartments, visualized the housing shortage, but the only solution the magazine showed was the single-family house. Photographs supplied the visual evidence for the claim that all Americans demanded suburban

else, were left further and further behind."⁹⁰ *Life*, like the government and private corporations, did not so much ignore social differences as argue that productivity would raise everyone to a higher level of affluence.⁹¹ This ideal of productivity pervaded the magazine's vision of social progress.

As part of a national corporation with its own direct political and economic interests, and as an institution with responsibilities to its investors and advertisers, *Life* supported government and business efforts to maintain a stable economy and political consensus. Toward that end, *Life* often cajoled its readers to be civic minded by spending more money. In a May 5, 1947, article entitled "U.S. Tackles the Price Problem," *Life* linked the ideal suburban family to the state by making the family accountable for economic prosperity.⁹² The article ends with a two-page spread on Ted and Jeanne Hemeke and their three children. The headline specifically associates consumption with civic responsibility: "Family Status Must Improve: It Should Buy More for Itself to Better the Living of Others." The editors use a popular photo-essay formula of a before-and-after narrative. The Hemekes appear first in their present home, an old frame house, then visiting a new suburban house. The text explains the latter as the vision of the future, "what life should be like in the U.S. by 1960."

In the foreground of the first picture, Ted Hemeke, having just returned from work, stands with his back to the camera holding a child's hand. The photographer's perspec-

tive encourages the viewer to identify with Hemeke's vision by putting us in his shoes. Following his gaze, we look past the foreground figures toward the house, observing the weeds and the grassless lawn as well as the poorly maintained house next door. In the background, Jeanne Hemeke stands in the doorway holding one child while another child sits on a barrel next to her. The other picture on this page shows Jeanne Hemeke using a large shovel to scoop coal into a "dirty coal furnace next to [the] stove" while her baby daughter sits on the floor nearby. This shot emphasizes the antiquated facilities of the old house as well as the woman's hard work.

On the facing page, two photographs parallel the ones on the previous page in composition, size, and layout. The first picture again shows the Hemekes in front of a house (*illustration 12*). This time, however, the wife stands in the doorway of a modern ranch-style house. By repeating the action of Ted Hemeke walking into the scene from the street, the visual narrative suggests that once again he is arriving home from work. Although the text explains that the Hemekes are visiting a model house, repeating the composition encourages a reading of economic progress from the old house to the new one. The Hemekes' attire underscores this narrative of upward mobility. In the first scene, Ted Hemeke wears heavy boots and a work jacket. His daughter does not wear a coat or socks. Here, he wears a suit and his daughter has on a coat, hat, socks, and dress shoes. The daughter in the back-

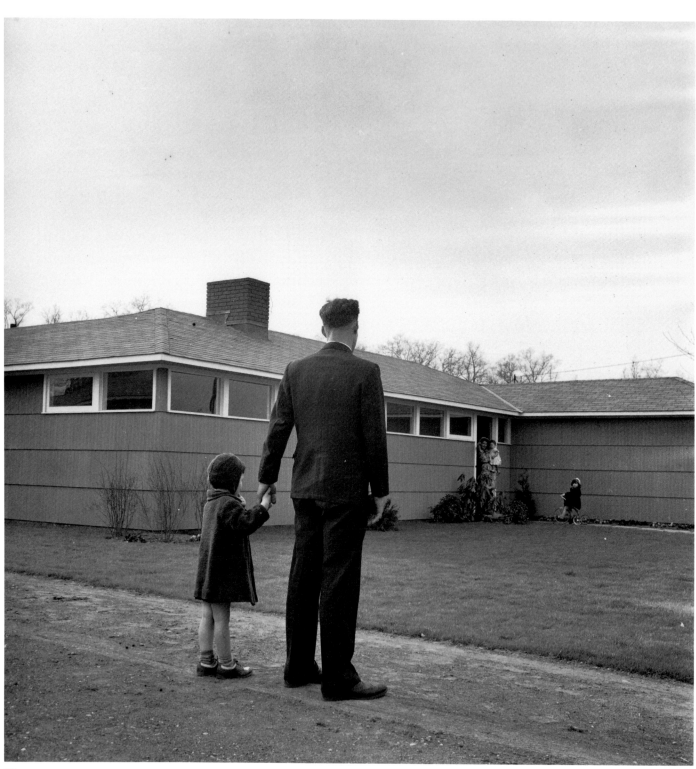

ground no longer sits on a barrel but rides a tricycle.

The second photograph of the alternative vision shows Jeanne Hemeke again in the kitchen but this time in a modern kitchen with gingham curtains and shiny new appliances. She stands at a counter with her hands on an electric beater, as if she were baking; behind her a kettle gleams on a gas stove. The baby no longer sits on the floor dangerously close to the furnace but plays with a toy in a high chair that has a bottle of milk on the tray. Visually, if not in actuality, Jeanne Hemeke and her family have attained these middle-class accouterments. The realistic *mise en scène* (for this is a staged performance by two different photographers) reinforces a reading that this woman is cooking in her own new kitchen. Here, domesticity constructs conventional gender roles by positioning the woman in the private space of the home. Moreover, placing her in a modern kitchen with new appliances, a composition frequently used in advertisements, objectifies her as an ideal consumer. Her husband, on the other hand, occupies space in the outside public world, signified by the sidewalk and the narrative journey from work. Visually and textually, *Life* presents a vision of America that characterizes people like the Hemekes through conventional gender identities and material possessions.

As with photo-essays on Romy Hammes and other representative families, here too *Life* locates the consumer ideal in the physical space of the suburbs, an isolated space in which no one else appears on the sidewalk. Thus, the magazine's vision of the nation integrates the ideals of social progress with ideologies of consumption and the private realm of domesticity. Indeed, the article claims that families have civic responsibilities based on their roles as consumers. At the conclusion of the story on the Hemekes, *Life* cites a Twentieth Century Fund projection study on the economy in 1960, stating that:

> To achieve a health and decency standard for everyone by 1960 each U.S. family should acquire, in addition to a pleasant roof over its head, a vacuum cleaner, washing machine, stove, electric iron, refrigerator, telephone, electric toaster and such miscellaneous household supplies as matching dishes, silverware, cooking utensils, tools, cleaning materials, stationery and postage stamps.

This prescriptive message presents a list of consumer goods as the minimum that families have not only the right to expect but the duty to acquire in order that everyone attain a decent standard of living. Concluding a story on inflation at a time when many still worried about an economic collapse, *Life*'s visual mediation of these fears takes on great ideological significance. In linking the family to the political economy, *Life* creates a portrait of the nation that legitimizes the social order by connecting moral authority to familial consumption.

In stories about people like the Hemekes, *Life* denied class distinctions when it pointed to consumption as evidence of upward mobility. Instead, the uniform domesticity that pervades photo-essays like this one offered a portrait of a national community of families with shared concerns. The political consequences of this nationalism are especially apparent in stories that explicitly linked domesticity to anti-Communist rhetoric. *Life* often supported the political tensions of the Cold War by contrasting the oppressive Communist state with the opportunities and freedoms of American families. For example, the January 1957 photo-essay on the Hungarian Csillag family (discussed in Chapter 1) recreates the deeply familiar story about progress through the layout. The narrative moves geographically and temporally from a "homeland," represented as a physical space of deprivation and fear (the refugees in a snowstorm), toward "America," the land of opportunity (pictures of consumer goods in a middle-class home).[93] This article is different from many news accounts of group immigration that raise the specter of invasion or violation of boundaries. The realistic pictures in this story of progress represent an assimilated nuclear family easily adjusting to its new surroundings.

Pictures of the Csillags settled in the United States combine domesticity and consumption to represent what the American nation offers these refugees. Three large photographs on a two-page spread offer evidence of that success by showing the Csillags standing in front of a table laden with food, having just arrived home from the grocery story.[94] The first photograph shows the Csillags with American relatives unpacking groceries. In the second photograph, a relative demonstrates how to use a tissue. In the third photograph, the adults are all laughing as Pal Csillag tries one. The Hungarians' awe at the consumer products destabilizes the norm of American consumption in order to foreground it as evidence of national ideals. The focus on consumption exemplifies the magazine's frequent Cold War strategy to contrast communism with American capitalism, assured that such comparisons easily demonstrated which culture was superior. The Csillags join an imagined community of families that defines social conventions in terms of gender divisions and political action in terms of Americans' consumer habits. The text underscores this position through unsubtle contrasts between the United States and the impoverished conditions of the Communist system the Csillags left behind. This narrative of immigrant assimilation submerges ethnicity as the Csillags become, as in Nixon's comment, the "kind of people who make good Americans" through the products they consume. Perhaps more than any other national narrative, this narrative of the successful immigrant enjoying the riches of capitalism embodies the American Dream.

Within the context of other media representations of the family, *Life*'s images of domesticity must be read as participating in the ongoing constructions of national social and political ideals in postwar America. The family's importance lies not only in its economic value in reproducing and maintaining the labor force or as a channel for socializing children, but equally important, in its role in reproducing cultural values.[95] *Life*'s narrative promoted the reproduction of a particular set of values and norms that formed a national culture around the dominant middle class.

Creating *Life*'s Audience

Life's narrative about consensus America did not merely reflect the trends of the baby boom or middle-class affluence. Instead, *Life* actively constructed meanings for its readers. This has significance for a postwar American society that was more heterogeneous than is typically imagined by stereotypes of postwar suburbanites, who were in fact a mixed group including returning GIs, second-generation immigrants, and working-class people.[96] Although the majority of *Life*'s readers were middle-class professionals, the letters to the editor indicate a degree of diversity among the magazine's audience. For instance, in response to the article on the internment of Japanese Americans at Tule Lake, a Nisei man used patriotic rhetoric to condemn "American fascists and race-baiters."[97] Similarly, a woman responding to a news article on a strike at a Detroit GM plant in 1946 identified with the striker, explaining that her husband was also on strike and therefore they could no longer afford her subscription.[98] Many in this heterogeneous group may have felt insecure about their place in the American Dream. Even 1950s television demonstrated

more social diversity; not all shows were middle-class family comedies, especially in the early days, with shows like "The Goldbergs," "The Honeymooners," and "Amos 'n' Andy." What united these shows, however, was a capitalist ethos that typically resolved problems of work, family, and politics through consumption.[99] Similarly, *Life*'s news reports worked to convince its readers just then moving into the suburbs that they too belonged to "America." An America, that is, that was upwardly mobile and consumer oriented.

Life's focus on the middle-class family occurred at a time when Americans were reorganizing social relations into nuclear families. Documentary photography, historically aligned with reform movements, had previously turned the camera's gaze on groups with lower status than the middle-class audiences viewing these images. *Life*'s contribution to photojournalism was to turn the camera's gaze on the middle class in an effort to mirror the readers' world. Readers saw in *Life* an optimistic vision of American society, which, they were told, was a reflection of their lives as homeowners. *Life*'s photo-essays invited viewers to make connections between a single family form and national interests through identification with signs of domesticity.[100] Realistic photographs of the family visualized socially constructed relationships, such as that between the breadwinner and housewife, in concrete and seemingly unmediated ways. Stories about individuals directed attention away from the political meanings embedded in representation by encouraging viewers to relate emotionally to the people in the news.[101] Like the letter writers who recognized their old sinks, readers frequently wrote in with pictures or stories that resembled the ones published in the magazine, fostering a climate that urged people to recognize the similarities.

Life addressed these readers through representational strategies in which seamless narratives present the working-class Hemekes, or even the Hungarian Csillags, as families just like other Americans. In this way, the photo-essay hails the reader into the signifying spaces of national identity, a space severely circumscribed by the patriarchal and racist ideals of domesticity. Underlying the clear anti-Communist message in the Csillag story, for instance, is a didacticism common in *Life*: both photographs and texts demonstrate "the kind of people who make good Americans." These immigrants are clearly not middle class. Rather, through a progressive narrative about characters who embody the American success myth, the story about the Csillags depicts, like the one about the Hemekes, the aspirations of Americans. Readers are urged to identify with the emotional efforts and achievements of an imagined community of like-minded families. Displacing class and ethnic differences, *Life* repeats a deeply familiar story of progress and achievement in stories as varied as Romy Hammes' auto dealership and the Csillags' escape from communism. In part, *Life* was so effective in this regard because realistic photographs promote

a reading of images as transparent mirrors of social reality.

In studying news stories that constructed an ideal of nationhood, it is also crucial to acknowledge who is left out of that ideal. In stories about representative Americans, ethnic differences were typically limited to Europeans, like the Hungarian Csillags. In contrast, people of color, including Latinos and Native Americans, appeared as representative of social problems but never to signify the American Dream. Moreover, some social groups, like Asian Americans after the close of the internment camps, were rarely seen. The one major exception, and we see how *Life* depicted them in Chapter 5, was African Americans and their struggle for civil rights.

The elderly were also notably absent from *Life*'s narrative of postwar family life. Suburban dwellers, at least in the pages of *Life*, did not live with elderly parents, much less aunts, uncles, or friends. When *Life* represented elderly people, it was typically in association with specific problems or issues. A June 1950 article on pension programs represents the elderly since they are the major recipients of these programs.[102] Photographs from a retirement settlement in St. Petersburg, Florida, include a group playing shuffleboard and an elderly couple smiling outside their cottage. In contrast, the final full-page picture depicts an old man in a county poorhouse. Seated on a wrought-iron bed showing signs of rusting, the man's unshaven face looks at the camera. Strong light from the window highlights his clenched hands while leaving his face in shadow. The text reassuringly notes that the surge in retirement plans will mean an "increasing scarcity of pictures of pathetic misery like that on the opposite page," yet the painful and disturbing photograph undermines any comfortable solution claimed by the text. The article praises retirement towns because the elderly there "entertain themselves, are a burden to nobody and best of all maintain the independence so cherished by old folks." The "nobody" evidently refers to the family relations who are not discussed. This story, which contains no photographs of children or relatives, identifies both the problem and the solution as socially and politically distinct from the ideals of domesticity. Life's first major treatment of aging, a July 1959 special series "Old Age," begins with an article titled "In a Dutiful Family Trials with Mother."[103] Unlike the earlier photo-essay, here the editors present aging as a problem for the family. Cornell Capa's photographs narrate the story of an elderly woman living with her son and his family. In one picture, Capa captures the situation through a grainy close-up shot of the daughter-in-law and a friend laughing at the kitchen table in a scene of intimacy and informality. The mother sits in profile in the background, spatially isolated and excluded from the conversation. Other pictures reveal cramped conditions, and two full-page pictures feature an emotional confrontation between the mother and her daughter-in-law. Most significant, in this first extensive report on the elderly, Life characterizes them as a problem that invades the family home.

Life's coverage of the elderly may have been limited, but homosexuality was beyond the representational limits of the magazine for most of the period. Postwar persecution of homosexuality and the homophobic currents in anti-Communist rhetoric are well documented, but in Life the denial of sexual difference, rather than an attempt to condemn it, was most prominent.[104] Homophobic rhetoric permeated the magazine, as did the heterosexual imperative that shaped its representation of social life. The limited visibility of different social and racial groups clearly shaped the news discourse to produce an extremely narrow portrait of "the kind of people who make good Americans."

For Life magazine, the task of constructing a unified nation out of a diverse polity depended on news presentations that advanced the twin ideologies of consumption and domesticity not just as goals of the nation-state but as the fulfillment of the democratic aspirations of the people in the nation. The family was a primary site through which Life hailed its audience as part of that unified nation. It is incorrect to assume, however, that there was a priori an audience of nuclear families for the magazine to address. Audiences are not typically unified but, rather, disorganized and disparate communities. Media producers, however, need to imagine an audience because communication is a dialogic process oriented "toward an addressee."[105] In other words, a text has to address a reader, however that reader is imagined. *Life* envisioned its readers to be midwestern, middle class, not very sophisticated, and definitely not intellectual. It is clear, moreover, from the forms of address in the photo-essays that *Life* conceptualized its readers as family members and as consumers. Seeking empirical evidence for these assumptions about its readers, the magazine's demographic studies determined the composition of its audience through extensive questionnaires on the age, gender, number in the family, and income level of its readers.[106] *Life* used demographic information to attract advertisers, as well as to shape its own discourse for a perceived audience. Nonetheless, common wisdom in the publishing industry until the 1960s insisted that magazines amass the broadest possible circulation.[107] Thus, *Life*'s vision both responded to a perceived middle-class audience, and yet sought to make a widely accessible product.

In constructing images to appeal to a mass audience, *Life* presented an ideal with which it encouraged its readers to identify. This does not mean that *Life* created nuclear families, for many Americans in these years lived in family forms resembling *Life*'s families. Yet, even these people lived complex and multiply constructed lives, and their identification with a specific ideological position, religion, political party, or ethnic group varied according to the context. Recognizing oneself as belonging to a nuclear family, therefore, comes about in the active process of reading and viewing.

Life urged its readers to identify with domesticity by focusing on the nuclear family as the representational ideal of American culture. As a form of representation, the nuclear family works so well because it blurs commercialism and consumer identity with seemingly voluntary ties of intimacy and affection.

Life's photographs of businessmen, politicians, and immigrants as self-made family men with their supportive wives and children constructed an ideologically meaningful portrait of the United States. Central to this vision was a narrative association between capitalism and democracy. Nationality often coalesces around ethnic or racial identities. In the United States, however, national identity is based on more abstract concepts of liberty, democracy, and citizenship. Family ideals and obligations function to mediate these abstract concepts and offer a source of identification because family is a site of emotional attachment and personal commitments. In the January 1953 special issue, which featured the cover photograph of Dale and Gladys Welling and their children, the editorial describes the American economy as "capitalism modified by democracy."[108] Complementing news stories about middle-class families, the editorial praises capitalism by labeling consumption as a democratic process. In this special issue, then, *Life* combines the family, democracy, and consumption in its portrait of the economic state of the nation. As Habermas suggests, *Life* turned to the patriarchal family and the American political tradition of democracy to legitimize the political economy at a time when it was undergoing significant transformations. Displacing political and social critiques, *Life* constructed an imagined community of middle-class families as the American nation.

When reporting on the intense social changes, political tensions, and economic upheavals of the postwar period, *Life* turned to an ideal of the middle-class family in order to direct a preferred reading about these events. Domestic ideology conceptualized the family as a private sphere distinct from the political arena. At the same time, *Life* continually relied on the family to represent domestic and political spheres. News photo-essays often negotiated ideological contestations between social conditions and consensus ideals through the intersection of these spheres. These intersections are explored in the next chapter, which examines the role of the public and private in *Life*'s news stories. Although public spaces and activities have more political weight in this society than activities centered around the home and family, the visual presence of the family in *Life*'s depictions of postwar America indicate that the public and private are interrelated rather than separate spheres.

CHAPTER 4

PUBLIC NEWS AND PRIVATE LIVES
The Politics of Merging Spaces

The ideal of domesticity has grown only more powerful as it has become less a matter of fact and more a matter of fiction, for the fiction of domesticity exists as a fact in its own right. It begins to exert power on our lives the moment we begin to learn what normal behavior is supposed to be. . . . In this respect, the most powerful household is the one we carry around in our heads.

—NANCY ARMSTRONG, *Desire and Domestic Fiction*, 1987

A Greek peasant woman wearing a dark cap and an old sweater sits in the opening of a railroad car holding a six-week-old infant in her arms (*illustration 13*). Sharp focus and strong light dramatically contrast the deep blacks of the background with the mother's highlighted face. The lighting directs the viewer's attention to her calm, untroubled expression as she looks out past the camera into an unidentified distance. Her stable, unmoving form in the middle of the composition further reinforces her calm demeanor. At the center of staff photographer Dmitri Kessel's picture, a tiny baby wrapped in blankets and securely nestled in the crook of its mother's arm cries vigorously. The woman's stoic figure connotes a maternal endurance that echoes countless Western images of mothers holding their children in just this pose. Indeed, the absence of any specific location (beyond the doorway of the railroad car) universalizes her as a symbol of motherhood.

This photograph appeared in a March 15, 1948, photo-essay on the Cold War entitled "The Showdown: Washington Belatedly Faces Up to Military Realities Abroad."[1] The article warns of the American military's lack of preparation in the face of a global Communist threat. Ignoring complex political realities, *Life* points to the Chinese revolution and the Greek civil war, from which these two figures were refugees, as evidence of Soviet aggression. The text advocates increased U.S. military intervention, stating that "unless we were prepared to abandon the free world to Stalin, the moment for the showdown had come." And yet, the photograph tells us nothing about the civil war in Greece. No evidence of war complicates the politics of this image, thereby naturalizing the mother's concerns as transhistorical. Compositional devices and iconographic codes in the photograph reproduce art historical conventions of the Madonna and child that symbolize maternity, the family, and the values of Christian society. Instead of the Stalinist menace or the ravages of war, *Life* presents an image of "why we fight."

Kessel's picture demonstrates the power of

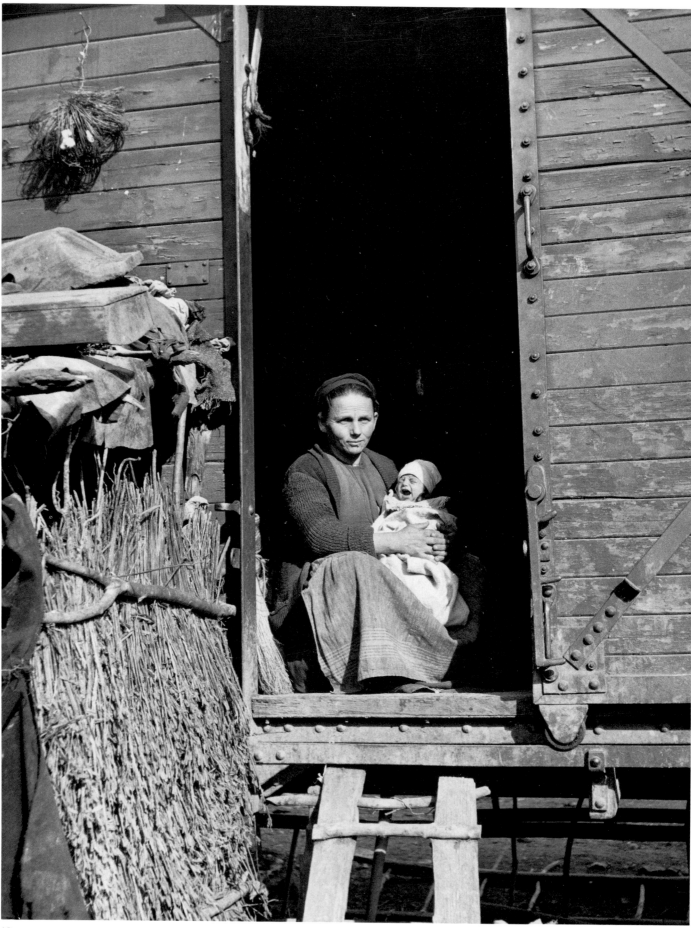

photojournalism to visualize what is at stake; American dollars should go to save the family as embodied in the ideals of the Madonna and child. In the middle of a story on Cold War political and military strategies, the photographer turns to the private sphere of the family to justify U.S. aid to Western allies. Defending foreign aid by using maternal imagery, the photograph resembles 1930s Farm Security Administration photographs of farm women and children that similarly relied on familial iconography to justify New Deal reform programs.[2] As in Dorothea Lange's famous "Migrant Mother" (1936), here too the caption informs the reader that the woman has other children and a husband. But, here too the rest of the family does not appear. Men and older children evoke different connotations, not the least of which is to raise questions about aid in the face of men's responsibilities as providers. Women's and children's traditional disassociation from politics makes them more easily invoked as symbols of higher ideals like morality, democracy, and freedom that *Life* used to defend Cold War politics.

Thus *Life* does more than construct an icon of maternity. In making the Greek mother the object of the viewer's gaze, the article displays her as a symbol of public policy. Throughout the postwar era, *Life*'s news stories about the public world repeatedly relied on photographs of the family to negotiate the conflicting demands of an unstable and changing society. In this picture, there is a merging of political and private spheres. These refugees who

recently lost their home in a guerrilla attack on their village sit in a train, a structure signifying physical movement through public spaces. At the same time, their temporary domicile's doorway locates them within an internal space. The train as both home and transportation metaphorically embodies the complex interactions between public and private spheres that challenge assumptions about the private nature of family life. Spatial ambiguities in turn suggest other merging politics. The camera's gaze denies any complexities of this woman's life by immobilizing her into an icon of motherhood. The refugee mother and child become a spectacle of need rather than people with family and community relationships who are also embroiled in political conflict. In addition, the mother's undirected gaze denies the viewer any knowledge about her historical concerns, because they are not visible. Within the context of the photo-essay, these figures become endangered objects that visualize the political demand for American paternalistic protection. In this way, the image of the woman and child, as a sign of domesticity, has the cultural power to articulate a political ideology.

Pictures like the Greek Madonna prompt a reevaluation of the concept of public and private spheres because *Life* did more than just promote middle-class domesticity. After all, women of color are implicated differently from white women in discourses about "public" and "private." Hence, representations that depend on dominant concepts of separate spheres not only reinforce gender ideals, but class and race privilege as well. The reliance on a narrow view of the private in pictures of public worlds, as in the picture of the Greek mother, conceals the experiences of the working class and people of color. By limiting the representation of women's roles in public arenas to maternity, the magazine ignores, for example, working-class women's public acts of resistance on the shop floor.

Nancy Fraser cautions feminists against referring to everything outside the familial as the public sphere; following Jürgen Habermas, she defines public spheres as "institutionalized arena[s] of discursive interaction" in which citizens deliberate about their common affairs.[3] In the twentieth century, mass communication systems increasingly replace face-to-face forms of communication as the sites of public deliberations. The news, for instance, maps out arenas for debate, identifying the topics and providing the perspectives for discussion. Ideals of objectivity and neutrality continue to remain relevant for many audiences who rely on the media to represent a newsworthy reality. Although in principle the public sphere is distinct from the state or official economy, the media, at least, are major corporate entities integrally wedded to both.[4] Thus, public discourses can support the state's efforts to secure hegemonic relations, but they can also foster democratic processes, allowing the personal to be spoken of as political and inviting political debate and contestation. The degree to which media encourage critical discourse and participation—by determining who is addressed and how—shapes the politics of representation, thus making public spheres crucial sites for the construction of social and political identities.[5]

Acknowledging Habermas's contribution to understanding the production and circulation of common concerns, Fraser and others nevertheless have criticized his historical analysis of the bourgeois public sphere as a neutral site where a common interest in the truth could (ideally) bracket out gender, race, ethnicity, and other social positions. Furthermore, they note that Habermas's claim of neutrality in the public sphere reinforces assumptions in liberal political theory that political discourse is autonomous and the private is nonpolitical.[6] Inequalities in supposedly gender- and race-neutral structures of discourse institutionalize racism and sexism by placing them outside allowable debate. Thus neither public nor private spheres are ever neutral, but replicate and reinforce the conditions of dominance and subordination that exist in society.

How do images of the private sphere reproduce cultural values that in turn reinforce social hierarchies and inequalities in public life?[7] As we saw in Chapter 3, *Life* linked a particular image of the middle-class breadwinner, homemaker, and small children to ideals of the nation by presenting this type of family as typical. *Life*'s strategy may appear to depoliticize the public sphere, but actually it politicizes it by representing America as a unified polity of families. Photo-essays that emphasize separate spheres as well as those that transgress those boundaries, like the one that features the Greek Madonna, indicate that the concept of spheres serves rhetorical and ideological purposes. Although I focus on the "seemingly private" images of families in public discourse, the concept of a public sphere is also related to the notion of domestic privacy. Ideals of privacy frequently exclude certain topics from public scrutiny by making them personal or familial, outside political debate. In the 1950s, issues like incest, alcoholism, or wife battering were for the most part invisible in the public sphere. Current political attention to these issues demonstrates that the divisions among spheres are not natural or given, but rather the outcome of political and social contestation that determines the public sphere's "common concerns," legitimating certain topics while silencing others.[8]

News reports about public affairs continually rely on social ideals and the concerns conventionally attributed to the private sphere. Fraser argues that public spheres produce consent by circulating discourses that construct the "common sense" of the day and by encompassing a broad enough spectrum of views that most people will recognize something of themselves in the discourse.[9] If the sentiments embedded in domestic images appeal to a large and diverse audience, they can be effective in securing audiences' consent to hegemonic rule. For instance, *Life*'s

big news story in the first issue of 1959 reports on the successful orbit around the earth of an Atlas ICBM.[10] A year after the Soviet launching of Sputnik, a technological achievement that had humiliated American leaders and heightened fears of a Communist attack, *Life* presented the Atlas orbit as "America's unique peaceful Christmas gift to itself and the world." Accompanying lengthy technical explanations of satellites, several pages show people including families, in London, New York, and San Francisco listening to the radio to hear news of the orbit, implying that these families share concerns about the Cold War.

Life's representation of private life visualizes an imagined community that merges personal and political symbols. In the only full-page color photograph, fireman Ed Oleksiak sits on a couch with his wife and daughter and listens to the radio. Oleksiak wears his hat and uniform, which identify his paramilitary status as a male protector not only of his family but of the (local) state as well. His son and two neighbor boys sitting on the floor in front of them play with toy missiles. The size, color, and location of the photograph focus attention onto this white nuclear family. The young boys in the foreground enact, like the father, the masculine drama of protection and military prowess. Like the Greek Madonna, this family becomes an emblem of why the United States needs orbiting Atlas missiles. Yet the photograph ambiguously captures both fear and reassurance since listening to radio news reports about a nuclear missile suggests a war mentality fearful of attack, despite the success of the launch, the boys' play, and *Life*'s rhetoric. Representing the ideal family, moreover, reveals the hegemonic power of the news to define social identities and align them with political concerns. Although the text claims that *Americans* are concerned about the nuclear threat posed by Sputnik, the photographs show only white families. This reveals racist currents in anti-Communist rhetoric since it ignores populations that would be most at risk in a nuclear attack. During the postwar years, military and political leaders worried that sites of nuclear production like Los Alamos, New Mexico, and Livermore, California, were most vulnerable to attack, but the Native American and Latino populations in these places were invisible in *Life*'s portrait of the Cold War.[11]

As this chapter shows, public and private spheres merge and interact in news stories to represent, legitimate, and at times struggle over the meanings of policies, actions, and social processes in public discourse. I am interested in the staged constructions of the representative "private" sphere as a means of political expression. My purpose here is to examine how *Life*'s representation of political issues relied on family imagery and the consequences of that reliance. At times, images of domestic life reified the division of spheres, thus legitimizing actions such as the Atlas orbit by focusing on private obligations. In other stories, families functioned as sites of struggle over defining social identities, in particular when the family itself was the source of social instabilities. Finally, *Life*'s photoessays used representative families to address the impact of political forces and conflicts on social life. The historical significance of *Life*'s family portraits lies in their active engagement in ideological struggles over defining social values and political ideals in postwar society.

Reevaluating the Public–Private Dichotomy

Postwar articles on politicians frequently contained seemingly trivial or unrelated pictures of wives and children that defined private spaces in contrast to men's public worlds. A February 1954 news story on Secretary of State John Foster Dulles attending a foreign ministers' conference in West Berlin contrasts the formal posed portraits of male diplomats with the private world of Mrs. Dulles.[12] The large central photograph in this two-page spread depicts the opening session of the conference. Delegates from Great Britain, the United States, France, and the Soviet Union stare somberly at the crowd gathered around a rectangular set of tables in this visual display of the public world of diplomacy. Another photograph shows Dulles on his way home from the meeting in the back seat of a car reading with the aid of a special light. Signifying a transitional space between home and work, this photograph demonstrates men's ability to move between public and private spaces. In contrast, Mrs. Dulles, who is never identifed by name, appears only in the last picture waiting for her husband's arrival (*illustration 14*). She looks out a window that frames and thus contains her within the home. This last photo tells the reader nothing about the foreign ministers' meeting, but it delineates the boundaries between public and private spheres, thus reinforcing prevailing ideologies of gender roles and domesticity by putting the woman "in her place."

The ideal of separate public and private spheres first appeared in its American form in the nineteenth century as bourgeois culture adapted to industrialization and new patterns of work.[13] As industrial production moved outside the home, middle-class culture relied on the concept of separate spheres to justify hierarchical gender, race, and class divisions. In this regard, capitalism played a crucial role in maintaining and consolidating the gender divisions that have made women economically and socially dependent on men. Although social production and reproduction remained vital work inside the home, the ideology of separate spheres legitimated the gender division of labor that separated tasks for middle-class men and women. Bourgeois culture represented middle-class women as biologically ill suited for the workplace and yet uniquely qualified to produce a domestic refuge removed from the competitive demands of the industrial world. This ideology defined the family as a unit of consumption and a site for the inculcation of dominant values about labor and leisure.[14]

As a middle-class, white ideal, the concept of separate spheres privileged the public male world of business and politics as it consolidated class and racial power. Specifically, middle-class white women who did not work for wages signified differences from other classes. In addition, the hegemonic ideal of separate spheres masked the various ways in which other groups organized social relations and coped with changing work conditions. Immigrants and poor people of color relied on alternative world views of family and community as their work demands created different experiences that did not divide work and family into distinct spheres.[15] Low wages and discriminatory practices in the industrializing United States made it necessary for poor women and children to work in order for the family to survive. Similarly, child care frequently remained a communal or extended-family practice that belies the ideal of the mother's sole responsibility for her children in the nuclear family. Piecework further challenged the concept of the private sphere as a haven, as women in the home worked extremely long hours for exploitative wages.

Ignoring social class and racial differences, domestic ideology justified the increasingly rigid segregation patterns in the workplace that forced working-class women into

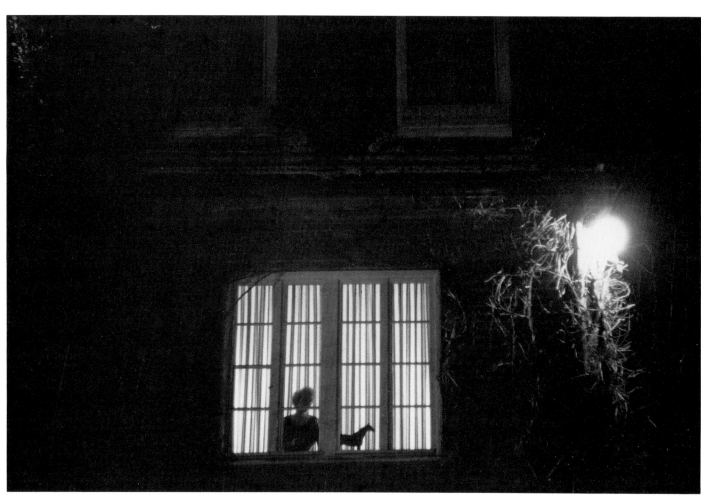

14

has been to increase the degree of public intervention in the private sphere through bureaucratic regulation of American families.[36] Social security, welfare, and education programs create a hybrid of the public and private, or what Donzelot refers to as the sphere of the social.[37] In a multitude of ways, the state actively participates in creating the family through tax policies, propaganda, education, and social-welfare rules and intervenes in family life by regulating marriage, divorce, child custody, abortion, and so forth. Intervention has taken different forms related to class and racial divisions. Housing subsidies for middle-class white families encouraged their migration to the newly built suburbs, while extensive welfare regulations have meant greater state intrusion into the lives of poor families even as they have been denied the federal housing loans offered white suburbanites.

Just as state intrusions deny a truly private space, so too concerns aligned with private life structure public spheres. Specifically, gender is not something merely inscribed in the home; it also structures the public world. If women have traditionally been identified with family and home, men's performances in public spheres—for example, education, business, politics, and sports—define masculine identity through promotion of such ideals as aggressiveness and independence. *Life*'s coverage of the Sputnik crisis exemplifies how the news constructed a white male public sphere. *Life* devoted over a third of its November 18,

1957, issue to this topic, and, with no white women or people of color, shows the public world of science and warfare as a world of white male scientists and politicians who have the ability to explain technology. The absence of women, family, and the private sphere from this coverage implies a distinct separation of worlds. As we saw in the 1953 article in which Dulles moves between home and the foreign ministers' meeting, however, news reports often rely on gender ideals to define both the public sphere of politics and the private realm of the family.[38] This suggests not only an interaction but an active participation of both spheres in constructing social identities. As Linda Nicholson notes, dividing public and private obscures the power dynamics common to both areas of social life.[39] In turning to family pictures to mediate political conflicts and tensions, news stories about the issues facing postwar Americans contradictorily reinforced and undermined the divisions of private and public.

Cold War Desires

Life's coverage of the Cold War justified an aggressive militarism by the United States through narratives that in part constructed a desire for war and violence based on ideals of sexuality and domesticity. Historians disagree about the origins and motives of the Cold War, but whether it originated from a fear of Soviet imperialism or from American hegemonic objectives in the international community, U.S.

foreign policies and political rhetoric demonized the Soviets as the enemy threatening American stability and security.[40] Actions at the end of World War II and immediately afterward led to increasingly hostile rhetoric and a rapid military build-up on both sides. The Soviet Union's consolidation of power in Eastern Europe, along with the Communist victory in China and the Soviet explosion of an atomic bomb, both in 1949, fueled American anticommunism and invigorated Cold War rationales. Colonial revolutions and other localized conflicts destabilized international relations, further heightening concerns about the United States' role in a global society. The United States kept information about the atomic bomb secret from the Soviets during World War II and afterward quickly became embroiled in local wars while directing new and more dangerous missiles at Soviet territories. Such actions fueled the superpowers' hostility and paranoid fears.

Anti-Communist rhetoric pervaded *Life*'s discourse as it pervaded other mass media. Except during the war years, *Life* from its beginnings cautioned against American political involvement with the Soviet Union. Immediately following World War II, the magazine began to espouse a strong anti-Communist position. For instance, in an often-cited November 1945 article, "The 36-Hour War," *Life* dramatized a scenario of a nuclear attack on the United States.[41] The article was based on a report written by General Henry H. Arnold, commander of the Army Air Forces.

In support of the general's call for increased military preparedness, the writer recalls the lack of preparation at the beginning of both world wars, and quotes Arnold's statement that security against atomic weapons "will rest on our ability to take immediate offensive action with overwhelming force." One drawing depicts bombs being launched from an enemy country located on the map in the vicinity of the Soviet Union, although the text states only that an unspecified enemy without warning launches an attack against the United States.

Government and media discourses frequently articulated the differences between American democracy and Soviet communism through gender-coded signs of power and weakness. Anti-Communist iconography elevated patriarchal emblems of masculinity into weapons necessary for the fight against communism, whereas stereotypes of dangerous women and effeminate men signified the threat of subversion. Such discourses presented femininity as threatening to the body politic unless, of course, it was contained within the home.[42] Although several scholars have analyzed "The 36-Hour War," they have not examined the visual images that depict the nuclear threat as a gendered threat that associates military strength with masculinity and weakness with femininity.[43] The first drawing is an aerial map of a city with a phallic-shaped shaft pointing downward, piercing the center of a blast site. The caption explains: "The 36-hour war begins with the atomic bombardment of key U.S. cities. Here a shower of white-hot enemy rockets falls on Washington, D.C." In this essay *Life* uses masculine pronouns to refer to the aggressor, in contrast to its usual convention of referring to sovereign nations with feminine pronouns.

The article sexualizes the threat of social disruption by representing the American defeat as a feminine loss. This nine-page essay depicts only one woman, and, not surprisingly, she is dead. A drawing of the enemy invading after the attack shows soldiers in gas masks cutting telephone wires. In the center of the picture, a telephone operator lies sprawled on the floor in front of her switchboard, clearly labeling her gender-specific work. She looks more like a pinup than the victim of a nuclear holocaust, with her blouse open and her blond hair in disarray. The woman's body is exposed to the male victors, and to the viewer. This spectacle of woman eroticizes destruction as the soldiers walk around her amid a scene of chaotic ruin, the objectified female representing the threatened weakness of the nation. Depicting the enemy as male, and the United States as female, intensifies Cold War dangers not only by conceding power to the enemy but by emasculating the signifier of the nation.

The final picture shows American technicians testing radioactivity on the steps of the New York Public Library. Although the city is in rubble all around them, the marble lions on the steps remain intact, signifiers of masculine strength. The imagery remains ambiguous because the lions and the technicians suggest survival despite the narrative of de-

feat. In the postwar period, many Americans placed great faith in expertise and technological superiority as the means with which to fight the Cold War.[44] Significantly, *Life* here represents masculinity in the form of scientific knowledge about radioactivity. Indeed, the text reassures the reader that the United States will win this war even though it offers no evidence to substantiate this claim. By framing victory and defeat in gendered terms, *Life* suggests that preparations for the fight against communism demand a revitalized masculinity, engendering national identity in the process.

As this article illustrates, in 1945 *Life* was still cautious about identifying the enemy. The magazine quickly dropped this reticence in articles like the one on the Greek civil war which named the Soviets as the Communist aggressors. *Life* supported government policies that fueled the Cold War, including the 1947 Truman Doctrine designed to offer military aid to countries identified as threatened by communism. This doctrine supplied the early Cold War rationale for American intervention in foreign affairs. Truman claimed that communism was a global Soviet conspiracy with international expansionist goals. Government officials developed a strategy of containment, which proposed that limited military involvement would halt Soviet expansion without embroiling the United States in full-scale war. Congress accepted Truman's exaggerated claim that the Soviets were backing the Greek civil war, and approved the administration's strategy of containment when it allocated to the president $400 million for aid to Greece and Turkey. The administration later justified the United States' involvement in the Korean War on the same basis, charging that the Soviets sponsored North Korea's invasion of South Korea in June 1950, and therefore posed a threat to American national security. During the Eisenhower administration, the Cold War waxed and waned. Eisenhower negotiated the peace in Korea, while military build-up of both conventional and nuclear weapons continued unabated. In addition, Eisenhower maintained the policy of containment in Southeast Asia and did little to stop the anti-Communist purges in the United States.[45]

Justifying American foreign policies, *Life* frequently showed its readers pictures of deserving allies as well as photographs of their military clashes with Communists. *Life* visualized the threat in extensive reports on such events as the riots between Communists and liberals in France and the Greek civil war. The Greek Madonna, for an example, offered visually credible evidence why Americans should fight Soviet insurgency around the world. This story, like many other news narratives, not only represented war as a gendered battle between a feminized enemy and a masculine America nation, but equally important, framed those gender divisions in familial terms. In "The Showdown," the text underscores the importance of domesticity to political rhetoric when it quotes an unnamed

military leader: "We ought to stop playing footsie . . . and come to the realization that any government opposed to Communism is on the team and deserves whatever support we are able to lend to the fight. . . . There will be time to deal with the family problems later." Turning allies into family members aligned against the "real" enemy positions Cold War antagonisms as the overriding concern of the public sphere, relegating "family issues" between political allies to a less important status. References to domesticity distinguish a Cold War hierarchy that privileges the male sphere of politics and in turn regulates the boundaries between the public and private. "The Showdown" envisions a polarized world in which sharp divisions confirm a binary opposition of good and evil through the entanglement of anti-Communist and domestic rhetoric.

Following conventions used frequently during World War II, *Life* routinely depicted American Cold War activities through pictures of clearly delineated separate spheres. Photographs of men fighting or planning strategy contrast with pictures of wives, mothers, and girlfriends waiting for them at home. During the Korean War, for instance, *Life* published stories on family reunions with returning GIs. "Marines Come Home from the Front," from March 19, 1951, opens with two photographs dividing the top half of the page.[46] One (a reprint of a picture previously published in a news story on the combat in Korea) is a photograph by David Douglas Duncan, one of the leading war photographers of his generation, of a soldier running through a field under fire. The other shows the same soldier arriving in San Francisco, thus demonstrating his masculine prowess at surviving warfare. These pictures contrast the active role of the returning male heroes with photographs of women standing in groups looking out anxiously into unspecified distances. At the end of the story, a six-photograph sequence depicts a woman waiting for her fiancé's arrival. Each photograph shows a different emotion as the woman first expresses nervousness, then frustration, then recognition, and finally excitement. Instead of showing the viewer what she sees, thereby acknowledging her subjective concerns through the power of her own gaze, the photographs detach the woman from the specific context. Once again, the woman's gaze, like those of the Greek Madonna and Mrs. Dulles, remains undirected, this time to represent the narrative of women waiting for men. The culminating image of the sequence, in which the woman buries her head in her fiancé's chest, obscures her face and denies her subjective perspective. In so doing, the visual narrative turns her into an object of heterosexual desire. Without the power to look that informs the reader of a person's perspective, women become signs that connote gender ideals and domesticity.

A 1957 story about the first nonstop flight around the world by B-52 bombers similarly divides social worlds into gendered public and private spheres.[47] Photographs depict various stages of the mission, including pictures of men in the cockpit, arriving back at the base and receiving medals from General Curtis LeMay. In contrast to this male world of activity, the final photograph shows a row of crewmen greeted by their wives, who had been flown to the base for this public relations occasion. The wives' faces are obscured as they hug their heroic husbands. As in the story about returning marines, *Life* combines pictures of both spheres to define public and private divisions through gender-specific active and passive roles. In addition, these stories reenact the drama of heterosexual romance in which women's identities are determined by their husbands' actions. The men look down at their wives who are visible only as bodies, turning them into spectacles of desire for the returning male heroes. Moreover, the absence of any pictures of people of color or female military personnel promotes a nationalist rhetoric that relies on the divisions of spheres to present white men as protectors of their families and the nation.

Photographs of women and families that visualize a distinctive domestic world often depoliticized war by focusing on the concerns and obligations of the private sphere as if this were outside the political arena. In an April 13, 1953, news story on the war, for instance, *Life* turns to the domestic sphere to represent the political dilemma of prisoners of war in Korea, a problem defying diplomatic resolution.[48] Instead of discussing the experiences of prisoners of war or diplomatic efforts to get them released, the editors use Robert Kelley's photographs to tell the story of one prisoner's wife, Dot Beale, and her three-year-old son Billy. The news report depends on visual conventions of both the gaze and the organization of space to signify domesticity. The photographic layout depicts Beale's daily activities, including pictures of her seated on a bed next to her kneeling son Billy, saying his prayers; at the dentist; standing next to the new car she bought; and reading a newspaper while Billy gets a haircut. The final photograph on this page shows Beale with her head bowed, in tears, as she sits on the floor next to a trunk full of her husband's papers and memorabilia. In this photograph, her emotional response results from her looking at his belongings. Unlike other pictures of women's undirected stares, this picture shows the reader what Beale is looking at. Nonetheless, her gaze remains framed by male authority, for she is reacting to her husband through his objects, which "act as memory traces of authority-in-absence."[49] Showing her desire through this memory trace secures heterosexual relations even when no man is present. Moreover, all of the pictures of Beale depict a world of domestic spaces and activities, thus limiting her role in this political story about prisoners of war to the care of her child and house. Like the story about the Greek Madonna, this one foregrounds domesticity to explain American involvement in the Korean War; in this instance, the husband has gone to war to protect the family.

The layout contrasts the domestic space that contains Dot Beale with masculine culture through pictures of men in public spaces. One photograph depicts Billy watching Navy cadets drill at The Citadel (*illustration 15*). Kelley positions the camera so that it looks down two rows of ramrod-straight cadets to the background where Billy stands looking at them. Like the boys playing with toy missiles in the Atlas orbit story, Billy is observing the rituals of his male elders, which visualizes the process of acquiring gender identity through learning proper masculine codes of behavior. Specifying his gaze defines the boy's subjectivity. Here the gaze is made concrete by the spatial conditions, for the photo-essay removes the boy from domestic spaces and places him in the world of the military.

Kelley's pictures depend on the realism of photojournalistic styles to make socially constructed relations appear natural. Mary Beth Haralovich notes that television's suburban situation comedies of the 1950s, like "Leave It to Beaver" and "Father Knows Best," used strategies of realism such as *mise en scène* and deep-focus photography to place the family within a suburban environment surrounded by material goods that middle-class viewers found convincingly realistic.[50] A similar strategy occurs in this photo-essay in which the photographs' sharp focus and conventions of space and gaze depict socially constructed gendered activities as normal behavior. Visual links between masculinity and the military draw on social conventions about boys playing war games, just as photographs of Dot Beale

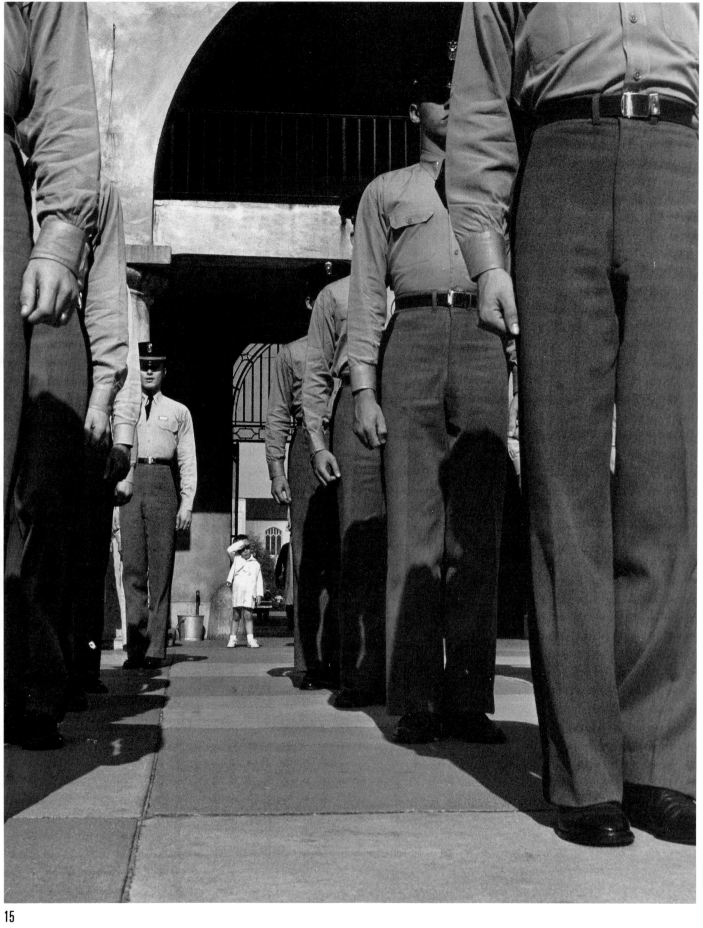

15

present women keeping the home fires burning. Realism acquires heightened legitimacy because the news turns the domestic narrative into an individualized story about one housewife's "actual" experiences.

The family functions here not only to establish the gender roles central to domestic ideology but also, at another ideological level, to displace politics by turning war into a personal crisis. In contrast to photo-essays on battles that visualize the need for a strong military, the Beale story diverts attention from politics to the private realm, thereby validating the war by never questioning its purpose. Life's focus on the private interests of the family relies on common-sense concerns rarely analyzed for their ideological content. The magazine explicitly associated privatization with national ideals in an April 1957 story of a wedding of a Czech and an American athlete, titled "Love Triumphs over Ideology."[51] The article assumes that only Communists have ideology; American values are implicitly depoliticized and aligned with "love." Such rhetorical strategies direct audiences' attention to domestic relations in order to reinforce a set of beliefs contained within the image of the ideal family. In this way, the family legitimizes the actions of the government by framing political issues as background to the central and familiar drama of domesticity.

The Family in Jeopardy

The prevalence of domestic portraits in postwar culture suggests that the family's ideologi-cal role extended beyond dividing the world into public and private spheres. Along with presenting the depoliticized family to justify actions in the public sphere, Life often used representative families as the focal point for explanations of changing social conditions. Frequently, the family as the signifier of national ideals embodied stability in an unstable world. Yet domestic life itself often became a source of postwar anxieties and insecurities, leading to stories in which the family becomes the concern of the public sphere.

Life's photo-essays on American economic news demonstrate how the metonymic use of representative families often located social issues as domestic instabilities. The magazine frequently reported on middle-class families as barometers measuring the health of the American economy. In this way, the magazine reinforced familial criteria used in economic calculations, such as single-family housing starts, identified as a leading economic indicator. In addition, Life's reliance on representatives of a particular social group, the white middle class, produced images of Americans that conflated the concerns of this social class with the concerns of the nation. In contrast, Life never discussed the conditions of ethnic groups or the working class when reporting on the overall state of the economy. These social groups remained outside the imagined community because they were not considered an integral part of the economic state of the nation. Instead, Life's coverage marked them off as isolated, special problems. To repre-

choose among a variety of products. *Life* conflated democracy and capitalism so that an array of consumer goods connoted liberty and freedom; in contrast the magazine represented communism as a totalitarian system that demanded conformity. These binary oppositions even more directly structured news coverage of Cold War events.

International political crises like the Korean War contributed to a climate of domestic repression that channeled Americans' concerns and anxieties into red-baiting campaigns that swept the nation. The spy trials of Alger Hiss and Julius and Ethel Rosenberg confirmed many people's fears of Communist infiltration. Domestic subversion seemed rampant as the House Un-American Activities Committee not only found "evidence" that exposed people's associations with the Communist party but persecuted witnesses who refused to name names. Other features of anti-Communist campaigns included demands that workers sign loyalty oaths; numerous firings of suspicious government workers; the McCarran Act, which required those deemed subversive to register as aliens; and the Smith Act, which led to the arrest of many Communist party members and leaders. Domestic anticommunism served diverse national political purposes, including the suppression of radical labor movements and the intensification of surveillance measures in the newly consolidated national security state.[59] For instance, debates leading up to the expulsion of three million Mexican workers under "Operation

Wetback" in 1954 included arguments by politicians and labor leaders that illegal immigration "served as a shield for communist infiltration."[60] The danger of subversion hung over the period, permeating discourses on domesticity, political factionalism, and the role of the United States in international affairs.

Virulent anticommunism campaigns attacked all types of political criticism and frequently found social difference itself to be evidence of Communist influence.[61] Unlike earlier anti-Communist attacks against immigrants, this Red Scare created a climate of fear in which the enemy was not visually recognizable by ethnicity or class and therefore could be anyone. Union activists, for instance, who challenged inequalities in the workplace faced tremendous harassment by the government and employers. This harassment was institutionalized with the passage of the Taft-Hartley Act in 1947, which required union officials to swear they were not Communists, thus sanctioning political purges and strengthening the power base of conservative union leaders. Civil rights and peace activists also encountered harassment by the government, frequently justified under the guise of anticommunism. Even differences not explicitly tied to anti-Communist campaigns, such as women's changing roles in work, education, and sexual mores that appeared to challenge men's authority, created concerns and fears about the social order. The strains, anxieties, and tensions in postwar social life manifested themselves in cultural discourses that often lacked coherence and remained contradictory despite efforts at narrative resolution. Dana Polan's study of 1940s cinema, for example, analyzes the breakdown of narrative authority in this period when films expressing dominant ideals competed with alternative filmic visions like *film noir* that destabilized the dream of totality, revealing society to be fragile and unstable.[62]

Life's attempt to turn an economic analysis of consumer spending into a family issue was a narrative solution common to a variety of postwar discourses, ranging from anti-Communist political attacks to Hollywood movies. For instance, Jackie Byars argues that in social-problem films that ostensibly address inequalities and problems in American society, such as *Come Back Little Sheba* (1953), narratives repeatedly focus on the problem of deviance from normal family life. These films did not challenge the status quo, but rather turned social issues into family problems that could be "solved only by a return to traditional family values and structures."[63] Throughout the decade, the media as well as popular critics worried about, even obsessed over, the conditions of family life. Media representations depicted the family not only as a haven secure from external dangers but also as the very source of social and political problems. In this regard, the photo-essay on credit exemplifies one of the central paradoxes of the period. On the one hand, the photograph of suburban life envisions the nuclear family triumphant in its suburban acquisitions; on the other, *Life* also depicted the family in danger in photographs such as the one of the debt-ridden family at the credit counselor's and the family exposed bereft of its material goods. Advertisements too responded equivocally to social instabilities. In the same issue as the story on Dot Beale, a Betty Crocker ad for milk carries the headline "What Will We Do with Nancy?"[64] The picture shows a little girl in a high chair deliberately spilling her milk while the text addresses parental fears about children's eating habits. The ad copy is structured as an advice column with highlighted questions, presumably from a worried parent, and answers by the expert who warns, "Don't scold her. It may be your own fault." Such ads generated unease and dependence on expert advice in order to encourage consumption as the solution to (maternal) fears. The ad implicitly addresses and blames women, although they are not specifically named, since the culture assigned mothers the task of childrearing.

In one characteristic narrative of the postwar cultural landscape, overpowering maternity or weakened masculinity posed internal threats to the family. First labeled by Philip Wylie in his *Generation of Vipers* (1942), "momism" laid the blame for the perceived weakened state of American males on sexually frustrated mothers who emasculated their sons with too much affection. A variety of films across several genres, including *Rebel without a Cause* (1955) and *Giant* (1956), created narrative conflicts about overbearing mothers who threatened their sons' masculinity.[65] A 1957 *Life* news story about a mass murderer in a small town in Wisconsin exemplifies this cultural current of blaming mothers.[66] Inquiring into how something so horrible could happen in a small farming community, the headline associates mental illness with obsessive maternalism: "Mother's Room, Neat amid Clutter, Gives Evidence of Ed Gein's Sick Mind." The writer uses this evidence to blame a "strong-minded woman who believed all other women were sinful. Ed was her favorite and she impressed her beliefs on him." The writer then generalizes that it "might have happened anywhere," but does not specify whether a mass murder or a "strong-minded" mother was what could happen anywhere. Nor does the text hold Gein or his father responsible for the problem, implying instead that overpowering women represent widespread danger. For Michael Rogin, "Momism is the demonic version of domestic ideology. It uncovers the buried anxieties over boundary invasion, loss of autonomy and maternal power generated by domesticity."[67]

Educators, the media, and popular writers blamed women for perceived disorders, ranging from juvenile delinquency to homosexuality to schizophrenia. Discourses on juvenile delinquency, for instance, identified a youth problem that threatened the middle-class family, and some critics specifically blamed working mothers for children's social maladjustments. This alarmist fear of the collapse of the family regulated social behavior, especially women's activities, by holding women responsible for the safety of the family.[68] Amid fears about powerful mothers and emancipated wives, critics began to worry that men's absences from the home (because of lengthy commuting schedules and career demands) would increase the likelihood that women would produce weakened sons. They urged men to be "Dads"—accessible role models who tended to the backyard barbecue and filled other manly domestic roles.

Misogynistic rhetoric warned of dangerous females who threatened not only the family but also the state by linking sexuality and subversion. Elaine Tyler May demonstrates that anti-Communist rhetoric often relied on domestic ideals and misogynistic hostilities to mediate between political tensions, social transformations, and cultural ideals. She argues that postwar culture often linked female sexuality and Communist subversion as threats that had to be contained.[69] The depiction of the female victim in *Life*'s dramatization of nuclear war, "The 36-Hour War," makes the connection apparent. The drawing locates this overtly sexual female in the paid work force—outside domestic bounds—and her fate in the narrative is death. Many discourses in the period attempted to regulate dangerous female sexuality through the family. In other narratives the family itself is the source of political danger and subversion. Rogin's study of postwar political rhetoric argues that narratives exposing family weaknesses not only "reveal troubles at the heart of American private life;

they explored those troubles in order to promote their cure." [70] In the 1950s the cure was frequently state intervention. Hollywood anti-Communist films, for instance, often centered on domesticity, representing a parent as the danger threatening the family. In films such as *I Was a Communist Spy* (1951) and *My Son John* (1952), the state, represented by the FBI or policemen, intervenes to rescue the family threatened by an overbearing mother or undermined by an ineffectual father. These films also justified national security practices that intruded on all aspects of private life as necessary for the protection of the family.

Like Hollywood films, the news media associated challenges to traditional gender roles and family relations with threats to the state. In a 1947 editorial, titled "The Family: In Western Civilization It Is Seriously Threatened and Needs Material and Moral Help," *Life*'s editors cite dangers to the family that include perceived higher divorce rates and declining birthrates and juvenile delinquency. [71] This obsessive concern with the family encouraged middle-class readers to scrutinize themselves rather than their relationships with and responsibilities toward other communities—for example, the forty to fifty million Americans Michael Harrington estimated were living in poverty during the decade of affluence. [72] Moreover, *Life* made this self-concern a political imperative by expressing the danger to the family in anti-Communist rhetoric, comparing the American divorce spree with "the record hung up by the 'Bolshe-

vik free lovers.' " As in Cold War films, here the editors justify national security intervention by explaining that the government exists "only to protect and support the family." Rogin points out that this rhetoric about state intrusions into the family in turn undermined any semblance of a private sphere. [73] In one reader's words, "Governments can help to maintain the family system by removing . . . the economic instability which threatens it." [74] This comment acknowledges American families' dependence on government support and configures economic fears as threats to the family. These explicit connections between the family and the state underscore the political significance of the domestic sphere in stories about public life, and recall the placement of the photographs of Mrs. Dulles and the Greek Madonna in the middle of stories about Cold War politics.

Many social critics worried not just about dangerous sexuality, but also about American society's consumption habits, fearing the rise of conformity in mass society. David Riesman's bestselling study, *The Lonely Crowd* of 1950, for instance, presents a view of a consumer society in which the demands of corporate businesses and the effects of affluence create a world of other-directed men, who are so sensitive to signals from the people around them and concerned with others' approval that they lose the individualistic ethos of the inner-directed personality. [75] Barbara Ehrenreich notes that Riesman's other-directed man resembles Talcott Parsons's description of the feminine personality, which further suggests that 1950s descriptions of social problems (like consumer culture and Communist subversion), were framed around fears of gender instabilities.[76]

Life published photographs of families in crisis, such as the picture of the family stripped of its consumer identity, amid social critics' warnings that consumer ideologies promoted bad judgment and excessive spending. To a society obsessed with consumption, the loss of goods carried implications of the loss of social identity. *Life* did not undertake critiques of materialism, but proposed to regulate consumer behavior, thereby regulating the family itself. The article's prescriptive message about proper borrowing is aimed at assuaging fears through pictures like the one of the honeymoon couple that associates borrowing with domestic bliss. Nonetheless, the text cannot completely erase the anxiety in this photo-essay, as the photograph of the family's loss touches on social fears that question, perhaps even destabilize, the dominant postwar narrative that equated affluence with family happiness.

In general, consumer culture produces problematic conditions because it challenges the authority of the family in its role as an institution of socialization. It distances Americans from traditional communities and reshapes them into predictable consumers with contained desires. In significant ways, fragmentation—not coherence—describes the experiences of middle-class families in the postwar period. Migrations separated families, and the elderly no longer had a recognizable political or social significance in a culture interested in affluent spenders. Furthermore, marketing strategies in the 1950s segmented youths into a teen culture in which peer identity was shaped by consumer culture rather than by community and family commitments.[77]

At the same time, consumption ideologies implicated the nuclear family in the reproduction of the political economy by replacing a truly private family with the ideal of the consumer-oriented family. The family is an effective ideological image because, in addition to being an institution regulating social behavior, the family holds out the promise of being a site of intimacy and affection sheltered from the aggressions of the marketplace. This promise of an intimacy that masks the imperatives of consumption ideologies sets up problematic tensions because the promise of the family as a location of desire is inadequately fulfilled through consumption.[78]

Contradictory messages in *Life*'s postwar narratives praised the family's ability to protect its members from outside threats and yet insisted on the need for state protection. These tensions reveal narrative struggles to define the "right" family distinct from other forms of family life. A June 1955 news article on the United Auto Workers' fight for a guaranteed annual wage displaces class and ethnic identities by characterizing economic instability and workers' demands for job security in terms of domestic consumer habits.[79] *Life* features a steel worker, John Michalewicz, and his family to illustrate the reasons for the UAW's fight for a guaranteed income. The photo-essay demonstrates economic upheaval by displaying the gifts the parents gave their children for Christmas. Evidence of a prosperous year appears in a snapshot of the children sitting on new bicycles in a manner reminiscent of advertisements. Another photograph shows a little boy standing in front of a television set; the caption explains that the family almost lost the set when shortened work weeks cut earnings. Family snapshots of Christmas gifts present the union's political drive for job security in terms of workers' desire and ability to purchase consumer goods. Class struggles are recast as families' consumption problems. One reader espoused this consumption-oriented perspective even more strongly by blaming Michalewicz: "It is a sad state of affairs when a man refuses to take the responsibility of putting away for the unforseen and, in the case of certain occupations, the inevitable lay offs and slack seasons."[80] Focusing on individuals instead of systemic conditions underscores the claim of inevitability or naturalness that the reader assigns to capitalist processes, including class exploitation.

Advertising also emphasized family instabilities when it turned consumption into a solution for personal concerns. A 1957 ad for Travelers Insurance uses photographic realism to demonstrate domestic anxieties.[81] A photograph of the interior of a car taken from the back seat shows a woman facing forward and a small boy next to her turned backward and smiling at the camera. Undermining the joyful qualities of the picture, the headline addresses the visually absent father: "With this much at stake." An ad for John Hancock Insurance in the same issue even more explicitly addresses men as breadwinners.[82] Underneath an extreme close-up of the worried face of a man with his head in his hands, the headline, "If Jane Had to Support Our Family," reveals the threat to domesticity. The ad copy then encourages the purchase of life insurance so Jane will not have to support the family. Meanwhile, a small inset photograph of the nuclear family of four smiling in a conventional posed portrait offers the reward for consumption.

Cultural discourses on domesticity represented social changes and anxieties as threats within the family at the expense of other explanations, such as gender oppression, class exploitation, or racial discrimination. These discourses functioned as forms of social regulation through their power to identify acceptable social behavior. Pictures of the family that negotiated the tensions between social changes and narrative ideals also reveal the struggles for hegemony that persist in representation. The image of family has significant power when it functions as a metaphor for the nation, but that power is tenuous because instabilities in families can appear to threaten the nation. Representations of domestic anxiety expose both the fragmenting qualities of postwar social life and the efforts to contain these changes within a coherent narrative.

Political Struggles in Domestic Dramas

Life's news section functioned as a public discourse that shaped and directed the conditions and terms of political debates. Multiple, even competing, messages in *Life*'s stories reveal the family to be a representational site whose instabilities mapped out conflicting political and economic alliances of the postwar world. For instance, a January 1958 news report on the Indonesian anticolonial revolution presents this event as a story about the effects of geopolitics on the white Dutch families forced to leave.[83] Accompanying text that repeats the Dutch warning that "Indonesians were not ready for liberty," the photographs combine domestic ideals with racial identities to divide the political world into good and evil. Pictures show Indonesian military rulers, strikers taking over a Dutch shipping firm, and three Indonesian men seated beneath an anti-Dutch slogan scrawled on a city wall. These images represent Indonesian opposition to white rule as a violent male revolt, for there are no pictures of Indonesian women rebelling against the Dutch. Such images reinforce Western stereotypes of men of color as violently threatening to civilization. The text underscores this theme through patronizing language that leaves unquestioned the legitimacy of colonial rule when it describes

"chip-on-the-shoulder Indonesian demands that resulted in retaliations for Dutch refusal to negotiate by seizing Dutch properties and by ordering Dutch nationals out." Meanwhile, photographs of white Europeans show families leaving Djakarta and others saying goodbye to family members who remained behind. The photo-essay visualizes the anticolonial uprising as a disruption of family life, literally separating husbands and wives, or fathers and children. As it did with the Greek Madonna, *Life* here positions the family as the stakes in geopolitical confrontations.

This type of story demonstrates another effect of merging public and private spaces in stories about families who metonymically signify social conditions. News articles about families caught up in geopolitical struggles narrate some of the processes by which the state intrudes into domestic realms. Such stories visualize in myriad ways the costs and effects of public policies and political actions. For instance, *Life*'s October 13, 1952, issue reported on a court battle for custody of an eleven-year-old boy, titled "The Story of Two Mothers."[84] In 1941, the Nazis incarcerated a Yugoslav woman at Auschwitz and separated her from her son, who was subsequently adopted by a German SS officer and his wife. The Yugoslav woman located her child after the war and in 1952 petitioned the occupation court for custody. The narrative dilemma revolves around the question of who deserves the child: the German parents who adopted him or his biological mother who was widowed during the war. In explaining these choices, the photo-essay conflates public and private spheres by symbolically playing out within the story of one child the major political and social issues confronting Europeans and Americans in the aftermath of World War II.

The conflict centers on the postwar realignment of political relationships among European and American allies, Germany, and the Soviet bloc. Along with coverage of Nazi trials, stories in *Life* about orphans, refugees, and displaced persons continued throughout the postwar period to address the political animosity toward Germany that persisted for years after the war. The biological mother symbolizes one side in these historical antagonisms as a victim and survivor of the United State's recent enemy. One of the occupation court judges who heard the case voiced this position when he decided in the Yugoslav woman's favor. He stated that to let the child stay with the German couple would suggest that an SS officer was a more worthy parent than a victim of Nazism. *Life* found itself in a contradictory position in such stories because it supported foreign policies fraught with Cold War antagonisms, especially with regard to reconstruction plans for Germany. The U.S. government formulated postwar foreign policies around economic needs for foreign markets, investment opportunities, and raw materials. The Marshall Plan (1947), for instance, attempted to stabilize the social and political situation in Europe, including the Allied occupied zones of Germany, as well as

to assist these countries in becoming profitable markets for American goods. Conflicts with the Soviets and the Warsaw Pact leading to the permanent division of Germany, however, complicated those reconstruction efforts. The United States offered to include Eastern Europe and the Soviet Union in the Marshall Plan, but the Soviets rejected this offer because it required that the Americans have an influential role in Soviet economic affairs and dominance in Eastern Europe.[85]

News stories about European affairs and American aid represented changes in political alliances as the Cold War shifted Germany's role in European reconstruction. The magazine addressed this dilemma explicitly in a February 1953 article covering a French trial of Nazis accused of massacring an entire town.[86] As elsewhere, the narrative frames political contestation in familial terms. The lead photograph shows an eight-year-old girl sitting with her mother at the trial with a dramatic headline above them stating "The Murderers of Her Father." The threat to the family posed by the Nazis, however, is contradictorily enmeshed in the political challenges posed by such trials as the subtitle dramatically states: "Or What Stands between France and Germany." *Life* explains that the French fear and hatred of the Germans endangered the rebuilding of Western Europe by interfering with economic reconstruction and political realignments. In news stories about postwar Europe, *Life* reworked the wartime narrative that the Nazis threatened family life into a new narrative that presented the continued hatred of the Germans as a threat to social progress.

Life addresses similar social, political, and moral dilemmas in the custody-battle photo-essay. The opening two-page spread places photographs of each mother on either side of a picture of the child. On one side, a photograph shows the shabbily dressed Yugoslav mother, Pavla Pirečnik, waiting outside the courtroom. On the opposite side, a picture depicts the German mother, Josefina Sirsch, seated at a sewing machine (an icon of domesticity as well as productivity) wearing a fashionable polka-dot, lace-collared dress. In the middle of the page between the two pictures, a photograph shows the boy Ivan-Dieter seated outside the judges' office staring into space, looking young and vulnerable in a chair so high his feet do not touch the ground. The opening layout thus visualizes the boy's social and ultimately political alternatives.

The photographs in this story juxtapose the German parents' middle-class domesticity, signifying Western democracy, with the Yugoslav's poverty and isolation, signifying Communist society. Pictures of Pavla Pirečnik on subsequent pages expose her poverty. One photograph shows her working as a janitor, sweeping a sparse room with a picture of Tito on the wall behind her, thereby linking her economic condition to the Communist state. The text underscores the theme of Pirečnik's poverty by pointing to her inability to make a decent living and her dependence on the state that supplied her with the train ticket to Germany. Underlying the more overt political messages in this photographic representation of Pirečnik lie cultural myths about Eastern Europeans as backward and ethnically inferior.

In contrast, photographs of the Germans visualize the "happy family." Pictures displaying the Sirschs' domestic life include the mother and son in a posed embrace, the son as a young boy dressed in fancy clothes seated on a rocking chair, and a portrait of the boy with a friend wearing their First Communion suits. These photographs associate the Germans' middle-class affluence with familial ideals by displaying their clothes alongside their physical intimacy and their religious values.[87] The text reinforces the visual construction of difference in the two mothers: *Life* describes Pavla Pirečnik as worn beyond her forty-two years by Auschwitz and grief, whereas Josefina Sirsch is "still buxomly youthful at 49." One reader clearly saw these pictures in similarly polarized terms sympathetic to the Germans, commenting that "to tear an 11-year old boy from his happy, loving parents, his dearest friends, and place him in a fatherless home in a strange country with a strange, poor, struggling mother is inestimably cruel."[88]

The pictorial drama of the two mothers contrasts class positions along with political ones. Pictures of happy, prosperous Germans link consumer imperatives to domesticity; pictures of the Communist mother emphasize her loneliness (there are no pictures of her with friends or family) and her poverty. Moreover, the Yugoslav nuclear family is no longer intact. By combining class position and family values, *Life* visually connects economic status with domestic loneliness or happiness. Not surprisingly, *Life* depicts the German parents, who represented American allies in the struggle against communism, in the same way it visualizes ideal American families. They appear comfortable and happy in their domestic settings. The layout reinforces this ideal through photographs of the German villagers who come out as a community to say goodbye to the boy and support the parents. These pictures reveal a town far different from early postwar pictures of a Germany devastated by war. Photographs of carefully tended houses and gardens envision economic recovery. The photo-essay sharply contrasts this image of prosperity, family, and community, with the Yugoslav mother's poverty. The Yugoslav mother can even be said to represent a threat to the unity of the nuclear family—a poor, single parent juxtaposed with the German couple, which represents domestic stability. *Life* visualizes this threat in the picture of the boy meeting his biological mother for the first time. Instead of a joyful reunion, the harsh lighting sharply silhouettes and isolates the figures whose shadows dance ominously on the wall behind them, reminiscent of cinematic techniques in *film noir*. This encounter between the mother and son raises the same specter of the dangerous mother that often appeared in *noir* and anti-Communist films. Such representational differences carry political meanings since the American economy depended on a productive reconstructed Germany, whereas, despite Yugoslavia's equivocal relationship with the USSR, most Westerners still saw it as part of the feared and hated Soviet bloc. *Life* quotes another occupation court judge at the trial whose Cold War stance echoes this visual message; since he would not want to live in a Communist state, he could not send a "helpless child" to live in one either.

Significantly, *Life* excludes the patriarch from this domestic drama in which the mother represents the family and such emotional attributes as parental love and grief. Although the German father makes an appearance in the essay, the headline, "The Story of Two Mothers," exclusively relates maternity to the family. Moreover, the first pictures in the layout, representing the main protagonists, depict the mothers but not the German father, who appears later in the essay but never in a large photograph or alone with the boy. *Life* resolves the dilemma of representing Germany as an American ally in view of its recent violent past by displacing the Nazi father from the text while keeping him visible enough to represent the intact nuclear family. The strategic absence of this husband recalls *Life*'s portraits of the Greek Madonna and the Korean POW's wife: women are more readily identified with the private world of emotion since their parental commitments are culturally assumed to be instinctual affinities.

Contradictory and unresolved messages in both the written and visual narratives reveal social struggles being waged through representation. Although the Yugoslav woman was a victim of Nazi persecution, geopolitical changes meant that she, as a representative of her country, no longer symbolized an acceptable ally. Further, *Life* reduces the various nationalities in Yugoslavia to "Yugoslav," which ignores the bitter partisan fighting that occurred during the war. The failure to identify Pirečnik's ethnicity demonstrates on a rhetorical level how postwar realignments subsumed national and ethnic differences beneath political determinants that lined up European nations on either side of the iron curtain.[89]

This custody battle addresses the dilemmas facing European reconstruction through differences in representation between the German and Yugoslav mothers. Germans were no longer America's enemies, and they were not presented that way. Contradictions, however, persist between the written text in which the Germans' war record indicates a tainted past and the photographs that present them as a loving and prosperous family. The visual representation of this drama might lead to an expectation that the German parents won custody of the boy. Instead, the court ruled in favor of the Yugoslav mother. Although the son returned to Yugoslavia, *Life* focuses on the

grief of the German family and village. Positioned as a conflict between the recent past and present demands, this grief is a social and political grief.

The photograph of the last encounter between the German mother with the boy dramatizes this political grief. Unlike the picture of the Yugoslav mother and son meeting for the first time, which suggests danger from the mother, the later image shows the son's arm stretched out of the car to touch his German mother as the car drives away, as if expressing his desire not to be taken from her. This photograph reveals another threat beyond that of the Yugoslav mother—the threat posed by the state, in this case the occupation court. This threat echoes ominously in a postwar climate of anti-Communist repression and surveillance. State-level politics led to the initial separation and adoption, and now once again the state takes the child from one of the mothers.

Instead of ending with the state's intervention, however, the story ends with Ralph Crane's photograph of the boy with his Yugoslav mother (*illustration 17*). The news, like fiction, imposes a narrative form that seeks to resolve social tensions within an acceptable ideological framework. Yet the persisting and unresolved tensions in this story reveal that social and political contradictions cannot be easily contained. The final picture shows the Yugoslav mother with her arm around her son; seated on a bed they are smiling at each other,

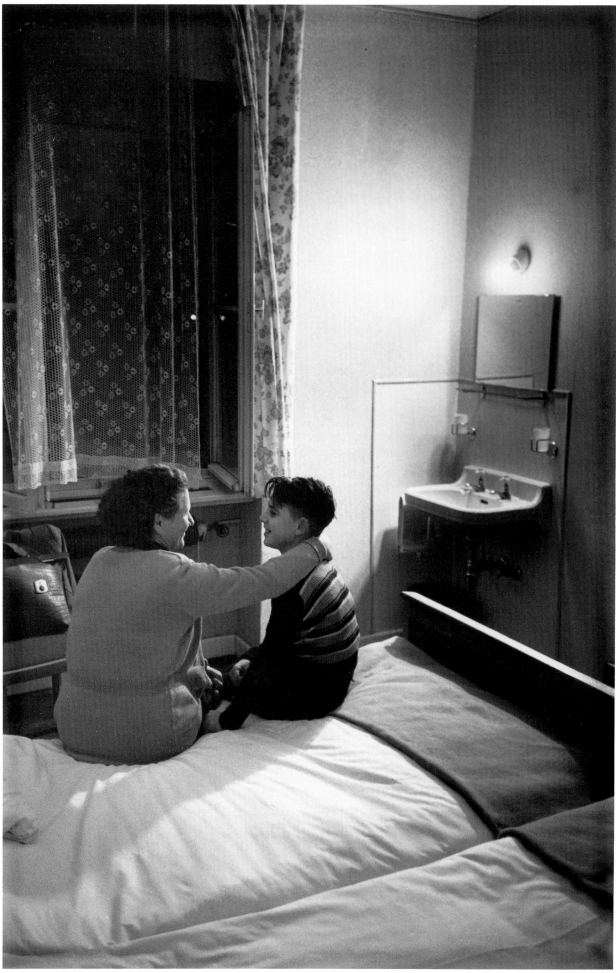

suggesting a happy ending. But, the camera also depicts the starkness of the surroundings. Crane shoots the scene from behind the two figures in order to look past them into the room, thereby directing the viewer's attention to the smallness of the hotel room, furnished with only a bed and a sink. The picture bleaches out subtle tones, creating harsh highlights against deep shadows; the sharp contrasts accentuate, if they do not exaggerate, the cramped conditions. In contrast to the earlier pictures of the German family's home, here the hotel's barrenness negatively represents the transition to the boy's new home, Communist Yugoslavia. The conclusion displaces the threat of state intrusion onto the mother, the impoverished Communist, who is taking the son away. Although this photo-essay addresses the conflicting political alliances of postwar society, the narrative lacks resolution, even coherence, because the Yugoslav is also a mother. The photo-essay exposes the constructed nature of maternal ideals because the narrative finds no "natural" mother to whom we can turn, neither the German mother with the tainted past nor the Communist mother who won custody.[90] "The Story of Two Mothers" reveals not only *Life*'s reliance on domesticity to represent postwar politics but some of the limits of this narrative ideal.

In response to this article, *Life* published six letters that reveal the contested nature of the politics embedded in this domestic drama. In contrast to the letter quoted earlier, other letters spoke of the cruelty of the Nazis and the horrors perpetrated on women and children. One writer commented that "the pain German women feel at losing adopted children is too small to compensate for the anguish which the German army, gauleiters, 'protectors,' Gestapo and extermination camps caused millions of mothers all over Europe." Opposing points of view demonstrate readers' diverse interpretations, which *Life*'s narrative focus could not completely control. A letter by a member of the French underground, for instance, imagines what would have happened if the SS had captured his wife and child. "What a thought that American judges would seriously consider, only seven years after the common victory, that my child could be brought up by the very murderers of its parents!" These remarks demonstrate the availability of familial language to different political perspectives, as well as the contested terrain of this political drama. On the letters page *Life* also published a photograph of Ivan and Pavla Pirečnik arriving at a train station in Yugoslavia and being greeted by a cheering crowd. The photograph challenges the more simplistic Cold War divisions presented in the article by offering a very different image of the consequences of state policy than the previously published, more ominous *film noir*–type photographs.

"The Story of Two Mothers" reframes the political issues at stake in postwar social relations by directing attention to the private sphere. As with much of *Life*'s news reporting in these years, the alignment between public concerns and family not only constructed a visual image of national identity but also supported immediate political needs. The consequences of this representational strategy, which was equally powerful in news reporting about other current political conflicts, are most apparent in news stories about working-class struggles. For instance, a January 21, 1946, feature story "CIO Forces Shutdown with Industry," includes a two-page spread about a striking worker and his family.[91] The magazine employs one of *Life*'s most common conventions, the "day in the life of an average person" narrative; the text features Andy Nabozny, a worker employed by Ternestedt Manufacturing Division of General Motors Corporation. The first paragraph introduces his representative status by referring to him as exemplary of the workers engaged in this strike. This formula encourages the reader to identify with actual people, thereby personalizing problems distant from middle-class Americans' experiences. Even though this is a story about striking auto workers, photographer Lisa Larsen directs the camera toward the private sphere.

The narrative begins with Larsen's posed portrait of Nabozny seated on a couch with his wife and youngest son between them and two other sons seated on the floor in front of them. An old-fashioned couch with an antimacassar on the back of it, lace curtains, and faded flowered wallpaper signify that the Naboznys' status is different from the middle class, with its modern decor as shown in advertisements and the Modern Living section of the magazine. Moreover, Nabozny's casual shirt and slacks contrast with the suits and ties worn by middle-class family men in other pictures.

The text, however, directs attention away from the family's class status by emphasizing ideals of consumption and domesticity. The caption states that "Andy Nabozny has a five-room frame house, a wife and three sons," an ordering that distinguishes him as a successful consumer. This is especially significant considering that the United States in 1946 faced a severe housing shortage. The priority given to acquisitions also suggests male ownership of the family. *Life* further displaces class politics because the text does not explain Nabozny's reasons for being on strike. Finally, the text ignores Nabozny's ethnicity, despite his Czech-sounding name and the concentration in Detroit and other northern industrial cities of Eastern European immigrants who worked in the automobile industry. Many of *Life*'s stories ignore the ethnic and racial identities of its representative individuals through discursive claims of their "normality" even as their names indicate social differences. *Life* includes the working-class Naboznys within a definition of the United States that champions domestic and consumer ideologies.

The inside cover of the same issue carried a Studebaker car ad that recalls an earlier era of craftsmanship represented as family traditions. Three color pictures depict three sets of fathers and sons working on machines together. Naming each representative, like a *Life* photo-essay, the ad describes the individual workers as "home-loving, home-owning family men themselves, these craftsmen have encouraged their own sons, through the years, to join with them in building Studebaker cars to the very highest standards of excellence." This nostalgia for a craft tradition hails a past that contradicts the contemporary strike movement protesting mechanization and loss of workshop control. In so doing, the advertiser denies the class interests of the workers in favor of domestic ideals.

Similarly, Larsen's photographs represent the working-class Naboznys as having "American" values, evidenced by the family portrait and consumption habits. At the same time, certain norms are violated because of the family's economic difficulties. In this regard, the text reveals interesting ambiguities as it negotiates between gender and class ideologies. Nabozny's wife, *Life* tells us, does not realize he has put in a full day working on strike duty because she makes him wax the floor, clean the living room, or even do the ironing. Thus, the writer identifies this family's differences, for the magazine almost never represented middle-class men doing household chores.[92] The text implies here that the strike threatens to emasculate men because it challenges the clear separation between work and domesticity, subjecting the man at home to the whims of women. On the other hand, Larsen's photographs do not visualize this threat, for none of the pictures shows Nabozny actually doing these chores. Instead,

pictures of Nabozny in meetings and on the picket line place him in public places; his wife remains exclusively tied to the home. Linking domesticity and consumption, the last photograph in the layout shows Nabozny putting the money from his relief check in his wife's outstretched hand. He stands over her as she sits on the couch. This composition visualizes the power relations embedded in the breadwinner and housewife roles, in a manner similar to the January 5, 1953, cover photograph, "The American and His Economy," discussed in Chapter 3. Larsen's photograph enacts the narrative of the man as provider, bringing home the money for his family even though Nabozny is on strike and the money comes from a welfare agency. Judith Williamson notes that photography provided "a form of representation which cut across classes, disguised social differences, and produced a sympathy of the exploited with their exploiters. It could make all families look more or less alike."[93] The photographs here reinforce a message of domesticity despite the political struggles and class tensions addressed elsewhere in the article.

Ultimately the photo-essay inscribes a narrative of assimilation that erases ethnicity and displaces Nabozny's working-class resistance, substituting in its place a consumer identity. If elsewhere the magazine depicted strikers as a threat to democracy and capitalism, as the letter writer Hunt suggests (in Chapter 3), here workers are figured as consumers. Nabozny's strike politics raise potential difficulties, but his family's gender roles and consumption habits visually conform to dominant ideals. Unlike "The American and His Economy" photograph, however, in this story there is a sense of unease rather than triumph. The surrounding text about class struggle destabilizes visual efforts to normalize the family. Moreover, Mrs. Nabozny looks unhappy as she receives the relief check, hinting at her economic troubles, which undermine the narrative assurance of consumer success.

This story was one of *Life*'s most sympathetic depictions of labor, mediating class tensions through the convention of "a day in the life" that personalized working-class struggles in terms of values promoted elsewhere in magazine. *Life*'s placement of the family at the center of a political and economic struggle renegotiates class and ethnicity through the gendered space of the home. The massive wave of labor disputes during this period made class a threatening, even dangerous, category of representation. So, it is perhaps not surprising that although the story ends with references to Nabozny's politics, stating that "he may be right or wrong, but he is going to stick by his beliefs," *Life* does not elaborate on these beliefs. Instead, the photo-essay privatizes a political crisis by focusing on a representative nuclear family to the exclusion of the communal political activism typical of strikers who, along with their spouses, frequently work collectively. Although several photographs feature Nabozny with other strikers, this story has

no pictures of women on the picket lines or of the family networks that assisted strikers. The narrative focus on the private world thereby blocks middle-class Americans' understanding of other social groups. Instead, the photographs encourage a personal empathy with the family from a middle-class perspective at the expense of articulating a class critique in the public sphere.

This article also denies differences in American social identities. In the postwar period, many white workers still identified with ethnic cultures, and increasing numbers of African Americans and Latinos migrated to urban industrial centers for work. *Life*'s focus on white workers as consumers, however, supported a trend toward a national popular culture that increasingly ignored ethnicity and race. The growing dominance and popularity of mass communications systems since the 1930s, which intensified after the war, led to the decline of regional cultural differences based in racial and ethnic identities in favor of a more uniform national culture, based on the ideals of white America.[94] *Life*'s photographs of the private sphere participate in efforts to define a unified social identity by presenting family pictures as evidence of that white public culture.

Life relied on a narrative of domesticity, therefore, even when discussing struggles that challenged the political center. The magazine's attempts to redefine social and political contestations as domestic desires put the interests of the middle class at the forefront of national concerns by promoting suburban homes and consumer goods as the concerns of every family, even those on strike. What was at stake in *Life*'s project was the power to define the social agenda for the public sphere, whether that was through stories about war, consumer credit, or American allies. Instead of representing the middle class in terms of its economic self-interest, therefore, *Life*'s focus on the nuclear family naturalized a middle-class consciousness as American.

More than merely reflecting postwar social changes, *Life* depended on the private sphere to present a public sphere structured by gender, race, and class ideals. In the postwar years, a historical moment of social change in the middle class, the ideal family proved to be a political representation with great power to negotiate these transformations. In winning out over other forms of representation, such as community organizations or kinship ties, the nuclear family turned political concerns into personal desires. The complex interactions between public and private spheres, however, indicate that along with this impulse toward privatization, domesticity was integral to news stories about political, social, and economic issues. In the 1948 Cold War article containing the photograph of the Greek Madonna, depictions of Chinese women refugees with their children also visualize the costs of war in familial terms.[95] Along with reproducing the paternalistic underpinnings of U.S. foreign policies, such stories depended on cul-

tural attitudes about the family to represent American allies as deserving of military and economic assistance. The fact that there are no photographs of Chinese male soldiers and only one of Greek men suggests that images representing male recipients of American aid might emasculate U.S. allies by showing them as unable to care for themselves.

Life's narrative, then, divides into two strains: one tending to depoliticize the public sphere by directing attention to domestic dramas, the other tending to politicize the private sphere by depending on domestic ideology in stories about political issues. Complex interactions, they thwart easy assumptions about the family's marginality as a private, nonpolitical space. For instance, domesticity confined middle-class women to narrow social roles as housewives while it provided a powerful representational tool for securing middle-class hegemony in postwar society. Such images reinforced the barriers to women's opportunities as well as upheld the great power women acquired through their social class.[96]

Encoding multiple and often contradictory messages, *Life*'s family photographs were unable to secure fixed meanings. These polysemic images were heavily mediated by textual strategies that sought to direct a dominant reading but they nonetheless include instabilities and contradictions. Beyond identifying dominant or resistant elements in popular culture, we need to consider the ideological workings of cultural practices by connecting texts to historical conditions in complex ways that explore the social constructions of cultural values in relation to histories of hegemonic formations.[97] Narrative tensions in *Life*'s news stories reveal the forces involved in struggles to achieve and maintain the power to represent postwar social and political agendas. That *Life* did not always succeed is the subject of the next chapter, which explores challenges to dominant social ideals within the magazine's own domestic narratives.

CHAPTER 5

RESISTING THE DOMESTIC
News Coverage of Social Change

They, and we, resist the only way we can by struggling with the contradictions inherent in these images of ourselves and our situation.

—LINDA WILLIAMS, "'Something Else Besides a Mother,'" *Cinema Journal*, 1984

The camera looks down a long, narrow railroad flat, revealing three rooms, one behind the other (*illustration 18*). In the foreground, an elderly Puerto Rican woman stands next to a young granddaughter seated on a bed in front of her. In the next room back, a boy stands with his arm around a younger brother similarly seated on a bed. In the back room, two other boys sit on a bed while behind them the mother and father stand facing the camera, each holding a baby. A dresser in the foreground partially blocks visual access to the background, defining the claustrophobic contours of this small apartment. The perspective recedes rapidly through the space, cutting off the sides of the rooms to emphasize further the apartment's narrow dimensions. The sharp focus of the image accentuates the barren, undecorated walls full of chips and cracks and the dirty conditions of the family's poor clothing. This picture by Albert Fenn concludes an August 25, 1947, photo-essay about the more than fifty thousand Puerto Rican immigrants who had come to the United States since the

end of the war, and were now living in poverty in overcrowded New York slums.[1]

The text represents America as the land of opportunity, despite scenes of poverty, explaining that immigrants come to the United States because of the lack of economic possibilities at home. The article's association of democratic ideals with claims of economic progress ignores postwar American neocolonial intervention in underdeveloped areas like Puerto Rico. Supported by government foreign policies, American multinational corporations after the war expanded their investments in third world countries in search of raw materials and cheap nonunion labor, intensifying a process of economic deterioration that in turn precipitated immigration to industrialized nations.[2] The photo-essay naturalizes the logic of capitalism as a shared social desire for economic progress by ignoring the historical conditions generating immigration. As it did so often, *Life* focuses on the private sphere to represent a public issue; here, however, the reliance on family undermines the ideal of consensus in postwar society.

This photo-essay ends, like many of *Life*'s articles, with a conventional full-page family portrait that provides narrative closure to the story. Several elements, however, place this representation of the family outside the

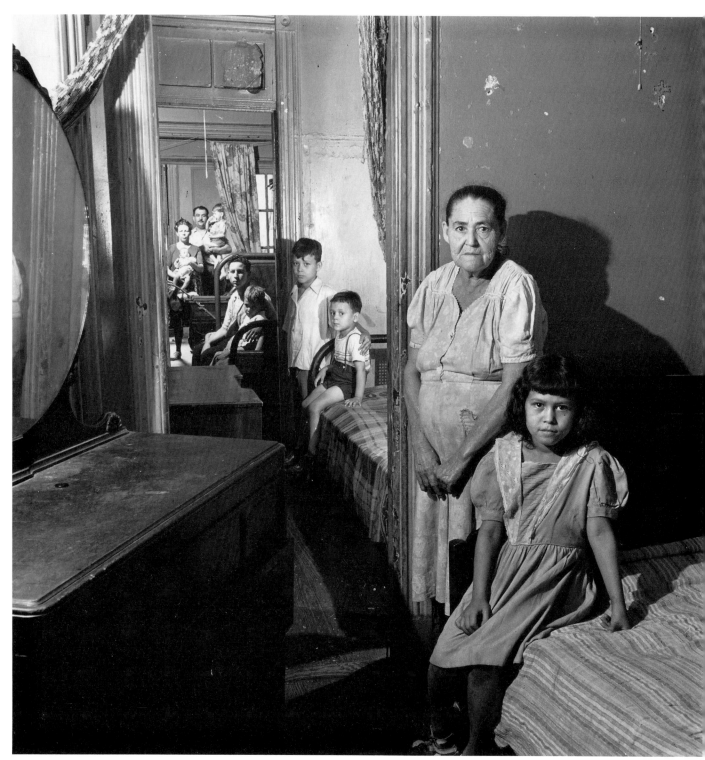

and after World War II, when African Americans fought a war for "democracy" and yet continued to face discrimination both on the home front and in the segregated army. War heroes experienced powerful contradictions when they returned to the United States only to be forced into segregated facilities and seated at the back of the bus.[18]

Broad social and economic changes supported and encouraged this political activism. Between 1950 and 1970, five million African Americans, mostly from the South, migrated to urban centers, lured by the promise of industrial jobs.[19] Instead of benefiting equally from the postwar economic boom, blacks faced discrimination in hiring as whites received preferential treatment in a job market tightening in response to automation and deindustrialization. Furthermore, urban renewal coupled with blatant racial discrimination in private and public housing forced blacks to crowd into older, declining parts of inner cities. In the context of forced segregation, African Americans organized communities of resistance against their exclusion from the promises of democracy. For all the stereotypes of postwar society as complacent and apolitical, the civil rights movement built its political constituency and made some of the most dramatic incursions against racism during the 1950s. Momentous landmarks like *Brown* v. *Board of Education* (1954) and the Montgomery bus boycott (1955) punctuated this decade of activism. African Americans

secured these achievements, however, at the cost of tremendous personal danger as violence escalated in opposition to social and legal challenges to racism.[20]

Life's coverage of struggles for racial equality supported social activism within a narrative that limited or masked critiques of systemic racism. From its inception, *Life*'s vision of American society as steadily progressing toward greater democracy included support for African American struggles for equality. The magazine frequently decried racial violence, condemned lynchings, and supported reform programs that sought to rectify racial inequalities. *Life*, however, did not include Native Americans, Latinos, or Asian Americans in discussions of racial inequalities or activism against violence and discrimination. Typically, coverage of these social groups, as in the story of Puerto Rican immigration, represented them only as social problems.[21] *Life*, moreover, framed support for the civil rights movement within a narrow concept of social reform and repeatedly admonished activists not to insist on rapid change. A March 1956 editorial, for instance, argued that African Americans had already accomplished a tremendous amount since the Civil War (ignoring the dismantling of African Americans' social and political rights after Reconstruction).[22] The editors urged blacks to be satisfied with their progress for the time being since Southerners could not be pushed too fast, echoing the Supreme Court's vacillation over race relations. A year after the *Brown* decision, the Court ruled that desegregation should proceed with "all deliberate speed," and returned the responsibility for reorganization to local school boards. The Court's ambiguous terminology enabled local governments to thwart federal laws.[23] As in many other instances, *Life*'s rhetorical and political strategy paralleled that of the federal government. This concurrence did not need to be consciously coordinated; rather it reflected the ideological continuity ensured by *Life*'s role as a central participant in a larger network of connected state and private interests.[24]

In general, the mass media in the twentieth century participate in political and social change because of their central roles in disseminating information. Ideologies of objectivity and impartiality as well as the imperative to acquire as wide an audience as possible necessitate media representations of social conflict and dissent. But it is crucial to understand *how* the news represents dissent because representational strategies determine the manner in which those Americans dependent on the news media perceive social change. News media generally depict a variety of social experience but they classify and order these experiences in terms recognizable to their audiences. Hence, news texts typically depict oppositional positions through terms that rely on dominant values and existing power relations.[25]

Just as *Life*'s representations of the economy relied on domestic narratives to legit-

imize economic policies and Cold War antagonisms, so too in covering race relations *Life* turned to the family. Here, the magazine directed the reader toward a preferred reading about social change that regulated knowledge about dissent. *Life*, for instance, presented a sympathetic portrait of political activism in the story on the Illinois housing project through photographs of families that signify domestic values, promoting reform within the framework of dominant social structures. An August 1, 1949, editorial, "Negroes Are Americans: Jackie Robinson Proves It in Words and on the Ball Field," combined this strategy with another common news convention of drawing boundaries between normative society and deviance in order to support a politics of liberal reform.[26] In 1947, Jackie Robinson achieved an important breakthrough by becoming the first African American to play major league baseball in the modern era. Even as *Life* champions this progress, however, the textual focus on dominant values perpetuates the status quo.

In the space of its weekly editorial, *Life* reprints Robinson's testimony before a congressional committee in which he criticized pro-Communist declarations by Paul Robeson, the actor and singer. The editors' introduction associates Robeson's political activism with communism, explaining that he had claimed the week before in Paris that African Americans would never fight for the United States against the Soviet Union. Linking civil rights to political dangers facing (middle-class) society raises the specter of racial difference itself as a threat. White supremacists reacting to legal efforts to dismantle Jim Crow laws in the South often mobilized anti-Communist rhetoric in an effort to discredit the civil rights movement. Throughout the 1950s, harassment of the NAACP took the form of security checks and libelous accusations of Communist infiltration.[27]

In an interesting maneuver, the editors used Robinson's congressional testimony to align anti-Communist rhetoric with liberal reform, as against more radical civil rights strategies. Robinson disavows the links between the black struggle and communism, insisting that efforts to end racism belong to the democratic traditions of the United States. Furthermore, he insists that African Americans deserve equality because they are respectable and religious people. To underscore these points, a small photograph dramatizes Robinson's heroic status as a participant in the all-American sport by depicting him stealing home.

Life mediates the radical threat further by turning to the family to reinforce a particular set of political values. In the text, Robinson depends on the family to define respectability. The baseball player rejects communism, stating that "I've got too much invested for my wife and child and myself in the future of this country . . . to throw it away because of a siren song sung in bass." The editors' introductory remarks underscore this position, characterizing Robinson as an "intensely respectable

man who takes proper pride in his handsome family and in his success as the first Negro admitted to major-league baseball."

Life visualizes the domesticity that connotes African American respectability on the facing page in a full-page photograph by Nina Leen (*illustration 20*). Robinson sits on the front stoop of his single-family home holding his two-year-old son, Jackie Jr., with his wife on the step below him. They, like the Puerto Rican family, look at the viewer, but here the well-dressed Robinsons smile for the camera. They appear to define the proper family, just like photographs of white nuclear families in similar poses. Leen's photograph displays the Robinsons' middle-class status, which gives them a visual legitimacy that in turn makes credible the politics of slow reform by demonstrating its benefits. The family mediates the threat of upheaval by visually associating certain political positions with the right kind of family. *Life*'s display of Robinson and his family as a spectacle of middle-class affluence equates economic progress with reform, in so doing committing the magazine to social change while distancing it from radical politics.

Life's support of civil rights had contradictory ramifications because its reliance on a domestic narrative often limited the representation of social and cultural differences. *Life*'s exclusive focus on the nuclear family in articles on integration and in the editorial on Jackie Robinson ignored the pivotal role of social and political alliances within black

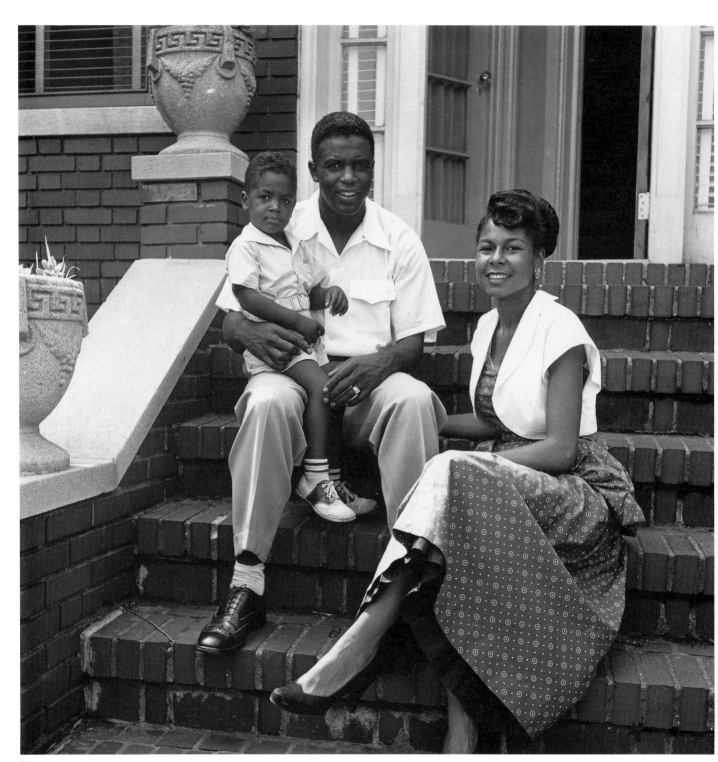

communities that sustained both organized and informal acts of resistance against racism. One of the remarkable features of any political struggle is the collective nature of that struggle. During these years, African American communities, often through the church, rallied together to fight racism. The Montgomery bus boycott, for instance, succeeded because of community organizing efforts that included a complicated network of car pools and weekly mass meetings in the churches to sustain activists against intimidation by the white power structure.[28] *Life*, of course, did print photographs of mass demonstrations; indeed, many notable photographs of the civil rights movement depicted crowds of African Americans united in protest. But in its representations of personal acts of struggle and courage, *Life*'s focus on domesticity ignored the community support and extended family networks prevalent in many African American communities. Such representations exemplify the political implications of the magazine's domestic narrative when it imposed a cultural ideal of the nuclear family on people whose lives differed from this ideal.

Life sometimes went even further, excluding blacks from photographic representation even when they were the main subject of the news report. Its coverage of one of the most celebrated lynching trials of the 1950s, the trial in 1955 of Emmett Till's murderers, demonstrates the political ramifications of the magazine's strategies for framing social contestation in domestic terms.[29] Emmett Till was a Northern fourteen-year-old black who went to Mississippi to visit relatives in the summer of 1955. Two white men kidnapped Till from his uncle Moses Wright's home one night and brutally beat him to death after he allegedly whistled at a white woman, Carolyn Bryant, the wife of one of the defendants. An all-white jury acquitted the two men because of a declared lack of evidence, despite eyewitness testimony.

The Till lynching received national attention as a result of civil rights activists' success in the 1950s in making racial violence and injustices of the legal system visible to the nation. News coverage exposed Americans around the country not only to civil rights struggles but also to the violent opposition by racists. The brutality of this murder of a child confronted the nation with the horrific conditions and dangers facing African Americans. The exposure of such racial violence led to international condemnation, and the murder became an issue in Cold War rhetorical battles. Critics of the government pointed to such racial violence as evidence of the hypocrisy in American anti-Communist propaganda promoting the country's democratic traditions.[30]

Life's article on the Till murder trial condemns the unjust verdict, pointing out that the "undertones of racial hatred in the case came out when the defense suggested that the whole thing was a plot by outsiders to help destroy 'the way of life of Southern white people.'" Despite this indignation, however, the photographs tell another story. The article contains no photographs of Till's family or of the African American community. The text does praise the courage of the black people who testified at the trial, an almost unprecedented occurrence in Mississippi in the 1950s. In addition, drawings of the courtroom events depict Till's uncle and mother testifying against the white defendants. But *Life* publishes no photographs of these people who testified at great personal risk. This absence has a powerful silencing effect in a magazine that typically depended on photographs of individuals to visualize political events.

Instead, *Life*'s photographs represent only the white defendants, and most significantly, these depict the men with their families. One close-up shows the defendant J. W. Milam holding his two-year-old son in his lap while his four-year-old son stands next to him. His wife sits at his right watching her husband talk with the children. The last photograph in the article shows the two defendants, Milam and his half-brother Roy Bryant, after the acquittal smoking cigars and hugging their wives. In the context of *Life*'s routine representations of the family as the foundation of society's stability, such editorial choices deny African Americans a presence in the narrative.

A March 1952 story, "Klan Is in Trouble," similarly demonstrates the effects of such silencing.[31] This report about an FBI crackdown on the Ku Klux Klan depicts no African American victims. Instead, photographs display whites who were beaten or whipped by Klan members for such transgressions of moral and sexual norms as irregular church attendance and adultery. The only image of African Americans shows a group of men looking through a door. The caption explains that these men are watching the Klan members being processed in jail. The image implies a reversal of power in which the blacks are free and the whites are captured. Yet the viewer does not see what the men see, so that the implications embedded in the gaze, the power to look at the Other, which would have visually reinforced the uncrowning of power, remain only suggested. Instead, *Life* characterizes the Klan as an extremist group concerned with social morality rather than a white supremacist organization committed to violent oppression of African Americans through lynchings and other forms of brutality. In that regard, articles such as this one demonstrate how the magazine's visual representations of race relations served to reinforce inequality rather than to question it. *Life*'s focus on white Americans turns the violence of the Till murder and Klan harassments into social aberrations, thus perpetuating a racist view of American society by directing the narrative away from social critiques.

Apparently *Life* found no way to represent the black family in the story of Emmett Till's murder trial that did not contradict its message of middle-class domestic life. The only alternative image is a photograph of Morris Wright's tenant shack, shown in the midst of a series of small pictures of the crime sites.

Unlike the American Dream home, the symbol of domesticity mentioned in Chapter 3, this shack visualizes the damaging effects of racial and class systems of oppression. *Life* printed no other visions of African American private life in the article; instead, attention remains on the white defendants as family men. In this way, *Life* includes them within its larger visual discourse on domesticity that legitimizes their private, and public, status. Such photographs reveal cultural representations to be the visual equivalents of power relations, demonstrating Fiske's argument that representation exists as a microcosm of the power structures existing in society. *Life*'s narrative of white middle-class domesticity mediates here, perhaps even undermines, its own efforts to critique violence by focusing exclusively on the white nuclear family.

Since most social experiences and events can be best represented through narrative, the ways in which modes of representation frame social realities are inherently ideological.[32] *Life*'s news stories about oppositional struggles attempt to structure social conflicts within the ideals of dominant society. Stuart Hall argues that "the circle of dominant ideas *does* accumulate the symbolic power to map or classify the world for others; its classifications do acquire not only the constraining power of dominance over other modes of thought but also the inertial authority of habit and instinct. It becomes the horizon of the taken-for-granted: what the world is and how it works, for all practical purposes."[33] *Life* encodes

dominant values into this photo-essay through family pictures like the one of the defendants with their wives that clearly rely on the "horizon of the taken-for-granted" (in other words, it is "natural" to show men with their wives). These representations do the ideological work of limiting a critique of systemic violence by directing the viewer's attention to domesticity.

Although *Life* structures dominant values into its texts, space for negotiation remains. The article's depiction of Southern rural poverty through a photograph of Morris Wright's shack challenges the suburban ideal of middle-class affluence. The picture may be small, even ultimately insignificant as the only photographic image of African American life in this story but still it exists to contradict the rhetoric of consensus. Dana Polan observes that the media contain both a "drive toward what we might call dominant narrative ideology *and* the possible fate(s) of such a drive in its interaction with the everyday life of a culture—fate(s) that can include perhaps the very impossibility of a complete or pure dominance."[34] Just as the photograph of the couple in the Illinois housing project watching the fire (*illustration 19*) opens up space for critical readings about the state's role in racist violence, *Life*'s coverage of the Till murder trial includes a photograph exposing poverty even as the driving logic of domesticity deflects attention away from this critique.

On October 10, 1955, the week following the article on the acquittal, the magazine published a photograph by Grey Villet that shows Emmett Till's mother, Mamie Bradley, standing atop a sound truck addressing a crowd of fifteen thousand in Harlem (*illustration 21*).[35] Villet uses a camera angle that looks out from behind Bradley toward the crowd, thus emphasizing her powerful stature. She stands in the foreground on the left side of the frame in three-quarter profile. Her straight, columnar pose, with her arm extended in a wave, provides the composition with a powerful T-shaped stability that accentuates her strength. This image of a strong African American woman appearing in public transgresses dominant white ideals of womanhood repeatedly visualized in ads and news stories about housewives. This is an ambiguous image because her challenge to conventional femininity can easily be reinterpreted within negative cultural stereotypes of African American women, like the myth of the powerful black matriarch who emasculates men. At the same time, the composition does not isolate Bradley as an outsider because her extended arm connects her to a community— the crowd to which she waves. Underneath the picture the caption reads " 'You have cried enough tears for me.' " The use of personal pronouns and direct address further links Bradley to a community aroused by this injustice. The gaze here is especially important. Unlike images of the Greek Madonna and Mrs. Dulles (in Chapter 4), which prevent the viewer from seeing what the women see, Villet's image is shot from over Bradley's shoulder; in this way, the composition associates her with a community that came out in

large numbers to support her. The photograph merges the public and private in an alternative social vision by connecting the intimacy of family grief with the politics of community activism.

Life published photographs like this one challenging racial and gender conventions alongside photographs about middle-class consumer culture. Yet the ways in which the magazine represented social differences also limited middle-class readers' knowledge of social conditions and political activism. Despite efforts to incorporate different points of view, *Life*'s commitment to domestic ideals often negated the complexities of social protest by framing political opposition or challenges to social conventions within the context of family imagery.

Anchoring Dominance

Life may often have resolved the difficulty of representing social protest by relying on family imagery, but it faced different problems when depicting social transformations within family life. In particular, the magazine published contradictory images of women in the public sphere who did not conform easily to normative ideals. *Life*'s struggle to retain credibility with its audience by reflecting the conditions of everyday life often conflicted with an ideological narrative that united the legitimacy of the state with the naturalness of one kind of family. Photo-essays about changes in women's social, work, and politi-

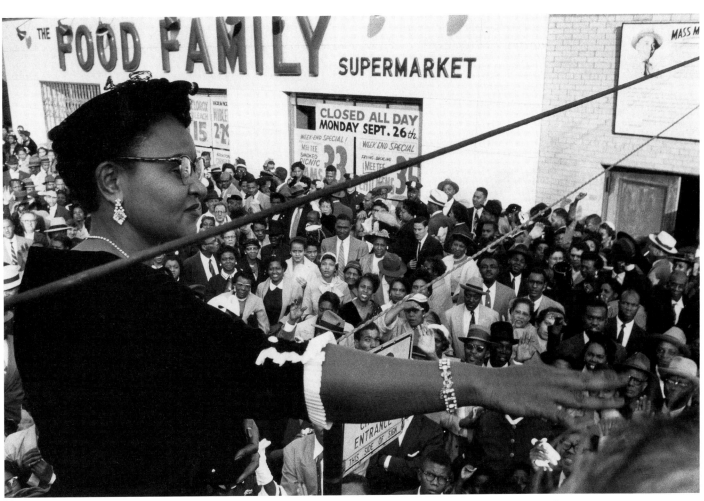

21

cal activities present an interesting portrait of negotiation over and containment of dominant gender norms. At the same time, these articles do not present any challenges to racial privilege or stereotypes since none of the representative women the magazine used to report on transformations in women's lives is a woman of color.

Women politicians were one group who seriously challenged the ideology of domesticity by participating in public affairs, often in leadership positions. Their involvement in the federal government, supported by the Roosevelt administration, declined in the postwar administrations of Truman and Eisenhower. Yet, despite a conservative climate, across the country women participated in local and state politics as elected officials and appointees to government posts. In 1950, for instance, 249 women held positions in state legislatures. Still a small number overall, women representatives in some states approached one-fourth of the total number. Women did not gain as substantially in national legislative positions as they did at the local level. Nonetheless, between 1940 and 1950, 22 women won seats in Congress. Other women meanwhile gained political experience through voluntary organizations like the League of Women Voters, the YWCA, the American Friends Service Committee, and other community service organizations.[36] Few women politicians articulated feminist critiques, but their political participation threatened social norms as they confronted patriarchal ideologies.

Life's photo-essays about women politicians addressed the social realities of white women's public lives within a narrative that accommodated the cultural ideals championed throughout the magazine, especially in advertisements addressing women exclusively in their roles as housewives and mothers. In the midst of complex and often competing codes, Life's representational strategies directed readers' attention toward a preferred reading. Photo-essays focused most consistently on women's femininity, framing these portraits in explicitly gendered terms. With varying degrees of success, Life's affirmations of traditional gender and patriarchal values contained the challenges posed by women active in public life.

News reports about women's political involvement in local government frequently assumed a patronizing tone that bordered on ridicule, labeling their activism "petticoat rule." In contrast, articles on local male politicians avoided such condescendion. In a September 18, 1950, photo-essay titled "Petticoat Rule Scores Again," the opening picture by Thomas McAvoy shows Mayor Dorothy Davis of Washington, Virginia, modeling her inaugural outfit for her daughter (*illustration 22*).[37] In a pretense of spontaneity, McAvoy positions the two figures in a manner that emphasizes Davis's femininity. Her outstretched arms mimic models' poses in advertising, thereby calling attention to her body. In the lower right corner, her daughter's pose and gaze function to bring the viewer into the

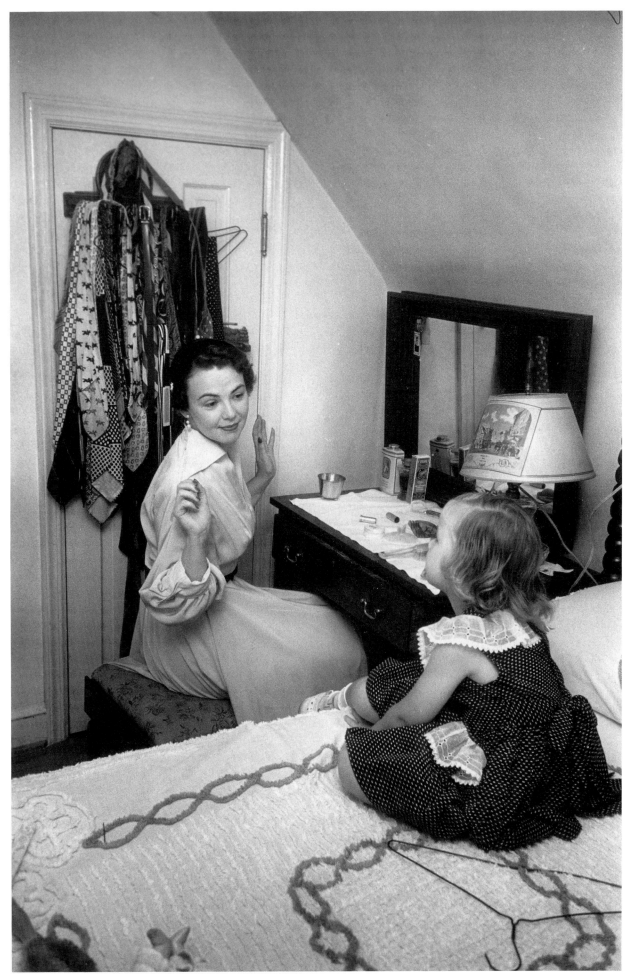

scene; in following her gaze we too gaze upon this woman. Emphasis on appearance and maternity through the daughter's presence identifies Mayor Davis first, and foremost, as a woman and a mother rather than as a politician. To support this visual attention to the feminine, the text surmises that "Mrs. Davis' good looks had swayed some votes." Moreover, the writer trivializes her political objectives. The text states that "the issues at stake were fewer, clearer and considerably more important than those in many a larger election. There were too many stray dogs on the streets, the weeds around town needed cutting, and a lot of the bulbs in the street lamps had burned out." These textual references anchor femininity to the photograph by offering seemingly natural confirmation of the photograph's veracity.[38]

Contradictions persist nonetheless, for along with this voyeuristic attention to Davis's "good looks," *Life* visually represents the mayor's political activism. In contrast to the opening image depicting the private sphere, on the facing page the photograph places Davis in the public arena, giving her inaugural address (*illustration 23*). McAvoy uses a low-angle camera shot to make her appear powerful as she looks down on her audience, and us, obviously in a position of leadership. At a time when pictures of women in responsible public positions were still rare, such photographs present an alternative to *Life*'s domestic ideology. Other signs, however, circumscribe this representation of a woman

politician within the confines of conventional femininity. McAvoy takes the picture from the side which reveals her legs; in a frontal view they would have been obscured by the podium. Within the context of pinups and other images of white femininity, the camera's attention to her legs makes the sexual body visible even when the primary focus is on the newly elected mayor giving a public address. The persistent textual and visual emphasis on Davis' femininity limits *Life*'s characterization of her role as a public official. Although the photograph cannot secure a singular meaning, femininity is a powerful ideology here reinforced by the text.

Life was not completely hostile to women's political activities. Rather, the magazine urged women to participate by influencing their families. An October 1946 editorial states that "politics, in a democracy with weak social traditions, shapes our customs and manners, as well as our laws. So if ours is to be a whole and healthy civilization, our politics needs the feminine touch. It needs our womanpower."[39] Public and private spheres intersect here as domestic ideals redefine the notion of "home" to allow women to participate in public arenas while still retaining their roles as mothers. Many political women accepted this domesticated version of their public roles. For instance, Mayor Davis in another context stated that if "the old-fashioned idea that a woman's place is in the home is correct, then it's my contention that home must extend beyond the front gate."[40] The gendered image

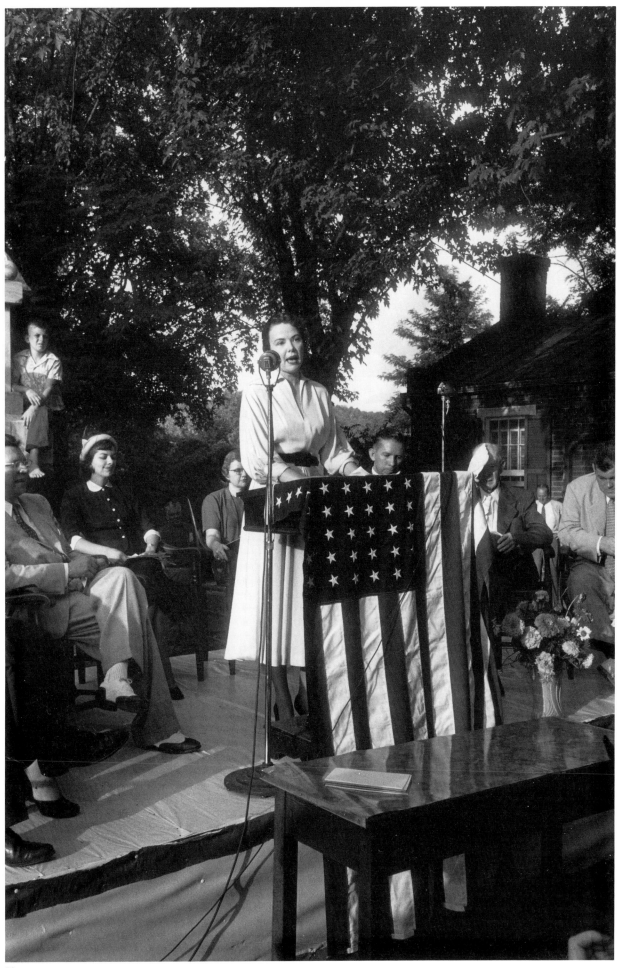

of extending the home into politics is a recurrent theme in American history, evident, for instance, in arguments about republican motherhood during the revolutionary period and efforts by late nineteenth-century reformers to create a "maternal commonwealth."[41] Such rhetoric identifies women's political importance in gender-specific terms that rely on their presumed superior morality, but it also provokes an essential paradox. Recognition of the importance of women's political responsibilities also envisions women in public arenas outside the home. *Life*'s dependence on domestic imagery in its news coverage of women politicians reveals how representational strategies negotiated this paradox by incorporating contestations over gender identities within a narrative of family life.

In the December 24, 1956, special issue, "The American Woman," an article on local and national women politicians focuses primarily on how these women find time in their busy schedules for domestic tasks.[42] One photograph depicts a Minnesota state representative giving her family breakfast; the text discusses her management of time but does not analyze her political beliefs. This story on women politicians concludes with three photographs of Washington, D.C., hostesses who, *Life* explains, make political contributions by throwing parties, thus blurring the boundary between public and private spheres by envisioning the tasks of women politicians as equivalent to those of party hostesses. Similarities also exist between representations of

women politicians and politicians' wives. Several photo-essays from 1956 to 1960 featured Jackie Kennedy as the consummate politician's wife, and she appeared on four magazine covers between 1958 and 1960.[43] Headlines proclaimed Jackie Kennedy a political asset while pictures of her and her children in the private sphere envisioned the nature of those assets. Representations of women politicians similarly focused on their maternal roles. A July 4, 1960, special issue titled "American Politics" includes only one story on a woman politician.[44] The last picture in the feature on State Senator Geri Joseph from Minnesota provides narrative closure through a close-up of Joseph hugging her son. Photographic attention to maternity, at the expense of women's political objectives, directs attention to the naturalized connections between women and the private sphere.

In addition to photographing women politicians as mothers, *Life* offered alternative visual representations of women's roles. Photographs in the 1956 special issue and the 1960 story on Joseph show women politicians canvassing voters and talking with male politicians amid the white columns and high ceilings of government buildings that signify official public spaces. The opening photograph of Joseph is a close-up head shot, a conventional portrait style used for male politicians as well. The caption comments, "A flashing smile is part of Geri Joseph's armory of political weapons, along with brains, charm and a lot of youthful energy." This articulates the conflicting messages that prevail in representations of women politicians for the writer immediately calls attention to the politician's femininity and yet also acknowledges her social and intellectual abilities.

Participation in politics was only one of many social changes for women in the postwar period. Women struggled between the demands of domestic responsibilities and involvement in public worlds as they pursued higher education and worked outside the home in increasing numbers. Such contradictory demands on women's lives provoked discontent and tensions that often met with stiff opposition.[45] From television sitcoms that praised ideal homemakers to stern warnings from women's magazines, the media admonished women that domesticity was their natural calling. Educators, sociologists, and politicians reiterated this message. In 1955, at a graduation ceremony at Smith College, Adlai Stevenson told women graduates that their role was to "influence us, man and boy," and to "restore valid, meaningful purpose to life in your home."[46] Yet, out of both necessity and desire, women continued in growing numbers to enter the paid labor force. For example, the percentage of married women working outside the home rose from 15 in 1940 to 30 in 1960. The most dramatic change in the period occurred for mothers with children between the ages of six and seventeen who increased by 39 percent their participation in the paid labor force; by 1960, they comprised one-third of all workers. This social develop-

ment dramatically contradicted the ideal of the happy housewife.[47]

Throughout the period, *Life* frequently discussed the situation of American women, including their problems and dissatisfactions. The magazine's most extensive treatment of this topic was the 1956 special issue "The American Woman: Her Achievements and Troubles." Even though the title and articles refer to American "women," it is immediately clear that this representation largely excludes women of color and working-class women. The cover photograph establishes the racial focus: a young, white woman leans her forehead against her blond daughter's head, and together they laugh in an intimate gesture. The caption identifies this woman as a "working mother," but the visual focus on her identity as a mother, rather than a worker, signals *Life*'s attention to women's domestic roles, which persists throughout the issue. A reader commenting on the special issue vividly captures the conundrum women faced in representations like this one: "If the American woman stays home and keeps house she is accused of being deadly dull. If she succeeds in the double duty of working woman-housewife, she is accused of neglecting her home and family. If she forgoes family life for a career she is accused of being unwomanly, frustrated and downright greedy."[48] In many ways, the special issue did not promote a simple return to domesticity but instead visualized these various contradictory roles for white women.

The editors' introductory comments emphasize visual appearance and maternal concerns by listing as women's major achievements their good looks and healthy babies. Feature articles include stories on domesticity and femininity. "Busy Wife's Achievements" describes a housewife's daily activities through photographs that show her in the kitchen talking on the telephone and serving refreshments at a Cub Scout meeting.[49] Another story, "The First Baby," contains pictures of a pregnant woman preparing a nursery in a single-family home, at a baby shower surrounded by friends watching her open presents, and at the hospital in labor.[50] The concluding photograph depicts the mother holding her newborn infant; the text explains that "of the accomplishments of the American woman, one she brings off with the most spectacular success is having babies." A third article, on domestic life, focuses on a teenage girl "growing up."[51] Growing up according to the pictures means the teenager has traded her tomboy interests in jeans and sports for skirts and her first date. These life-cycle stories about women's activities and interests concentrate attention on traditional gender roles in the middle-class world of domesticity, presenting the interests and concerns of these white women as the concerns of all American women and creating an imagined community that aligns an ideal of gender and race with an image of a unified national culture. Indeed, these pictures of women in domestic settings seem familiar and even routine because *Life* so fre-

quently depicted women in private spaces. This familiarity encourages an acceptance of constructed gender roles as commonplace norms, an acceptance that rewards the reader, as Fiske notes, with the pleasure of recognition and privileged knowledge.[52] One letter to the editor articulated an imagined community of women's shared domestic concerns: "Your special issue . . . was truly valuable. I read it cover to cover feeling as if each article was written especially for me." Another letter writer commented that "I now find that each day's experience with my children, my husband and my friends can have true meaning and significance. . . . It also requires the woman's quiet guidance and direction of the family's hours together. Most of all must come a reaffirmation of one's faith in God. The results can be magnificently rewarding." Letters like these, written apparently by ordinary readers, reaffirm the magazine's representation of femininity by reiterating one social ideal as if it were the only one. None of the letters in response to the special issue offered a feminist perspective or argued that women work because of necessity. Women subscribers undoubtedly had a range of opinions, but either they did not write letters or *Life* did not publish them.

The types of stories as well as forms of representation privilege heterosexuality and maternity in this imagined community of middle-class women, as when the editors describe women's interests as "their life in the suburbs, their preferences in spouses . . .

their abiding faith in love." The reference to suburban life also reproduce the discriminatory experiences of women of color. For example, by the end of the 1950s, whites outnumbered blacks in American suburbs by a ratio of thirty-five to one.[53] Although three photographs in an article on working women show women of color, the photo-essays devoted to life-cycle stories about being a housewife, growing up, and widowhood depict only white women. The one story about working women includes pictures of working-class women in factories and on assembly lines, but the text never discusses women of this class or women of color.[54] The issue's repeated emphasis on suburban housewives as well as a story on women in charitable volunteer organizations further underscores how *Life* addresses women of a particular economic class.

The special issue's story on women's public accomplishments reports on women's wage-work experiences.[55] According to *Life*, women held one-third of the jobs in the nation. Consistent with the issue's focus on traditional femininity and domesticity, however, the photographs featured gender-segregated jobs, such as sales personnel, nurses, teachers, and garment makers. Even though the text states that a million women were business owners or executives, the photograph representing this group depicts women executives at a fashion show. This story implicitly addresses class relations in the sense that the layout places photographs of working-class women on assembly lines next to pictures

of teachers and businesswomen. However, as with the 1947 story on housing shortages when *Life* depicted houses in different price ranges without discussing who could afford them,[56] the article shows different types of jobs without discussing class-based determinants that affect job distributions. Moreover, the text does not address the class and racial discrimination that confronted postwar female workers. Instead, *Life* constructs a portrait of the United States where choice prevails and women's natural instincts extend into the public sphere.

In representing women's work commitments as a choice, *Life* defined work itself in terms of middle-class cultural ideals. In this special issue, *Life* repeatedly comments that women do not *have* to work, but instead work because they like it or to augment the family income. The story "My Wife Works and I Like It" dramatizes the daily routine of Jennie Magill.[57] The text quotes her husband, Jim Magill, who states that her full-time job is good for her, for him, for their children, and for the household budget. The reference to the budget reflects social conditions of the period as middle-class women increasingly worked to maintain their family's class status.[58] Photographer Grey Villet depicts the couple paying bills, which underscores how Jennie Magill's work benefits the family, that is, the consumer-oriented family. The text reinforces the association between domesticity and consumption by quoting Magill's husband who comments that her paycheck supplements the family budget so that "now when we see a piece of furniture we want, we can buy it." Thus, *Life* legitimizes woman's work in terms of consumption ideals. Such circumscribed representations of working women serve in important, although inconclusive ways, to contain rather than give voice to opposition to patriarchal ideals.

Life further narrows its portrait of working women by choosing a woman in a gender-specific occupation. Magill runs the bridal service in a local department store. Only one picture—a close-up of her talking with a woman wearing a bridal veil—shows her working, and two others—one with her husband riding down the department store's escalator after work, the other eating lunch with fellow workers—show her in public spaces. The minimal representation of work lessens the visual threat of women engaged in work activities. Moreover, Villet's photograph of Magill on the escalator places her in the same space and pose as the shoppers. Visually, *Life* characterizes her as a consumer rather than a worker.

Significantly, Jennie Magill does not speak in the narrative. *Life* only quotes Jim Magill, thereby giving the husband the power to speak for his wife. This reproduces traditional notions of male power that silence women, yet it is nonetheless a contradictory representation because he repeatedly extols the benefits of his wife's work. Elsewhere in this issue, an article on divorce claims that working women's selfishness causes grave psychologi-

cal damage to husbands and children.[59] In contrast, here a male authority, the husband, argues that women's wage work benefits the family.

Contradictory messages about gender and economic roles also compete visually in this essay. For example, in the center of the two-page layout, a photograph of Jennie Magill shows her standing in the kitchen holding her two-year-old son who is pointing at a cake he helped the housekeeper make. This picture of a woman with a young child is problematic because mothers of small children were more vigorously discouraged by employers and the media from working than any other group. Villet captures these tensions by including in the photograph the housekeeper whose presence appears to question if not undermine Jennie Magill's maternal role in the kitchen. The caption underscores the cultural divisions between work and home when it comments that Magill takes "over the family reins when she gets home," which suggests at least a temporary loss of maternal authority during her working hours. At the same time, the picture directs the viewer's attention to this woman's status as a mother; similarly the cover also features Jennie Magill as a mother, this time with her daughter. The power of photographs to be persuasive works here to emphasize domesticity to the exclusion, visually at least, of work. These images also reveal the inherent instabilities in the domestic narrative because depictions of intimacy can show, as happens in the photograph of the Puerto Rican immigrants (*see illustration 18*), that familial affection exists outside the ideal of middle-class domesticity.

The special issue acknowledges social tensions surrounding American women's public status, yet the texts reposition these difficulties as domestic problems caused by women. The introduction, for instance, tells readers that women are unhappy because they do not cherish their privileges, defined as femininity, beauty, and the ability to bear children. *Life* describes American women's problems as domestic concerns in stories about a teenage girl becoming a woman, women's marital problems, the "lifelong task" of staying young and beautiful, and the loneliness of widowhood. This implies, although it remains unstated, that the male gaze determines women's concerns. The list of problems could be rephrased as a teenager trying to be attractive for her first date with a boy, keeping the man happy at home, staying beautiful for a man, and coping with loneliness when he is gone. The stories in this issue reveal the tensions created by changes in women's activities, but the prominence of dominant gender ideals validates normative patriarchal relations. Moreover, this class-determined narrative of domesticity limits viewers' understanding of working-class women or women of color. This is reminiscent of the narrow way in which *Life*'s family narrative envisioned African American culture. *Life*'s representation of the problem of middle-class white women's discontents in this special issue participates in broader cultural trends managing or regulating social behavior.

Photo-essays about families that did not conform to domestic ideals, namely nonnuclear families, similarly relied on dominant cultural values to frame the narrative. A November 30, 1953, news report tells the story of an unmarried Navy officer who adopts a Korean War refugee.[60] The photo-essay differs from standard representations of domestic life because the lack of pictures of women or the home underscores the absence of the nuclear family. *Life* contains any threats to patriarchal ideals posed by the absence of women by focusing on codes of masculinity. The first photograph shows the Korean boy wearing a navy uniform standing with his uniform-clad new father as they "enter" the United States. Outdoors, in the public sphere, the father and son walk purposefully toward the camera. The boy's uniform here connotes both his Americanness and his masculinity. The photograph directs attention away from his ethnic difference to codes signifying his adoption of American values. In the last photograph, the father swings the boy in the air by the seat of his pants as they walk down a public street (*illustration 24*). Here, the boy wears a cowboy outfit complete with toy guns in a holster around his waist. Iconography about the mythic West combining masculine and nationalistic codes presents this Korean child as an American boy, or as the Other tamed.

Life responded to challenges to domestic ideals posed by working women or single

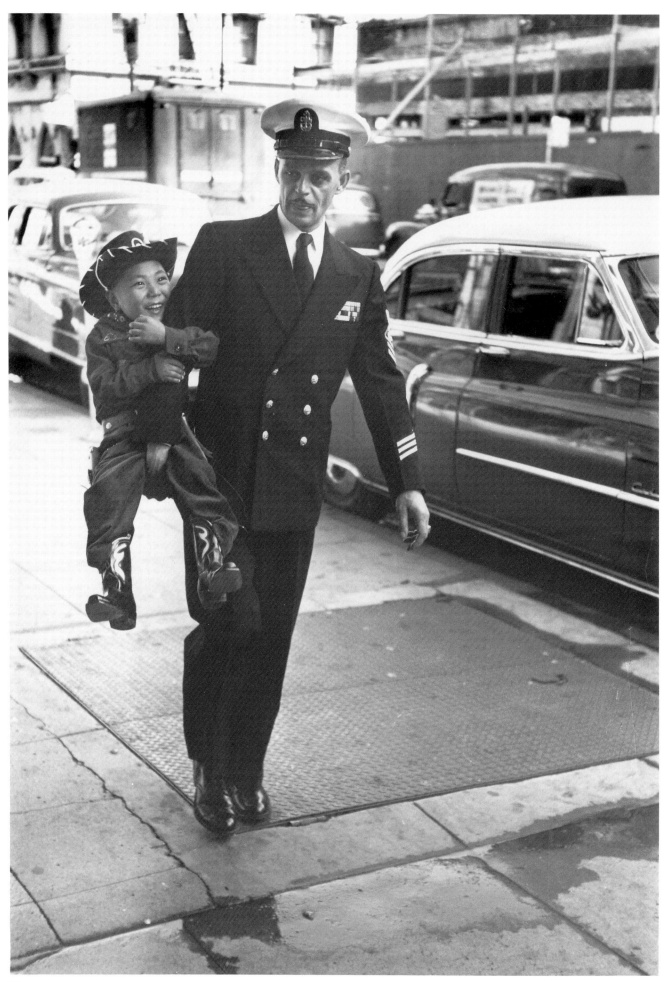

male parents with anchoring mechanisms that encoded gender and family ideals into the text. Representation, however, is never totally contained by these signifying codes nor can meanings be made entirely predictable because combinations of codes frequently offer contrasting meanings. Indeed, the greater the number of codes, the greater the instability of connotation.[61] For instance, the need to assert that "my wife works and I like it," speaks to the contradictions between women's work experiences and a dominant ideology that makes this quote stand out as extraordinary in postwar American popular culture.

V. N. Voloshinov uses the concept of multiaccentuality to explain such instabilities. He argues that because there are no distinct languages associated with different classes, various groups use the same set of signs for ideological communication—but inflect them with differently oriented accents.[62] Ruling classes, as we have seen in *Life*'s domestic narrative, struggle to impart an eternal character—a single accent—to ideological signs. Michael Denning recommends that we assume the "multiaccentuality" of all signs, so that such attempts cannot succeed in concealing "the struggle, and thus the meaning of the ideological document."[63] Indeed, as we find in *Life*'s photojournalism, ambiguities persist. In the production process, writers, photographers, and editors represent social realities from their own contradictory social positions, and similarly, readers accent their readings from their historical perspectives.

Despite the editorial logic in *Life* promoting a unified postwar culture, the magazine's representational strategies could not fully contain or suppress differences. Even representations of the most dominant and seemingly univocal concept, namely masculinity, contain multiple codes that can be accented differently depending on context and reader. Although *Life*'s news reports, especially on the military, at first glance appear to valorize men, codes reinforcing male authority exist in an unstable environment with other codes competing to define masculine identity.

Resisting the Ideal

Masculinity, like femininity, is not a stable or fixed ideal but a contested arena that continually changes amid social challenges to gender conventions. In many ways, masculine bravado dominated cultural discourses of the postwar era. This bravado supported Cold War politics by dividing the world into spheres of masculine power and feminine weakness. Military exploits during the postwar years, especially the Korean War, presented *Life* with the opportunity to depict fighting men protecting the United States. A September 18, 1950, lead news story, "This Is War," for instance, featured a series of photographs by David Douglas Duncan of American troops fighting in Korea.[64] In one picture a group of marines lies on the ground in an open field, rifles pointed at the unseen enemy, while one marine stands, having just tossed a grenade. Another photograph shows marines with clothes caked in mud, running through a field past an enemy corpse. Pictures of white men in action define masculinity by signifying the marines' strength and courage. Moreover, this visual portrait of war shows a public world completely devoid of women, thus avoiding the danger of feminizing the collective spirit of male action.[65] The narrative of war is central to the photo-essay's construction of masculinity, yet the war itself is strangely absent since the photographs do not depict Korean villagers or enemy soldiers engaged in combat. Only two small pictures in this photo-essay depict Asians: one shows a group of prisoners, an image that serves to display American prowess and superior fighting capabilities; the other depicts a group of South Koreans carrying a wounded marine. The absence of any further historical context turns the war into an occasion for white men to act bravely and courageously as they disregard danger and poor conditions.

Masculine rhetoric may have been prevalent in *Life*'s coverage of the Korean War, but the magazine also published photographs that challenged these gender codes. Unexpected contradictions sometimes occurred when competing signs destabilized the discursive boundaries of the magazine's gender ideals. The first and last photographs in "This Is War," for example, tell a different story from the others. In the opening picture, Duncan moves the camera in to take a close-up shot of a white marine in half-length profile, dressed in fatigues and a helmet. Although the pose creates a stable, columnar composition, the close-up reveals the man's dirty and unshaven face. He looks exhausted as he stares blankly, a single tear rolling down his cheek. Blurred against the picture plane in the foreground, his right hand gestures upward almost as if in supplication. During both World War II and the Korean War, *Life* occasionally published pictures of soldiers' anguish. The image of a man crying in the context of war connotes another aspect of war than photographs of soldiers firing rifles or throwing grenades. Pictures of male emotions reveal the hardship and pain of war and thus the soldier's courage to endure. Duncan's portrait suggests through the lone tear the frustration and anguish of war rather than an emotional breakdown. The caption underscores this interpretation by explaining that the marine had just fought in a grueling battle with heavy losses to his unit. The surrounding context of other photographs of brave soldiers further limits any threat of weakness. Paradoxically, the one safe place *Life* found to represent men's emotions was in war.

The man's grief and exhaustion speak to the horrors of a war that is visually absent without even a hint of landscape in the totally indistinct background. Duncan removes the soldier from the historical context of the war to turn his portrait into a universal expression of suffering. Like decontextualized portraits of mothers with children signifying maternity, this marine becomes "everyman" suffering in an ultimately apolitical realm. The most obvious effect of this decontextualization is to displace any political critique of the Korean War. Photographs like this one tell the viewer nothing about the conditions of the war, much less the reasons for this marine's presence in Korea.

Yet this visual moment also addresses emotions that pose a threat to stereotypes of masculinity. The image of a man overcome by physical and emotional exhaustion contradicts the masculine codes typical in media portraits of soldiers as strong and independent, unemotional and powerful. The dirt, the suffering, and the pain contrast with the glamorous depictions of war seen elsewhere in *Life* or romanticized by Hollywood cinema. Notably, the last photograph in the photoessay shows a wounded marine crying out in pain. He appears dirty and exhausted as his right arm reaches over to support his bandaged left arm. The close-up makes visible his pain through both the cry of distress on his face and the left hand clenched at his chest in the center of the composition. Behind him, a worried-looking soldier in a jeep moves to help him. Pictures like these offer visual alternatives to such masculine ideals of war as strength, toughness, and emotional detachment and expose masculinity itself as a culturally constructed ideal, not inherent or natural behavior.

Challenges to masculine ideals in Duncan's photographs also open up spaces in which to critique the political actions taken in the name of masculinity. *Life* defended the Korean War as an action in the interests of national security, an argument grounded in gendered assumptions about American men protecting their women and children. Alternatives to dominant male gender ideals potentially make problematic the military actions legitimized on the basis of those same ideals. Conflicting codes in a June 17, 1957, news report of an accidental shooting of a Japanese woman by a GI in Japan similarly challenged assumptions about the legitimacy of the American military's international role.[66] The most prominent photograph in the story is not a picture of the soldier, who represents American interests, but a portrait of the dead woman's family seated around a table with a space left by her absence. The ideal of American masculine protection of civilians is undermined in this story because here masculinity also signifies danger to domestic life. The photograph of the family resonates with social values familiar to *Life*'s readers; in the process of recognizing one set of values, the article destabilizes assumptions about the American military's paternalistic claims that justified its continued presence in Japan. In "This Is War," the photograph says nothing about why these marines are in Korea and the text gives only an account of war maneuvers. Yet, the men's anguish raises questions about the events and policies that led to this situation. *Life* reproduces images critical of dominant ideologies because, as Fredric Jameson argues, the mass media must address the hopes and anxieties of their audiences in order to capture their interest and sell products effectively. While appealing to audiences' desires, mass culture must also contain these desires in order to legitimate the social order.[67] In this regard, Duncan's marines address emotional anxieties current in postwar social life. The frustrations, the anger, and the suffering implied in these pictures may have resonated with *Life*'s audience, many of whom undoubtedly participated in World War II or Korea or knew someone who had been in the military.

Semiotic complexities in these photographs present the potential for multiple readings by *Life*'s audience but only within the specific historical context of reception. Representations do not have infinite meanings; instead historical memories and social conditions form the horizon limiting viewers' interpretations.[68] Linda Williams argues in her discussion of female spectators of 1940s Hollywood melodrama that audiences recognized alternative subject positions even within the ideologically containing frameworks of patriarchal narratives.[69] Her argument suggests that viewing consists of more than just the desire to dominate the Other of the image. Visual imagery can also encourage sympathetic readings based on recognition of familiar emotions. Viewers, however, are historical subjects who read within the contexts of the social spaces they occupy, and therefore we need to examine the historical context within which readers would have seen this picture.

President Truman justified American in-volvement in the Korean War by claiming that first Soviet and then later Chinese aggression provoked the conflict. Insisting that communism's objective was global domination, the administration made Korea a key site for implementing its "strategy of containment," arguing that limited military intervention would contain the spread of communism. Strategists assumed American military and political superiority, pointing to the United States' success in World War II and its military position at the end of the war, as well as its early monopoly of the atomic bomb and the tremendous economic productivity of American industry. In addition, racism pervaded Americans' expectations about the feasibility of military encounters; the assumption was that superior military capabilities would enable Western forces to overrun quickly the industrially backward North Koreans.[70]

The American public, however, did not easily accept military involvement in Korea, finding it difficult to substitute an ideal of unconditional victory for the more limited aims of containment. Indeed, many found humiliating the United States' inability to crush the Communists swiftly. One of the most frustrating aspects of the war was that it dragged on, despite early promises that it would be easy to win. In fact, in the first months of the war, the presumably inferior North Korean troops pushed the UN and South Korean troops all the way to the southern tip of the peninsula in Pusan. Not until the end of September 1950 did General Douglas MacArthur launch UN troops in a counteroffensive. Such setbacks did not bode well for a war that concluded through diplomatic negotiations.[71]

Life published "This Is War" while American troops were still in retreat, and one might read the two portraits of the marines as exemplifying the frustrations of the United States' humiliating military position. Images of suffering potentially speak to the confusion over the weak position of the Americans and the implied threat of Communist domination. Beyond this specificity, photographs of men crying present alternative emotional responses to the masculine bravado underlying anti-Communist rhetoric and common to ideologies justifying corporate demands on workers, namely the breadwinner ethic. Despite media portrayals of domestic life as happy and fulfilling, many Americans, including white middle-class males, had difficulty adjusting to the demanding conformity of consumer culture. The consumer-oriented family, having replaced other forms of private life, could not always make people happy.[72]

Bestselling novels like Sloan Wilson's *The Man in the Gray Flannel Suit* (1955) examined this discontent among middle-class men and women who found themselves unfulfilled by the promises of corporate life.[73] Other popular media explored alternative expressions of sexuality that challenged traditional ideals of masculinity and family roles. Rock and roll questioned bourgeois sexual relations in music and lyrics that celebrated physical intimacy and the body's sensuality. At the same time, Hollywood movies about teenage rebellion examined family and gender conflicts, including sexual frustrations, generational clashes, loveless marriages, and alienated adolescents. In *East of Eden* (1955), for example, James Dean's powerful performance explores a young man's struggles to define a masculine identity in the face of his domineering father's demands.[74] Amid such myriad and often incompatible examinations of sexuality and gender roles, Duncan's photographs of male emotions undoubtedly resonated with readers' social experiences.

On yet another level, the photographs challenge dominant culture, for images of men crying in a homophobic society like postwar America threaten to feminize the men. Homosexual communities became more visible in the postwar period, largely as a result of World War II experiences, when gays and lesbians met in gender-segregated wartime organizations both in military service and on the home front. There, they built communities that toward the end of the period began to gain a political foothold in society. In general, however, postwar media found homosexuality so threatening that they rarely dealt with the issue directly. During the years of this study, *Life* did not publish any news stories on gay or lesbian communities. At the same time, homophobia intensified in the media, which often linked homosexuality with political threats to the state.[75]

"This Is War" protects these images from homophobic fears of weakness or emasculation, by placing the photographs showing male emotions alongside pictures of men fighting in battle. Furthermore, the written text relies on patriotic rhetoric and a "masculine point of view."[76] It describes how this unit suffered many casualties in an attack made worse by rain, lack of communications, and a low supply of ammunition. The narrative then resecures American superiority, explaining that "the action had been won by that eternally fundamental principle of war—man against man. The marines had proven themselves better fighters than the North Koreans who outnumbered them." The author frames the military success as a masculine triumph of man against man. In addition, an undercurrent of racism persists in characterizations of the weaker enemy, also referred to as "the Reds." Despite the machismo of the accompanying text, *Life* could not completely negate the emotions visualized here. In a layout that begins and ends with images of suffering, Duncan's close-ups of the marines' emotions represent the contradictions underlying Western definitions of masculinity. The men's suffering signifies the demands of war and men's courage in battle, but at the same time, the photographs visualize the suffering experienced in the name of masculinity. By focusing on human pain, visual representations like these legitimize personal feelings and inform viewers about the sufferings of others. In struggling over meanings, however, Duncan's photographs do not present a political analysis but rather depict complex foreign

policies and domestic politics in terms of individuals that ultimately leave questions about Cold War actions and responsibility unexamined. Although they articulate hardship and pain, images such as these direct political awareness away from historical critique. At the same time, Duncan's marines offer alternative views of masculinity at a time when Americans were negotiating gender and social relations and when responses to the Korean War were equivocal.

The issue in which this photo-essay appeared further challenges gender ideals through the spatial relationships created by the layout. A departure from typical advertising that portrays women as consumers occurs in an ad for Western Electric preceding "This Is War." The advertiser uses a color drawing of a woman testing dials on an assembly line to represent the reliability and credibility of the company. Immediately following Duncan's photo-essay was the article on Mayor Davis, "Petticoat Rule Scores Again." Placing the ad, the marines, and the woman politician one after the other indicates how layout and design contribute to the openness of visual representation and the possibilities for reading against the grain. This suggests that *Life*'s efforts to secure a hegemonic reading succeeded only provisionally. A rare photograph of women soldiers similarly demonstrates how contradictory images can challenge gender conventions, even those traditionally associated with military power. A report on Israel's birthday from May 1958 includes a photograph of women in uniforms and helmets carrying guns.[77] Women lined up in rows on parade stride forward forcefully into the foreground and toward the viewer. A rarity, this image stands out against the preponderance of images of male soldiers and challenges the assumed natural association between masculinity and military power. Although we cannot know what individuals thought of these pictures, potential readings indicate the possibility of seeing gender differently, just as the powerful photograph of Mamie Bradley presents an alternative vision of race and gender.

These complexities and incompatibilities expose the limits of ideological unity in *Life*'s vision of postwar society, even in the context of the magazine's patriotic representations of American military forces. Laura Mulvey observes that disruptive desires frequently occur in cultural forms within an integrative and arguably conservative context. These disruptive gestures, emblems, and metaphors can "provide an almost invisible breeding ground for a language of protest and resistance," for one cannot simply revert to the dominant order. As Mulvey argues, "The problems, contradictions and irreconcilable demands made by the acquisition of sexual identity, family structures and historical conditions surface in collectively held desires, obsessions and anxieties. This is the shared, social dimension of the unconscious . . . [that] erupts symptomatically in popular culture."[78] No matter how hard discursive strategies work to secure a preferred reading, images such

as Duncan's portraits of the marines and the Japanese family mourning its loss persistently force viewers to confront pain and suffering just as they had to confront poverty in the picture of Emmett Till's uncle's shack. *Life*'s representations are a dialogic terrain that addresses the social and political contestations of the postwar period, and the magazine's attempts to frame these representations within dominant ideals are necessarily indeterminate and contingent. Horace Newcomb points out that "even when the most powerful, controlled messages are dominant, they must still face the answering 'word' of the viewer and the world of experience."[79] In this way, readers' critical interpretations of war and traditional masculine imperatives can coexist with or even replace more dominant ideals about American society.

How, we might ask, could a picture of a man crying, a woman working, and a Latino family in its apartment threaten the hegemony of dominant culture? Such images challenge the transhistorical claims of dominant society by exposing the constructed terms of seemingly natural gender, race, and class identities. Changes in the narrative of family life, apparent in the relations among Puerto Rican immigrants, or between a working woman and her family, contest *Life*'s cultural ideal of domesticity. Representations of difference threaten to expose the narrative assumptions that mask and justify social hierarchies and oppression.

News media report on the experiences of

the public sphere, in particular on topics dealing with social dissent or conflict. The means by which the news narrates events and issues of social concern reveal the powerful structuring mechanisms of these narrative discourses. The news repeatedly depicts conflict and discord because showing excess, deviance, and revolt establishes boundaries between a consensus society and outsiders.[80] Political struggle is nonetheless difficult to represent for challenges to social legitimacy contain codes that may resonate differently with readers' experiences.

In the photographs and texts of *Life*'s narrative of domesticity, there are possibilities for envisioning a world different from that of the nuclear family. *Life*'s photo-essays reporting on the public world of postwar America, whether civil rights struggles, racist violence, women politicians, or war, revealed the public world to be more conflictual than the narratives imposed on them. The contradictory nature of *Life*'s discourse encompassed a variety of positions in which no single reading could ever be absolutely ensured. Looking involves negotiations between the viewer and the text where viewers interpret polysemic codes within their own historical conditions. In these texts, however, the persistent, perhaps overwhelming ideology of domesticity seems to win out through the logic of narrative and the pleasurable rewards of closure. Or does it? Since we cannot predict in advance any one response, differences within texts may be as important as the dominant

message secured through narrative closure.[81] The media appeal by presenting the tensions and desires of their audiences. Therefore, media texts always retain the potential for resistance because in identifying with the text, viewers then locate themselves in a world that is contingent and negotiable.

The stereotype of a complacent postwar middle class does not conform to historical realities. Instead, middle-class Americans faced significant changes in this period, including economic changes, demographic shifts that isolated them from family and friends, and political strife that included the threat of nuclear attack. *Life*'s middle-class audience read about a world that was unstable and full of competing political and social objectives, a world in which hegemony was never absolute but had to be secured and could then be challenged. Representations of social struggles potentially fostered empathy in competition with other signs, for *Life*'s targeted middle-class readers could also locate themselves in the space of struggle, even perhaps imagining alternative communities.

Despite the powerful domestic ideologies encoded in *Life*'s narrative, its depictions of social change undermined the universality of one type of domesticity, and its association with national identity. Photographs enabled middle-class readers to perceive flaws in the social order as well as in domestic ideologies. In addition, *Life*'s dominant narrative was itself internally contradictory and unstable. This narrative offered a story of private comfort and satisfaction, yet it was a story that could never be fulfilled completely because it called into being a family that was less a voluntary affectionate unit or a repository of tradition than a locus of consumption and production. Thus, the possibilities for change rested even within the most powerfully dominant representations.

The politics of representation revolve around issues of polysemy and closure in texts that affect readers' perceptions of their worlds and other worlds around them. *Life* frequently portrayed a consensus about the family and about nearly everything else in American society. The magazine, however, could not successfully represent as unified and unproblematic all the social changes occurring in the 1940s and 1950s. With varying degrees of success, *Life* contained ideological challenges and legitimated state power by praising traditional domestic values. Yet these struggles also reveal the limits of *Life*'s representational strategies, and the contradictions within domestic ideals in postwar America. In these years, consensus was an ideal continually contested and never totally achieved.

CHAPTER 6

CONCLUSION

But the instant the criterion of authenticity ceases to be applicable to artistic production, the total function of art is reversed. Instead of being based on ritual, it begins to be based on another practice—politics.

—WALTER BENJAMIN, "The Work of Art in the Age of Mechanical Reproduction," 1968

Red Scare campaigns throughout the postwar period blamed Communist subversives for such political and military losses as the Communist takeover in China, the Soviet expansion of its atomic arsenal, and the humiliating settlement in Korea. In 1953, for example, Eisenhower signed an executive order instituting extensive loyalty checks on federal employees, the government declared J. Robert Oppenheimer a security risk, and forced Charlie Chaplin to give up his re-entry visa. On June 19, 1953, this political hysteria culminated in the execution of Julius and Ethel Rosenberg who had been convicted of selling atomic secrets to the Soviets.[1] Amid the political witch hunts and only two months before the Rosenbergs' execution, on March 30, 1953, *Life* explicitly visualized anti-Communist fears. The big news story features a dramatic photograph of a house exploding, flying debris, and a roof lifting off (*illustration 25*).[2] The text ominously explains that "the first house on the American continent to be destroyed by atomic energy has been reduced to char and radioactivated kindling." This frightening image envisioned one of the most terrifying fears facing postwar Americans: a nuclear attack on the United States.

Fortunately for people living in the United States in 1953, this was a simulated test by the Atomic Energy Commission (AEC) and the Federal Civil Defense Administration (FCDA). These government agencies built two houses, at the cost of $18,000 each, which they located 3,500 and 27,500 feet from ground zero. The government intended to demonstrate the effects of a nuclear attack in order "to inject an overdue sense of urgency into its [civil defense] campaign to organize a sensible defense of American cities." Four sequential photographs show the progressive destruction of a six-room, colonial-style house by an atomic blast. At 0 seconds, eerie light and dramatic shadows illumine the house. At $11/24$ of a second, the heat of the explosion scorches the window frames and doorway of the side facing the blast. At ¾ of a second, the entire front of the house is "engulfed in flame and billowing black smoke." Then, at $1\,19/24$ seconds, the house is fully ablaze. Each photograph is roughly twice the area of the previous one,

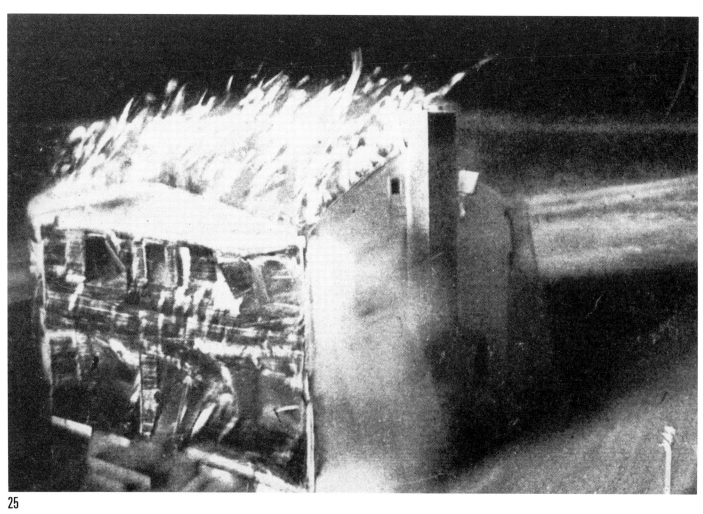

25

thereby bringing the destruction ever closer to the viewer. The viewer then turns the page to see the final picture in the sequence, a two-page photograph of the house at 2⅓ seconds, blowing apart from the shock waves. Despite the simulation, the photographs have a frightening credibility underscored by the relentless temporal progress of this destruction. The visual absence of the bomb creates a powerful metaphoric sign reinforcing the warnings commonly issued by anti-Communists that subversives were invisible and could be anyone, even one's neighbor.

In stories like this one, *Life* supported civil defense efforts to mobilize public sentiment by fueling popular fears about the imminence of a nuclear attack. These fears pervaded the period as Americans practiced air raid drills and built bomb shelters. The question is, who was under attack? The test does not simulate the destruction of an urban center despite the stated purpose of designing a defense for cities. Instead, the test blows up two single-family houses. In both houses, themselves signifiers of middle-class suburban affluence, the FCDA and AEC positioned mannequins to simulate further the effects of an attack. The final photograph in the article shows four mannequin victims from house no. 2 lying beneath the debris from the collapsed building (*illustration 26*). The text explains that in house no. 2, "where the mannequins had been disposed in domestic contentment, there was now only chaos and confusion. The family group has been scattered to the four corners

and the blonde ejected from her bed." Chaos and confusion, as much as death and destruction, threaten the white mannequin family in this single-family suburban house. Sexuality is also central to this image of nuclear holocaust, as it was in "The 36-Hour War." Both articles envision American destruction through the icon of femininity, the blond woman. Here, she has been propelled from her bed, which further eroticizes the violence. Meanwhile, photographs of the ruined living room furniture and the destroyed family car also depict the destructive force of the bomb. The class status of the family destroyed in the blast suggests that affluence, the hallmark of middle-class culture, faced external threats. The photo-essay taps into cultural fears of the decade as war, sexuality, and domesticity mingle in the photographs of the destroyed family.

The photo-essay exemplifies *Life*'s strategy of linking domesticity and consumption to matters of grave concern, demonstrating the integral relationship between public and private spheres in twentieth-century American culture. In this instance, though, the state, rather than *Life*, directed attention to the family. During the postwar period, both the media and the government defined society and measured the effects of political policy in domestic terms. Conflating political antagonisms with private concerns justified Cold War politics in the name of preserving domesticity.

Photographs' cultural status as evidence here competes with the story line on atomic

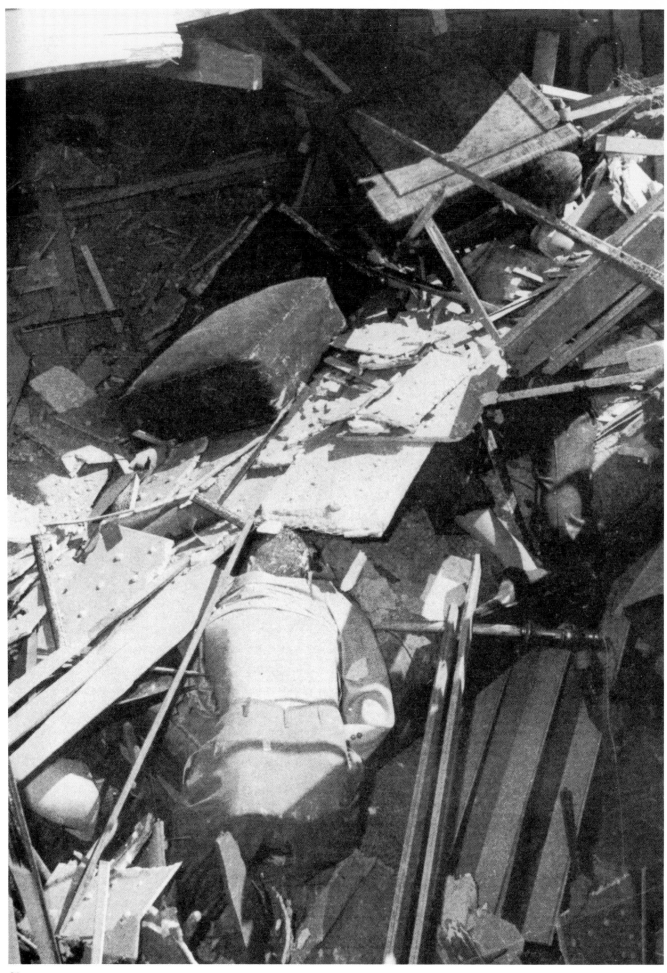

testing. The photographs' credibility overwhelms the textual explanations of a simulated test because the viewer "sees" the house being blown apart by an atomic bomb. Tensions between the seeming transparency of photojournalism and the simulated nature of the event bring into sharp relief what happens on a more routine, even mundane, level each time viewers encounter photographs. Although the ideological power of photojournalism derived from narratives that addressed the concerns of postwar middle-class readers, photographic realism enhanced this ideological power by making the stories credible because they seemed "real." Nonetheless, realism is a narrative style, a means of representing complex social experiences within a particular narrative framework. Instead of criticizing or praising the media for their degree of realism, it is more productive to examine how narratives rely on realism to frame social experiences.

News media play a crucial role in twentieth-century American social life because they inform their audiences both about their own world and about societies distant from their daily lives. How the media tell these stories of difference and similarity, of conformity and dissent, is a crucial determinant of what Americans know about themselves and other people. *Life*'s representations of domesticity contained great ideological significance because news events in themselves cannot signify but depend on narrative structures for meaning. Photographs of both ordinary and famous families, therefore, were not trivial but essential to the magazine's legitimation of middle-class culture.

Life presented a specific vision of postwar America that promoted as normal and commonplace a particular social class, defined through gender and race ideals as well as class status. Photo-essays praising the middle-class family's consumer habits naturalized a class-based affluence and its accompanying ideology of consumption as a defining characteristic of American society. *Life* often equated democracy with consumption, arguing that the right to choose which goods to buy signified American freedom. Yet *Life* also admonished its readers that responsibilities accompanied this freedom, that it was their patriotic duty to purchase goods to stimulate the economy. Even in the story on civil defense, the text links the family of a particular social class with the welfare of the nation. Domesticity was a powerful narrative defining cultural norms that had political ramifications for how middle-class Americans perceived the postwar world.

Life's persistent attention to the family corresponded to, and supported, dramatic shifts in postwar social life. By championing consumption ethics and suburban lifestyles, *Life* encouraged the trend toward privatization that increased middle-class Americans' isolation from extended family and community ties. *Life*, like other postwar media, supplied the cultural justifications for privatization by promoting nuclear-family life as the solution to social problems. Capital accumulation depended on the seemingly private world of individual choice which deflected attention from the state's increasing intervention and regimentation of society on behalf of capital. But in fact, government actions—from programs like the FHA, to urban renewal, to foreign policies that protected multinational investments in foreign markets—shaped these very choices. Privatization, for instance, tied the nation's prosperity to "family-oriented" subsidies for the construction of highways and single-family houses. Subsidies for mass transit and public housing would also have involved massive state intervention in the economy and generated higher wages and full employment, but would in addition have built up public transportation systems and supplied badly needed public housing. Instead, a host of government programs, including credit plans for consumers and tax abatements to large corporations, subsidized privatization. This support was most apparent in subsidies that stimulated private automobile travel, destroying mass transit systems and replacing them with the highways that now crisscross the nation.[3] Domesticity was a narrative ideal that did more than just divide the world into public and private spheres; it presented a vision of private life that met the needs and served the interests of dominant political and economic sectors. Cultural discourses that suppressed other family narratives—narratives about families tied to community and social responsibilities—in favor of this domestic ideal

supported political and economic policies that strengthened capitalist accumulation.

Life played a crucial role in postwar culture by envisioning the benefits of privatization and aligning this portrait with national ideals. The power of this narrative vision was that it placed its readers at the center of the postwar world. This helps explain *Life*'s popularity, for the magazine urged its readers to locate themselves in a world that praised middle-class norms, values, and consumption patterns as democratic and American. Through narratives that relied on family pictures to legitimize public policies and economic demands, the magazine merged domestic ideals with capitalist ideologies. This, however, created an essential contradiction because consumer spending alone cannot satisfy personal needs and alleviate the alienation produced by advanced capitalism. Consumer ideologies fragmented and isolated the nuclear family from other social relations so that this family could never fully offer the intimacy and affection it promised.

Life's narrative of domesticity provoked another contradiction because the magazine also asked readers to locate themselves in a world that was bigger, more complex, and more contested than the suburban private home. Photo-essays reported on a world of crisis and conflict, albeit within a reassuring narrative that framed the news in terms of middle-class family values. In so doing, *Life*'s own narrative proved to be unstable.

Representations of domestic intimacy among families who were not the right kind of family exposed the ideological construction of the seemingly natural link between family happiness and middle-class affluence.

In offering its readers the most extensive visual portrait of postwar American society, *Life* also established characteristics prominent in contemporary news media. Television retains *Life*'s focus on the middle-class family as one of the primary subjects of the news, and news media frequently focus as much attention on the president's family as on his politics. Likewise, television news depends on the experiences of "ordinary" families to explain topics ranging from inflation (visualized through scenes of the family of four coping with increased food bills) to reactions to the 1991 Gulf War (when local news stations interviewed soldiers' family members). Even the seemingly unposed and candid scenes often seen in television news reports have precedents in *Life*. Spontaneity is no more possible under the heat of lights and scrutiny of the television camera than it was for Mayor Davis with a *Life* photographer in her bedroom (*see illustration 22*).

Life was in no way alone in establishing popular acceptance of photographs as evidence. Cultural and legal practices first turned to the camera in the nineteenth century to depict the social world. Reliance on photography gained momentum in the 1920s with the introduction of new technologies that made photographic reproduction economically viable. Nonetheless, *Life* played a pivotal role at mid-century by familiarizing a national audience with visual news and turning Americans into consumers of visual culture through its weekly pictorial view of the world, which accustomed its audience to seeing social life in visual terms. Subsequent television news claims about film's transparency rely on viewers' ready acceptance of film as a mirror of the real world.[4]

For about thirty years, *Life* dominated the news media by committing tremendous financial power and personnel resources to the depiction of events from around the world. During the 1950s, *Life* began to face competition from television; by 1960, almost 90 percent of American households had at least one television set and watched an average of five hours a day.[5] Despite television's dramatic growth, the medium did not initially devote financial resources to news gathering. But, by 1963, when television changed from fifteen-minute to half-hour news shows, the medium was well on its path to preeminence in news reporting; in 1965, when the medium went to color, for the first time a majority claimed television as their chief source of news.[6] *Life*'s political and social importance declined in the 1960s as it faced changing audience habits and was beset by economic difficulties. The magazine lost many advertisers to the new medium, which commanded far greater audiences, when it found itself increasingly unable to compete with television for fast-breaking news events. In addition, rising production costs and declines in subscriptions plagued the magazine. In 1972, *Life* closed its doors.[7] Although the magazine restarted as a monthly in 1978, it has not regained the cultural dominance it had in the postwar period.

Since World War II, privatization, consumption ethics, mobility patterns, and the fragmentation of communities increasingly have affected American family life. Since the baby boom peaked at the end of the 1950s, media began responding to shifting attitudes toward social life and political objectives with more varied representations of family life. News coverage more frequently makes visible some of the manifestations of domestic fracture, including divorce rates, spousal and child abuse, and men's abandonment of their families.[8] Despite the many and varied contributions of the modern feminist movement, evidence indicates that many women still work a double shift by retaining child-care and housework responsibilities while working outside the home. Moreover, teenage pregnancies continue to confine women and their children to conditions that trap them in inescapable poverty. Economic and social conditions in the work place have contributed to the instabilities in Americans' personal lives. Women entering the work force in the expanding sales and service areas face persistent cultural messages that they are women first and workers second, a definition that functions to lower their wages and worsen their

working conditions. The lack of cross-gender unity also hurts the working class by preventing workers from uniting to protect themselves against declining wages. The result has been the need for almost twice as many workers to bring home the same real income. In addition, the eclipse of community and public services means that people work as individuals to pay for their own transportation and child care instead of pooling the costs through taxes, a factor that also strains "families" by adding to the burdens of work.

In the 1970s and 1980s, cultural responses to these economic and social stresses were equivocal. On the one hand, examples exist of social and political responses to alternative forms of family relations—in some states, for instance, gay and lesbian communities' increased political and economic power has forced the legal recognition of same-sex marriages and adoption of children. On the other hand, the ideal of domestic family life persists as an important narrative through which Americans conceptualize social structures, political responsibilities, morality, and justice. Popular culture abounds now with talk about shared parenting responsibilities and house husbands, yet the latter, at least, pose a paradoxical situation because men at home challenge traditional gender assumptions and also reinforce domestic ideals. The emphasis on a parent giving up outside commitments for the sake of childrearing perpetuates the ideal of the private nuclear family at the expense of explorations into alternative social and community solutions to the conflicting demands of work and home. The political ramifications of this family ideal became apparent in the 1980s when domestic ideology became the cornerstone of conservative political rhetoric with Ronald Reagan and members of the New Right lionizing the middle-class family while attempting to dismantle abortion rights and child-care support systems.

At the start of the new decade, in his 1990 State of the Union address, President George Bush once again championed domesticity, relying on rhetoric about private life to map out his political agenda. Toward the conclusion of his speech, Bush mentioned his newly born grandchild, stating that "when I held the little guy for the first time, the troubles at home and abroad seemed manageable, and totally in perspective." Bush framed his vision of the world in familial ideals that he presented as natural and transhistorical.

> Yet, all kids are alike. The budding young environmentalist I met this month, who joined me in exploring the Florida Everglades. The Little Leaguers I played catch with in Poland, ready to go from Warsaw to the World Series. . . . But, you know, when it comes to hope and the future every kid is the same: full of dreams, ready to take on the world, all special because they are the very future of freedom.[9]

Avoiding differences enables Bush to substitute for a political agenda clichés that appeal because of their apparent naturalness. The power of this rhetoric rests in its ability to hail its audience. Who, after all, would

deny the right of every child to dream, and every parent the ability to care properly for his or her children? Photographs of families appeal to audiences because they touch emotional needs and desires about intimacy, moral values, and social concerns. But to say that all children or all families are the same ignores the political and economic conditions that have a determining effect on social life. Historical events, political repression, and economic deprivation distinguish the Polish Little Leaguers from the Florida environmentalists. Certainly, suffering and joy can be shared across these boundaries, but they do not transcend different outlooks and political objectives. Bush's strategic attention to the family directs his speech away from political accountability and programmatic solutions to the problems facing Americans at the end of the century and toward transcendent ideals that associate the family with the health of the nation and the world. This rhetorical strategy focuses attention on an ideal in which holding a grandchild can turn overwhelming social troubles like unemployment and poverty into manageable issues.

The power of domesticity as a cultural ideal rests in its ability to invoke our desires and needs for intimacy and affection in a world woefully lacking in community and personal commitments. Family narratives address emotions not often acknowledged in the increasingly rationalized world dominated by multinational corporations and competitive consumption. On the other hand, political and cultural attention to the specific form of the middle-class nuclear family serves a positive function for the state by making particular public actions and policies more legitimate. Dependence on this family narrative gave *Life*, and continues today to give cultural and political discourses, the power to determine whose stories are legitimate. As Benjamin notes in the epigraph to this chapter, the function of artistic production in the modern age lies not in ritual but in politics. The politics of familial imagery rests in its ability to establish specific economic and political objectives as the national social agenda by reframing them as personal relations. Domestic imagery has the power to attract middle-class Americans' attention to AIDS, racism, homelessness, and a host of other crises facing the United States by presenting these problems in familiar terms that encourage audiences to care. It also, however, shapes that attention in highly politicized ways that often blame the people victimized by social policies for not conforming to middle-class ideals. The contradictory meanings embedded in this domestic narrative, that is, emotional sentiment competing with the hegemonic power of this political ideal, are perhaps *Life*'s most significant legacy.

NOTES

CHAPTER 1: Documenting the Ordinary

1. "They Pour in . . . and Family Shows Refugees Can Fit In," *Life*, January 7, 1957, 20–27.

2. For an excellent analysis of the gender and consumption ideologies in the kitchen debates, see Elaine Tyler May, *Homeward Bound: American Families in the Cold War Era* (New York: Basic Books, 1988), 16–20.

3. For two now-classic discussions about the politics of popular culture, see Fredric Jameson, "Reification and Utopia in Mass Culture," *Social Text* 1 (Winter 1979): 130–148, 139; and Stuart Hall, "Notes on Deconstructing the Popular," in *People's History and Socialist Theory*, ed. Raphael Samuel (London: Routledge and Kegan Paul, 1981), 227–240.

4. See *N.W. Ayer and Son's Directory, Newspapers and Periodicals* (Philadelphia: N.W. Ayer and Son, annual volumes 1945–1960).

5. I examined The Week's Events section as well as advertisements and letters to the editors for all issues of *Life* from 1936 to 1960. In addition, I studied all the special issues devoted to a single topic. These issues occurred intermittently throughout the calendar year, and since they usually did not include a news section, I examined them in their entirety.

6. For a comparison of *Life* and *Look*, see James Guimond, *American Photography and the American Dream* (Chapel Hill: University of North Carolina Press, 1991), chap. 5.

7. For a discussion of television news in the 1950s, see Erik Barnouw, *Tube of Plenty: The Evo-* *lution of American Television*, rev. ed. (New York: Oxford University Press, 1982), 101–103, 168–172.

8. See William Adams, "Visual Analysis of Newscasts: Issues in Social Science Research," in *Television Network News: Issues in Content Research*, ed. William Adams and Fay Schreibman (Washington, D.C.: Television and Politics Study Program, School of Public and International Affairs, George Washington University, 1987), 156–157, for a discussion of scholars' lack of attention to visual images. For an important exception, see Gaye Tuchman, *Making News: A Study in the Construction of Reality* (New York: Free Press, 1978).

9. See, e.g., Vicki Goldberg, *Margaret Bourke-White: A Biography* (New York: Harper and Row, 1986); and Ben Maddow, *Let Truth Be the Prejudice: W. Eugene Smith, His Life and Photographs* (Millerton, N.Y.: Aperture, 1985). Photographic histories have also discussed the contributions of photojournalism; for example, see Beaumont Newhall, *The History of Photography from 1839 to the Present*, rev. ed. (New York: Museum of Modern Art and Little, Brown, 1982). Douglas Crimp, however, critiques art historical perspectives that aestheticize the photographic discourse by removing it from the social context of production; see "The Museum's Old/The Library's New Subject," in *The Contest of Meaning: Critical Histories of Photography*, ed. Richard Bolton (Cambridge, Mass.: MIT Press, 1989), 3–13. See also Christopher Phillips, "The Judgement Seat of Photography," 14–47, in the same volume, for an analysis of the role of the museum in this aestheticizing process. For a recent study that examines photojournalism in the context

of a longer documentary tradition, see Guimond, *American Photography*.

10. This work has been influenced by recent trends in photographic history by scholars like Jan Zita Grover, Peter Hales, Allan Sekula, Sally Stein, and John Tagg, who examine the semiotic and material processes through which visual images construct social identities, act as forms of regulation, and function as sites of negotiation or resistance. Two excellent recent anthologies are Bolton, ed., *Contest of Meaning*; and Carol Squiers, ed., *The Critical Eye: Essays on Contemporary Photography* (Seattle: Bay Press, 1990). For theoretical analyses of photographic representation, see, e.g., Allan Sekula, "On the Invention of Photographic Meaning," in *Thinking Photography*, ed. Victor Burgin (London: Macmillan, 1982), 84–109; idem, "The Traffic in Photographs," in *Modernism and Modernity*, ed. Benjamin H. D. Buchloch, Serge Guilbaut, and David Solkin (Halifax: Press of the Nova Scotia College of Art and Design, 1983), 121–154; and John Tagg, *The Burden of Representation: Essays on Photographies and Histories* (Amherst: University of Massachusetts Press, 1988).

11. Robert T. Elson, *Time Inc.: The Intimate History of a Publishing Enterprise*, vol. 1: 1923–1941 (New York: Atheneum, 1968), 279.

12. For an analysis of how this visual imperative constrains television news, see Adams, "Visual Analysis of Newscasts."

13. Quoted in Loudon Wainwright, *The Great American Magazine: An Inside History of LIFE* (New York: Alfred A. Knopf, 1986), 33, who comments that Luce had help writing this prospectus from various people including Archibald MacLeish. Edward G. McGrath, "The Political Ideals of LIFE Magazine," Ph.D. diss., Syracuse University, 1962, credits Daniel Longwell, who became managing editor in the 1940s, with writing this prose, 23.

14. John Fiske, *Television Culture* (New York: Routledge, 1987), 293–296; and John Hartley, *Understanding News* (London: Methuen, 1982), 115–118.

15. See, e.g., Fredric Jameson, *Signatures of the Visible* (New York: Routledge, 1990); and Donald M. Lowe, *History of Bourgeois Perception* (Chicago: University of Chicago Press, 1982). For discussions on the historical developments of photographic realism, see Sekula, "Traffic in Photographs"; John Tagg, "The Currency of the Photograph: New Deal Reformism and Documentary Rhetoric," in *Burden of Representation*, 153–183; and Maren Stange, *Symbols of Ideal Life: Social Documentary Photography in America, 1890–1950* (Cambridge: Cambridge University Press, 1989).

16. See Fiske, *Television Culture*, chap. 3, for a discussion of mass media's reliance on realism.

17. Ibid., 291–293, discusses the news as metonymy; see also Sekula, "Invention of Photographic Meaning," for a similar discussion of the metonymic function of the photographic image. For a discussion of the news convention of "vox pop" or voice of the people, see Hartley, *Understanding News*, 90, 109.

18. For a discussion of visual discourse, see Sekula, "On the Invention of Photographic Meaning"; see also Tagg, *Burden of Representation*; and Fiske, *Television Culture*, 14–15, and 41–42.

19. Fiske, *Television Culture*, explains that "ideology is mapped onto the objective world of 'reality,' and the accuracy of realism's representation of the details of this 'real' world becomes the validation of the ideology it has been made to bear," 36.

20. Allan Sekula, "The Body and the Archive," in *Contest of Meaning*, 342–388, esp. 377–379.

21. Stuart Hall, "The Toad in the Garden: Thatcherism among the Theorists," in *Marxism and the Interpretation of Culture*, ed. Cary Nelson and

Lawrence Grossberg (Urbana and Chicago: University of Illinois Press, 1988), 51–53.

22. For discussions of the news media's relationships with the state, see, e.g., Stuart Hall, "Culture, Media and the 'Ideological Effect,'" in *Mass Communications and Society*, ed. James Curran, Michael Gurevitch, and Janet Woollacott (Beverly Hills: Sage, 1976), 315–348; Hartley, *Understanding News*; and Michael Gurevitch et al., eds., *Culture, Society and the Media* (London: Methuen, 1982).

23. George Lipsitz, "The Struggle for Hegemony," *Journal of American History* 75, 1 (June 1988): 146–150.

24. Hall, "Culture, Media and the 'Ideological Effect,'" 333.

25. See Chantal Mouffe, "Hegemony and Ideology in Gramsci," in *Culture, Ideology and Social Process*, ed. Tony Bennett et al. (London: B.T. Batsford, 1981), 219–234; and Hall, "Culture, Media and the 'Ideological Effect,'" 344–346.

26. See Robert Karl Manoff and Michael Schudson, eds., *Reading the News* (New York: Pantheon, 1986), for a recent volume of essays on American news media whose often insightful critiques do not consider the role of gender in any substantive way.

27. Fiske, *Television Culture*, chap. 15.

28. Joan Wallach Scott, *Gender and the Politics of History* (New York: Columbia University Press, 1988), 46.

29. See, for instance, Henry R. Luce's much-cited editorial that articulates this position, "The American Century," *Life*, February 17, 1941, 61–65.

30. See, e.g., Paul Hartmann and Charles Husband, *Racism and the Mass Media: A Study in the Role of the Mass Media in the Formation of White Beliefs and Attitudes in Britain* (Totowa, N.J.: Rowman and Littlefield, 1974); Carolyn Martindale, *The White Press and Black America* (Westport, Conn.: Greenwood Press, 1986); and Glasgow University Media Group, *More Bad News* (London: Routledge & Kegan Paul, 1980).

31. David Roediger, *The Wages of Whiteness: Race and the Making of the American Working Class* (London: Verso, 1991), and Alexander Saxton, *The Rise and Fall of the White Republic: Class Politics and Mass Culture in Nineteenth-Century America* (London: Verso, 1990), offer two excellent studies of coalition building around whiteness in the nineteenth century.

32. Fiske, *Television Culture*, 293–294, cites Stuart Hall on this point.

33. Steven Mintz and Susan Kellogg, *Domestic Revolutions: A Social History of American Family Life* (New York: Free Press, 1988), xiii–xx.

34. See Hall, "Culture, Media and the 'Ideological Effect,'" 344.

35. For an overview of consensus and revisionist histories, see Lary May, "Introduction," in *Recasting America: Culture and Politics in the Age of Cold War*, ed. L. May (Chicago: University of Chicago Press, 1989), 1–16.

36. See, e.g., George Lipsitz, "The Meaning of Memory: Family, Class, and Ethnicity in Early Network Television Programs," *Time Passages: Collective Memory and American Popular Culture* (Minneapolis: University of Minnesota Press, 1990), 39–75; Mary Beth Haralovich, "Sitcoms and Suburbs: Positioning the 1950s Homemaker," *Quarterly Review of Film and Video* 11, 1 (1989): 61–83; and Lynn Spigel, *Make Room for TV: Television and the Family Ideal in Postwar America* (Chicago: University of Chicago Press, 1992).

37. See, e.g., Christine Gledhill, ed., *Home Is Where the Heart Is: Studies in Melodrama and the Woman's Film* (London: BFI Publishing, 1987); and Jackie Byars, *All That Hollywood Allows: Re-*

Reading Gender in 1950s Melodrama (Chapel Hill: University of North Carolina Press, 1991).

38. Elaine May, *Homeward Bound*, 26–28.

39. Horace M. Newcomb, "On the Dialogic Aspects of Mass Communication," *Critical Studies in Mass Communication* 1 (1984): 34–50.

CHAPTER 2: Looking at *Life*

1. "U.S. Normalcy: Against the Backdrop of a Troubled World 'LIFE' Inspects an American City at Peace," *Life*, December 3, 1945, 27–35.

2. Allan Sekula, "On the Invention of Photographic Meaning," in *Thinking Photography*, ed. Victor Burgin (London: Macmillan, 1982), 86.

3. Maureen Honey, *Creating Rosie the Riveter: Class, Gender, and Propaganda during World War II* (Amherst: University of Massachusetts Press, 1984).

4. Stuart Hall, "The Determinations of Newsphotographs," *Working Papers in Cultural Studies* 3 (Autumn 1972): 77.

5. Roland Barthes, *Mythologies*, trans. Annette Lavers (New York: Hill and Wang, 1972), 109–159; see also Hall, "Determinations of Newsphotographs," 79–85, for an application of Barthes's theories to news photographs.

6. See Sekula, "On the Invention of Photographic Meaning," 84–85; and Stuart Hall, "Culture, Media and the 'Ideological Effect,'" in *Mass Communications and Society*, ed. James Curran, Michael Gurevitch, and Janet Woollacott (Beverly Hills: Sage, 1976), 343.

7. For examples of this debate, see Alan Trachtenberg, ed., *Classic Essays on Photography* (New Haven: Leete's Island Books, 1980). Sekula, "Traffic in Photographs," 122, argues that "photography is haunted by two chattering ghosts: that of bourgeois science and that of bourgeois art."

8. For analyses of institutional uses of photography for surveillance and control, see Sekula, "The Body and the Archive," in *The Contest of Meaning: Critical Histories of Photography*, ed. Richard Bolton (Cambridge: MIT Press, 1989), 342–388; John Tagg, *The Burden of Representation: Essays on Photographies and Histories* (Amherst: University of Massachusetts Press, 1988), chaps. 2, 3, and 5; Roberta McGrath, "Medical Police," *Ten:8* 14 (1984): 13–18; and David Green, "A Map of Depravity," *Ten:8* 10 (1985): 36–43. See Pierre Bourdieu, *Photography: A Middle-Brow Art*, trans. Shaun Whiteside (Stanford: Stanford University Press, 1990), who argues that people consider photography realistic and objective because "it has been assigned *social uses* that are held to be 'realistic' and 'objective,'" 74.

9. Peter B. Hales, *Silver Cities: The Photography of American Urbanization, 1839–1915* (Philadelphia: Temple University Press, 1984), 163.

10. Maren Stange, *Symbols of Ideal Life: Social Documentary Photography in America, 1890–1950* (Cambridge: Cambridge University Press, 1989), chap. 1, esp. 23; see also Hales, *Silver Cities*, 163–217.

11. For a comparison of Riis and Hine, see Alan Trachtenberg, "Ever the Human Document," in *America & Lewis Hine: Photographs 1904–1940*, ed. Walter Rosenblum, Naomi Rosenblum, and Alan Trachtenberg (Millerton, N.Y.: Aperture, 1977), 131; for a discussion of Hine's expressiveness, see Sekula, "On the Invention of Photographic Meaning," 103–108.

12. Stange, *Symbols of Ideal Life*, 65.

13. Dan Schiller, *Objectivity and the News: The Public and the Rise of Commercial Journalism* (Philadelphia: University of Pennsylvania Press, 1981), 87–95.

14. R. Smith Schuneman, "Art or Photography: A Question for Newspaper Editors of the 1890s,"

Journalism Quarterly 42 (1965): 43–52; Rune Hassner, "Photography and the Press," in *A History of Photography: Social and Cultural Perspectives*, ed. Jean-Claude Lemagny and André Rouillé (Cambridge: Cambridge University Press, 1987), 77–78.

15. Walter Benjamin, "The Work of Art in the Age of Mechanical Reproduction," in *Illuminations*, ed. Hannah Arendt, trans. Harry Zohn (New York: Harcourt, Brace and World, 1968), 238.

16. See, e.g., Hall, "Determinations of News-photographs"; for a specific analysis of American news practices, see Robert Karl Manoff and Michael Schudson, eds., *Reading the News* (New York: Pantheon, 1986).

17. Michael Schudson, *Discovering the News: A Social History of American Newspapers* (New York: Basic Books, 1978), chap. 3, identifies the development at the turn of the century of two modes of journalism, informational journalism, which promoted a rational, intellectual discourse, and story journalism, which concentrated on emotion and unpredictability. The tabloids clearly fit the story-journalism mode.

18. John D. Stevens, "Social Utility of Sensational News: Murder and Divorce in the 1920s," *Journalism Quarterly* 62, 1 (Spring 1985): 53–58; John R. Brazil, "Murder Trials, Murder, and Twenties America," *American Quarterly* 33, 2 (Summer 1981): 163–184.

19. Raymond Smith Schuneman, "The Photograph in Print: An Examination of New York Daily Newspapers, 1890–1937," Ph.D. diss., University of Minnesota, 1966, 102–109.

20. Ibid., 308–314.

21. Roland Barthes, *Image—Music—Text*, trans. Stephen Heath (New York: Hill and Wang, 1977), 21. On composographs, see Kenneth Kobre, *Photojournalism: The Professional's Approach* (New York: Curtin and London, 1980), 17–18.

22. Robert Sidney Kahan, "The Antecedents of American Photojournalism," Ph.D. diss., University of Wisconsin, Madison, 1969, 195; John Tebbel and Mary Ellen Zuckerman, *The Magazine in America, 1741–1990* (New York: Oxford University Press, 1991), 227.

23. Sally Stein, "The Graphic Ordering of Desire: Modernization of a Middle-Class Women's Magazine, 1919–1939," in *Contest of Meaning*, 146.

24. David Halberstam, *The Powers That Be* (New York: Alfred A. Knopf, 1979), 12–17.

25. For a general discussion of these developments, see Gisèle Freund, *Photography and Society* (Boston: David R. Godine, 1980), 115–160; for a discussion of German photojournalism, see Tim N. Gidal, *Modern Photojournalism: Origins and Evolution, 1910–1933* (New York: Macmillan, 1973).

26. James L. Baughman, *Henry R. Luce and the Rise of the American News Media* (Boston: Twayne, 1987), 78–81.

27. Ibid., 82–88; Vicki Goldberg, *Margeret Bourke-White: A Biography* (New York: Harper and Row, 1986), 106, 172–174.

28. For a discussion of the prehistory of *Life*, see Robert T. Elson, *Time Inc.: The Intimate History of a Publishing Enterprise*, vol. 1: 1923–1941 (New York: Atheneum, 1968), 270–280.

29. See Terry Smith, *Making the Modern: Art and Design in America* (Chicago: University of Chicago Press, 1993), 340–350, for an analysis of images of modernity in *Life* during the late 1930s, including a discussion of the November 23, 1936, issue.

30. " 'The Birth of a Baby' Aims to Reduce Maternal and Infant Mortality Rates," *Life*, April 11, 1938, 33–36; see Loudoun Wainwright, *Great American Magazine: An Inside History of LIFE* (New York: Alfred A. Knopf, 1986), 96–98, for a discussion of the controversy that surrounded this article; and "The First Baby," *Life*, December 24, 1956, 57–63; this article was published in a special issue

titled "The American Woman: Her Achievements and Troubles." See Chapter 5 for an analysis of this special issue.

31. For a discussion of this relationship, see Carl Fleischhauer and Beverly W. Brannan, eds., *Documenting America, 1935–1943* (Berkeley: University of California Press, 1988), 8–9.

32. For analyses of FSA photography, see F. Jack Hurley, *Portrait of a Decade: Roy Stryker and the Development of Documentary Photography in the Thirties* (Baton Rouge: Louisiana State University Press, 1972); Fleischhauer and Brannan, *Documenting America*; Wendy Kozol, "Madonnas of the Fields: Photography, Gender, and 1930s Farm Relief," *Genders* 2 (Summer 1988): 1–23; Tagg, "Currency of the Photograph," in *Burden of Representation*, 153–183; James Curtis, *Mind's Eye, Mind's Truth: FSA Photography Reconsidered* (Philadelphia: Temple University Press, 1989); and Stange, *Symbols of Ideal Life*, chap. 3.

33. See Stange, *Symbols of Ideal Life*, chap. 3, and Curtis, *Mind's Eye, Mind's Truth*.

34. Kozol, "Madonnas of the Fields."

35. *Life*, January 18, 1937, 9–15.

36. Louis Liebovich, *The Press and the Origins of the Cold War, 1944–1947* (New York: Praeger, 1988), argues that none of the news groups he studied, including *Time*, supported the Roosevelt administration during the 1930s, "a time when the press in the country was separated philosophically from mainstream United States on political matters," 22.

37. See, e.g., Tagg, *Burden of Representation*, 14.

38. Reprinted in Curtis, *Mind's Eye, Mind's Truth*, 105. For a discussion of the FSA's pictorial representation of an ideal America that includes analyses of Lee and Rothstein's photographs, see chap. 5; and Alan Trachtenberg, "From Image to Story: Reading the File," in *Documenting America*,

esp. 56–57. Several FSA photographers, including Carl Mydans, Arthur Rothstein, and Esther Bubley, went on to careers in photojournalism at *Life* and *Look*.

39. Wainwright, *Great American Magazine*, 81, 179.

40. Tebbel and Zuckerman, *Magazine in America*, 244–245.

41. A. J. van Zuilen, *The Life Cycle of Magazines: A Historical Study of the Decline and Fall of the General Interest Mass Audience Magazine in the United States during the Period 1946–1972* (Uithoorn, Neth.: Graduate Press, 1977), 80.

42. Elson, *Time Inc.*, 276; Ben H. Bagdikian, *The Media Monopoly*, 3d ed. rev. (Boston: Beacon Press, 1990), 131–132, 137–138; and Tebbel and Zuckerman, *Magazine in America*, chap. 12.

43. Quoted in van Zuilen, *Life Cycle of Magazines*, 25.

44. This proved financially disastrous at first because advertising deals made prior to publication protected initial subscribers from rate increases the first year. *Life* lost about $3 million in the first year. See Baughman, *Henry R. Luce*, 92–94.

45. After 1956, the magazine's circulation rates and advertising revenue began to decline. By 1965, advertising pages were down to sixty-four pages per issue; see van Zuilen, *Life Cycle of Magazines*, 247.

46. Robert T. Elson, *The World of Time Inc.: The Intimate History of a Publishing Enterprise*, vol. 2: 1941–1960 (New York: Atheneum, 1973), 283, 341–342.

47. John Fiske, *Television Culture* (London: Routledge, 1987), 101.

48. See Bagdikian, *Media Monopoly*, 8, 154.

49. *Life Study of Consumer Expenditures*, conducted for *Life* by Alfred Politz Research, Inc. (New York: Time Inc., 1957), vol. 2, 10.

50. Curtis Prendergast, *The World of Time Inc.: The Intimate History of a Changing Enter-*

prise, vol. 3: 1960–1980 (New York: Atheneum, 1986), 40.

51. Van Zuilen, *Life Cycle of Magazines*, 117-119. *Life* paid Churchill $750,000 for the magazine rights to his war memoirs and $500,000 for a deal with the Mercury astronauts in 1962. See Wainwright, *Great American Magazine*, chap. 12; and Prendergast, *World of Time Inc.*, 57–59.

52. Baughman, *Henry R. Luce*, 115; and Elson, *World of Time Inc.*, 431–433; see also Edward G. McGrath, "The Political Ideals of LIFE Magazine," Ph.D. diss., Syracuse University, 1962, 27–29, for a discussion of Luce's role in editorial decisions.

53. Quoted in Wainwright, *Great American Magazine*, 173.

54. "Brief, Very Brief Birthday Thoughts," *Life*, November 26, 1956, 2.

55. Baughman, *Henry R. Luce*, 170–171.

56. Quoted in Wainwright, *Great American Magazine*, 181.

57. Ibid., 110–111, 218–219. Shooting scripts were also used extensively by the FSA; see Curtis, *Mind's Eye, Mind's Truth*, 83, 103, for a discussion of how the scripts directed the photographers' perspectives.

58. Baughman, *Heny R. Luce*, 97; Wainwright, *Great American Magazine*, 174.

59. Elson, *World of Time Inc.*, 44–45, 286. See also Barbara Rosenblum, *Photographers at Work: A Sociology of Photographic Styles* (New York: Holmes and Meier, 1978), 59–60.

60. Bylines were generally reserved for photo-essays that ran for four or more pages, which tended to feature the work of the famous photographers. *Life* did list photographers' credits, but in small print, usually on or near the table of contents page. For a discussion of Bourke-White's battles with *Life* over credit, see Goldberg, *Margaret Bourke-White*, 194–195. Disputes over editorial control led both David Douglas Duncan and W. Eugene Smith to

resign; see Wainwright, *Great American Magazine*, 149–150.

61. Quoted in William Scott, *Documentary Expression and Thirties America* (Chicago: University of Chicago Press, 1973), 130.

62. See, e.g., Wilson Hicks, *Words and Pictures: An Introduction to Photo-journalism* (New York: Harper, 1952), 3; for a more recent example of this argument, see Beaumont Newhall, *History of Photography from 1839 to the Present*, rev. ed. (New York: Museum of Modern Art and Little, Brown, 1982), 259–260.

63. Goldberg, *Margaret Bourke-White*, 192; for a similar comparison, see Stott, *Documentary Expression*, 219–223.

64. Kozol, "Madonnas of the Fields," 19–21.

65. Kobre, *Photojournalism*, 21–26; Colin Osman and Jean-Claude Lemagny, "Photography Sure of Itself," in *A History of Photography*, 166–168.

66. For a discussion of the classic Hollywood narrative style, see David Bordwell, Janet Staiger, and Kristin Thompson, *The Classical Hollywood Cinema: Film Style and Mode of Production to 1960* (New York: Columbia University Press, 1985).

67. Curtis, *Mind's Eye, Mind's Truth*, 76–82. For a discussion of documentary film, see Erik Barnouw, *Documentary: A History of the Non-Fiction Film*, rev. ed. (New York: Oxford University Press, 1983).

68. Hicks, *Words and Pictures*, 41–43; Elson, *Time Inc.*, 304.

69. *Time*, which adapted fiction techniques to the news, was an important source for *Life*. Obviously unable to compete with the timeliness of either radio or newspapers, *Time* instead sought to sum up the week's news through quickly readable stories. For a discussion of *Time*'s narrative style, see John Kobler, *Luce: His Time, Life and Fortune* (New York: Doubleday, 1968), 162–163; and Halberstam, *Powers That Be*, 62.

70. Quoted in *Photojournalism*, rev. ed. (Alexandria, Va.: Time-Life Books, 1963), 134. Carl Mydans similarly wrote, "I wanted to tell these stories, and because I was a photographer I became a storyteller in pictures." See Mydans, *Carl Mydans, Photojournalist* (New York: Harry N. Abrams, 1985), 6.

71. James Guimond, *American Photography and the American Dream* (Chapel Hill: University of North Carolina Press, 1991), 161.

72. For a more detailed discussion of this issue, see Chapter 3.

73. For a discussion of how texts anchor meanings, see Barthes, *Image—Music—Text*, 38–41.

74. George Lipsitz, *Class and Culture in Cold War America: "A Rainbow at Midnight"* (South Hadley, Mass.: Bergin & Garvey, 1982).

75. Kaja Silverman, *The Subject of Semiotics* (New York: Oxford University Press, 1983), 194–236.

76. Stanley Rayfield, *How LIFE Gets The Story: Behind the Scenes in Photojournalism* (Garden City, N.Y.: Doubleday, 1955), 6.

77. "Letters to the Editor," *Life*, December 24, 1945, 7.

78. M. M. Bakhtin, *The Dialogic Imagination*, trans. Michael Holquist and Caryl Emerson (Austin: University of Texas Press, 1981), 270.

CHAPTER 3: "The Kind of People Who Make Good Americans"

1. Steven Mintz and Susan Kellogg, *Domestic Revolutions: A Social History of American Family Life* (New York: Free Press, 1988), 184.

2. John H. Mollenkopf, *The Contested City* (Princeton, N.J.: Princeton University Press, 1983), 28.

3. Juan Ramon Garcia, *Operation Wetback: The Mass Deportation of Mexican Undocumented Workers in 1954* (Westport, Conn.: Greenwood Press, 1980), 23–36; Teresa L. Amott and Julie A. Matthaei, *Race, Gender, and Work: A Multicultural Economic History of Women in the United States* (Boston: South End Press, 1991), 79–80, 274–279.

4. David Halberstam, *The Powers That Be* (New York: Alfred A. Knopf, 1979), 60.

5. John Hartley and Martin Montgomery, "Representations and Relations: Ideology and Power in Press and TV News," in *Discourse and Communication: New Approaches to the Analysis of Mass Media Discourse and Communication*, ed. Teun A. van Dijk (Berlin: Walter de Gruyter, 1985), 260.

6. Among the growing theoretical literature on nationalism, see Anthony D. Smith, *The Ethnic Origins of Nations* (Oxford: Basil Blackwell, 1986); E. J. Hobsbawm, *Nations and Nationalism since 1780: Programme, Myth, Reality* (Cambridge: Cambridge University Press, 1990); and Benedict Anderson, *Imagined Communities: Reflections on the Origin and Spread of Nationalism*, rev. ed. (London: Verso, 1991).

7. Mary Layoun, "Telling Spaces: Palestinian Women and the Engendering of National Narratives," in *Nationalisms and Sexualities*, ed. Andrew Parker et al. (New York: Routledge, 1992), 411.

8. Anderson, *Imagined Communities*, 6–7; he argues that nationalism is not an ideology, but rather, that concepts of nation, like those of gender or kinship, are neither inherently reactionary or progressive. Eve Kosofsky Sedgwick similarly defines nationalism as an "underlying dimension of modern social functioning that could then be organized in a near-infinite number of different and even contradictory ways"; see "Nationalisms and Sexualities in the Age of Wilde," in *Nationalisms and Sexualities*, 238.

9. Anderson, *Imagined Communities*, 25.

10. Hobsbawm, *Nations and Nationalism*, 142.

11. Anderson, *Imagined Communities*, 144.

12. Stuart Hall, "Toad in the Garden: Thatcherism among the Theorists," in *Marxism and the Interpretation of Culture*, ed. Cary Nelson and Lawrence Grossberg (Urbana: University of Illinois Press, 1988), 35–73, esp. 58.

13. See John Taylor, *War Photography: Realism in the British Press* (London: Routledge, 1991), for an analysis of family imagery used by the British press during wartime. The American media also promoted family ideals during World War I but did not continue to use this iconography to the extent or with the cultural resonance that occurred after World War II.

14. Loudoun Wainwright, *Great American Magazine: An Inside History of LIFE* (New York: Alfred A. Knopf, 1986), 122.

15. "U.S. Joins War in Africa," and "Men Who Fought in Solomons Come Home Wounded," *Life*, November 16, 1942, 42–43.

16. This policy changed as it became clear that the United States and its allies would win the war. The first photograph in *Life* of dead American soldiers was George Strock's September 20, 1943, Picture of the Week of dead soldiers lying face down on a beach at Buna.

17. Anderson, *Imagined Communities*, 144.

18. Robert Westbrook, "'I Want a Girl, Just Like the Girl That Married Harry James': American Women and the Problem of Political Obligation in World War II," *American Quarterly* 42, 4 (December 1990): 587–614.

19. "Missing in Action," *Life*, July 6, 1942, 15–21.

20. See Michael Renov, "Advertising/Photojournalism/Cinema: The Shifting Rhetoric of Forties Female Representation," *Quarterly Review of Film and Video* 11, 1 (1989): 1–23, for an analysis of the image of woman in wartime advertising and its impact on film and other visual media during the 1940s.

21. Ad for Oneida Community Silverware, *Life*, June 14, 1943, 14.

22. "Letters to the Editor," *Life*, October 16, 1944, 2–4.

23. Westbrook, "'I Want a Girl, Just Like the Girl That Married Harry James,'" 599. For a discussion of *Life*'s depictions of the Japanese during the war, see Karen Huck, "Seeing Japanese: The Constitution of the Enemy Other in *Life* Magazine, 1937–1942," paper presented at the annual meeting of the American Studies Association, New York, 1987.

24. *Life*, September 25, 1944, 75–76.

25. "Home: It's the Same as Ever," *Life*, September 25, 1944, 86–89.

26. "Coast Japs Are Interned in Mountain Camp," *Life*, April 6, 1942, 15–19. For a discussion of the photographs and conditions at one of these camps, see John Armor and Peter Wright, *Manzanar* (New York: Time Books, 1988).

27. "Tule Lake: At This Segregation Center Are 18,000 Japanese Considered Disloyal to U.S.," *Life*, March 20, 1944, 25–35.

28. Among the extensive literature on this topic, see, e.g., Eleanor Straub, "United States Government Policy toward Civilian Women during World War II," *Prologue* 5, 4 (Winter 1973): 240–254; Susan M. Hartmann, *The Home Front and Beyond: American Women in the 1940s* (Boston: Twayne, 1982); and Karen Anderson, *Wartime Women: Sex Roles, Family Relations, and the Status of Women during World War II* (Westport, Conn.: Greenwood Press, 1981).

29. D'Ann Campbell, *Women at War with America: Private Lives in a Patriotic Era* (Cambridge, Mass.: Harvard University Press, 1984), 113–116; see also Hartmann, *Home Front and Beyond*, chap. 5.

30. The OWI joined forces with the War Manpower Commission to launch national campaigns to acquaint the public with the problems caused by the labor shortage. The national promotion, titled "America at War Needs Women at Work," employed all the major mass communications media including advertising, film, radio, magazines, newspapers, leaflets, posters, and brochures. For more on this campaign, see Maureen Honey, *Creating Rosie the Riveter: Class, Gender, and Propaganda during World War II*, (Amherst: University of Massachusetts Press, 1984); and Leila J. Rupp, *Mobilizing Women for War: German and American Propaganda, 1939–1945* (Princeton, N.J.: Princeton University Press, 1978).

31. Honey, *Creating Rosie the Riveter*, 179.

32. People section, *Life*, June 15, 1942, 44.

33. Honey, *Creating Rosie the Riveter*, esp. 97–108.

34. "Soldier's Wife at Work: Peoria Girl Takes Over Her Husband's Business," *Life*, September 7, 1942, 39–42.

35. Honey, *Creating Rosie the Riveter*, 23.

36. For instance, the government only allocated $1.5 million for child-care services during the war. For a detailed discussion of the issues of child care and support services, see J. F. Trey, "Women in the War Economy—World War II," *Review of Radical Political Economics* 4, 3 (July 1972): 40–57; and Anderson, *Wartime Women*, chap. 4.

37. Hartmann, *Home Front and Beyond*, 24; William H. Chafe, *The American Woman: Her Changing Social, Economic, and Political Roles, 1920–1970* (New York: Oxford University Press, 1972), 180.

38. Hartmann, *Home Front and Beyond*, 189.

39. Henry R. Luce, "The American Century," *Life*, February 17, 1941, 61–65.

40. For a discussion of the debates between isolationists and interventionists, see Robert A. Divine, *Second Chance: The Triumph of Internationalism in America during World War II* (New York: Atheneum, 1967). Even before Pearl Harbor, interventionists justified immediate military commitments by equating current objectives with future global objectives. Personnel at Time Inc. were among the intellectuals, politicians, and economic leaders who explored planning for a postwar society. In May 1947, for instance, *Fortune* published several pamphlets on postwar planning; see Robert T. Elson, *World of Time Inc.: An Intimate History of a Publishing Enterprise*, vol. 2: 1941–1960 (New York: Atheneum, 1973), 17–20.

41. David W. Noble, *The End of American History* (Minneapolis: University of Minnesota Press, 1985).

42. By June 1942, the conversion to war production had resulted in a 29 percent drop in the production of consumer goods. The projected loss of business to the advertising industry was 80 percent. In response, the advertising industry formed the War Advertising Council to work with the government. Consumer businesses, constrained from selling goods, were interested in cooperating with the government, as advertising enabled them to keep their name in the public eye—indeed the war effort offered companies a perfect opportunity to associate their name with national goals. Publicity also continued to stimulate consumer desires. The Treasury Department assisted businesses by allowing war contractors to deduct publicity expenses from taxable income. This meant that businesses engaged in government contracts could run propaganda ads partially underwritten by the government. For an in-depth analysis, see Honey, *Creating Rosie the Riveter*, 31–36.

43. Published in *Life*, January 22, 1945, inside cover.

44. Published in *Life*, October 9, 1944, 9. See Roland Marchand, *Advertising the American Dream:*

Making Way for Modernity, 1920–1940 (Berkeley: University of California Press, 1985), for a discussion of advertising typologies; and Bruce W. Brown, *Images of Family Life in Magazine Advertising: 1920–1978* (New York: Praeger Special Studies, 1981).

45. Kenneth T. Jackson, *Crabgrass Frontier: The Suburbanization of the United States* (New York: Oxford University Press, 1985), 273.

46. *Life*, September 3, 1945, 30–33.

47. Hartmann, *Home Front and Beyond*, 24, 92.

48. "U.S. Success Story 1938–1946: Auto Dealer Romy Hammes, Whom 'Life' Looked at in 1938, Is Now Going Like a House Afire," *Life*, September 23, 1946, 29–35.

49. *Life* was not alone in equating the automotive industry with the nation's economy. In what has become one of the most famous clichés of the period, Eisenhower's Secretary of Defense Charles Wilson testified before Congress that "what was good for our country was good for General Motors, and vice versa"; quoted in John Patrick Diggins, *The Proud Decades: America in War and Peace, 1941–1960* (New York: W.W. Norton, 1988), 130. See Lary May, "Introduction," in *Recasting America: Culture and Politics in the Age of Cold War*, ed. L. May (Chicago: University of Chicago Press, 1989), 5, for a discussion of the shift in postwar nationalistic rhetoric from an antimonopolistic to procorporate position.

50. Lynn Spigel, *Make Room for TV: Television and the Family Ideal in Postwar America* (Chicago: University of Chicago Press, 1992), chap. 4, esp. 116.

51. See, e.g., David Riesman, *The Lonely Crowd: A Study of the Changing American Character* (New Haven: Yale University Press, 1950); William H. Whyte, *The Organization Man* (New York: Simon and Schuster, 1956); and Ferdinand

Lundberg and Marynia F. Farnham, *Modern Woman: The Lost Sex* (New York: Harper and Bros., 1947).

52. Barbara Ehrenreich, *The Hearts of Men: American Dreams and the Flight from Commitment* (New York: Anchor, 1983), 11.

53. See Julia Hirsch, *Family Photographs: Content, Meaning and Effect* (New York: Oxford University Press, 1981), 21, for a discussion of the visual convention of representing the family as a possession.

54. *Life*, September 21, 1959, 31–37.

55. Hirsch, *Family Photographs*, 101, 120.

56. "It Couldn't Have Happened Anyplace Else in the World," *Life*, February 2, 1953, 14–23.

57. Rosalind Coward, *Female Desires: How They Are Sought, Bought and Packaged* (New York: Grove Press, 1985), 163–171, observes that the British royal family similarly represents nationhood through domestic values.

58. "New Leaders, New Zeal: Take 'Old' Out of G.O.P.," *Life*, July 21, 1952, 14–27.

59. "Barkleys' Become Capital's No. 1 Guests," *Life*, February 13, 1950, 29–33.

60. "Letters to the Editor," *Life*, March 6, 1950, 4.

61. Hartmann, *Home Front and Beyond*, 66–70.

62. Robert Coughlan, "Changing Roles in Modern Marriage: Studying Causes of Our Disturbing Divorce Rate, Psychiatrists Note Wives Who Are Not Feminine Enough and Husbands Not Truly Male," *Life*, December 24, 1956, 108–118. Throughout this period *Life* often pointed to divorce as evidence of a crisis in the family despite statistics that revealed the 1950s to have the lowest divorce rate in the century.

63. Mary P. Ryan, *Womanhood in America: From Colonial Times to the Present*, 3d ed. (New York: Franklin Watts, 1983), 260–261.

64. For discussions of postwar cultural attitudes

toward fathers, see Elaine Tyler May, *Homeward Bound: American Families in the Cold War Era* (New York: Basic Books, 1988), 145–149; and Ehrenreich, *Hearts of Men*, chap. 2. Margaret Marsh, "From Separation to Togetherness: The Social Construction of Domestic Space in American Suburbs, 1840–1915," *Journal of American History* 76, 2 (September 1989): 506–527, argues that by the late nineteenth century, the suburban ideal had recast domesticity. Previously an ideal defined by women and the family, domesticity in its new version emphasized family togetherness, including men. For discussions of 1950s television representations of the family see, e.g., Mary Beth Haralovich, "Sitcoms and Suburbs: Positioning the 1950s Homemaker," *Quarterly Review of Film and Video* 11, 1 (1989): 61–83; and Spigel, *Make Room for TV*.

65. "The Nixons in Their Backyard," *Life*, September 22, 1958, 43–46.

66. The color photographs and Nixon's status as Vice President would appear to give him a cultural advantage over John Kennedy (anticipating the 1960 election) in this staunchly Republican magazine. News stories about politicians, however, used the same format regardless of party affiliation. In fact, even as a junior senator, Kennedy's charms, good looks, and young family made him a frequent subject of sympathetic photo-essays in *Life*.

67. Haralovich, "Sitcoms and Suburbs"; and Lynn Spigel, "Installing the Television Set: Popular Discourses on Television and Domestic Space, 1948–1955," *Camera Obscura* 16 (January 1988): 11–46.

68. Allan Sekula, "The Traffic in Photographs," in *Modernism and Modernity*, ed. Benjamin H. D. Buchloch, Serge Guilbaut, and David Solkin (Halifax: Press of the Nova Scotia College of Art and Design, 1983), 136–143.

69. For a recent articulation of this position, see Diggins, *Proud Decades*, 181.

70. Elaine May, *Homeward Bound*; see also Andrew J. Cherlin, *Marriage, Divorce, Remarriage* (Cambridge, Mass.: Harvard University Press, 1981), who argues similarly that scholars must combine cohort studies with analysis of the historical conditions of the period.

71. Jürgen Habermas, *Legitimation Crisis*, trans. Thomas McCarthy (Boston: Beacon Press, 1975).

72. Quoted in Wainwright, *Great American Magazine*, 165; see Clifford E. Clark, "Ranch-House Suburbia: Ideals and Realities," in *Recasting America*, 171–191, for a discussion of how suburban architecture represented cultural ideals.

73. "$15,000 'Trade Secrets' House," *Life*, January 5, 1953, 8–15.

74. Jackson, *Crabgrass Frontier*, 209–218.

75. Marty Jezer, *The Dark Ages: Life in the United States 1945–1960* (Boston: South End Press, 1982), 179.

76. Mollenkopf, *Contested City*, 41.

77. Jackson, *Crabgrass Frontier*, 190–245.

78. *Life*, December 17, 1945, 27–35.

79. "Letters to the Editor," *Life*, January 7, 1946, 6.

80. George Lipsitz, *Class and Culture in Cold War America: "A Rainbow at Midnight"* (South Hadley, Mass.: Bergin and Garvey, 1982).

81. "The Great Train Strike: Railroad Shutdown Brings Wrath of People Down on All U.S. Labor," *Life*, June 3, 1946, 27–33.

82. Ibid., 32.

83. *Life* also uses this strategy on the first page of the essay when the writer quotes a dentist from Des Moines who said, "Labor is like a kid who gets too much money from his parents."

84. Hunt's attention to proper behavior is reminiscent of the relationship between respectability and nationalism that developed in conjunction with the rise of the bourgeoisie in modern Europe. See George L. Mosse, *Nationalism and Sexuality: Respectability and Abnormal Sexuality in Modern*

Europe (New York: Howard Fettig, 1985), 8–9, who argues that respectability played a crucial role for the middle class by distinguishing it from both the aristocracy and lower classes, as well as providing stability amid the upheavals of industrialization and modernization.

85. "Letters to the Editor," *Life*, June 24, 1946, 6.

86. Jezer, *Dark Ages*, 119–122; Douglas F. Dowd, *The Twisted Dream: Capitalist Development in the United States since 1776* (Cambridge, Mass.: Winthrop, 1974), 65–75, 105–107.

87. Hartmann, *Home Front and Beyond*, 8.

88. Jezer, *Dark Ages*, 120.

89. Hartmann, *Home Front and Beyond*, 7–8.

90. Jezer, *Dark Ages*, 203.

91. Charles S. Maier, "The Politics of Productivity: Foundations of American International Economic Policy after World War II," *International Organization* 31, 4 (1977): 607–633.

92. *Life*, May 5, 1947, 27–33.

93. "They Pour in . . . and Family Shows Refugees Can Fit In," *Life*, January 7, 1957, 20–27.

94. In an excellent discussion of Tom Wesselman's Pop Art images of "the economy of domesticity," Cecile Whiting analyzes an image that bears a resemblance to these pictures in their display of consumer goods on the kitchen table; see "Pop Art Domesticated: Class and Taste in Tom Wesselman's Collages," *Genders* 13 (Spring 1992): 43–72.

95. See Judith Williamson, *Consuming Passions: The Dynamics of Popular Culture* (London: Marion Boyars, 1986), 115–116, who discusses the family in relation to Gramsci's concept of political and civil society, arguing that the family participates in both sectors.

96. Jezer, *Dark Ages*, 192–193.

97. "Letters to the Editor," *Life*, April 10, 1944, 4.

98. Ibid., *Life*, February 11, 1946, 4.

99. George Lipsitz, "The Meaning of Memory: Family, Class, and Ethnicity in Early Network Television," *Time Passages: Collective Memory and American Popular Culture* (Minneapolis: University of Minnesota Press, 1990), 39–75.

100. This reading of how photographs secure identification derives from Judith Williamson's *Decoding Advertisements: Ideology and Meaning in Advertisements* (London: Marion Boyars, 1978), 44–45. She argues that advertisements work by combining unrelated signifiers, like a product and an actress, leaving the reader to make meaningful connections between the two. Thus, the advertisement draws the reader into the space of the signified so that the reader identifies with the message.

101. John Fiske, *Television Culture* (New York: Routledge, 1987), 169.

102. "GM Paces the U.S. Pension Parade," *Life*, June 5, 1950, 21–25.

103. The article appeared in *Life*, July 13, 1959, 16–25, as part of a series of articles titled "Old Age: Personal Crisis, U.S. Problem." The title indicates the perspective the magazine took on this topic.

104. See Lee Edelman, "Tearooms and Sympathy, or, The Epistemology of the Water Closet," in *Nationalisms and Sexualities*, 263–284, for an excellent discussion of Cold War attacks on homosexuality and the role of the media in promoting virulent homophobia. He examines *Life*'s first photo-essay on gays and lesbians, "Homosexuality in America," which appeared on June 26, 1964, 66–80.

105. John Hartley, "Invisible Fictions: Television Audiences, Paedocracy, Pleasure," in *Television Studies: Textual Analysis*, ed. Gary Burns and Robert J. Thompson (New York: Praeger, 1989), 223–243; see also Horace M. Newcomb, "On the Dialogic Aspects of Mass Communication," *Critical Studies in Mass Communications* 1 (1984): 34–50.

106. See, e.g., *Life Study of Consumer Expenditures*, vol. 1–6, conducted for *Life* by Alfred Politz Research, Inc. (New York: Time Inc., 1957).

107. Curtis Prendergast, *The World of Time*

Inc.: The Intimate History of a Changing Enterprise, vol. 3: 1960–1980 (New York: Atheneum, 1986), 53–54.

108. "What Makes the Economy Tick? Capitalism Modified by Democracy Has Room for Lots of Incentives—Including Money," *Life*, January 5, 1953, 16.

CHAPTER 4: Public News and Private Lives

1. *Life*, March 15, 1948, 31–39.
2. See Wendy Kozol, "Madonnas of the Fields: Photography, Gender, and 1930s Farm Relief," *Genders* 2 (Summer 1988): 1–23.
3. Nancy Fraser, "Rethinking the Public Sphere: A Contribution to the Critique of Actually Existing Democracy," *Social Text* 25/26 (1990): 57.
4. For a discussion of the media as global media conglomerates and the consequences for communications in contemporary society, see Ben H. Bagdikian, *The Media Monopoly*, 3d ed. rev. (Boston: Beacon Press, 1990).
5. See Craig Calhoun, "Introduction: Habermas and the Public Sphere," in *Habermas and the Public Sphere*, ed. C. Calhoun (Cambridge, Mass.: MIT Press, 1992), 1–48, for an analysis of Jürgen Habermas, *The Structural Transformation of the Public Sphere: An Inquiry into a Category of Bourgeois Society*, trans. Thomas Burger and Frederick Lawrence (Cambridge, Mass.: MIT Press, 1989).
6. See Calhoun, *Habermas and the Public Sphere*, and Fraser, "Rethinking the Public Sphere." Fraser also criticizes Habermas's exclusive focus on the bourgeois public sphere because it does not consider "counter publics" or competing public spheres. As she notes, for instance, "the view that women were excluded from the public sphere turns out to be ideological; it rests on a class- and gender-biased notion of publicity, one which accepts at face value the bourgeois public's claim to be *the* public,"

61. There were important counter publics during the postwar period that competed with the official public sphere represented by *Life*. Although my focus is on understanding the power and implications of the official or dominant sphere, these counterpublics did offer an alternative to *Life* and other hegemonic discourses. For analysis of certain counterpublics that addressed gender issues, see Joanne Meyerowitz, ed., *Not June Cleaver: Women and Gender in Postwar America* (Philadelphia: Temple University Press, 1994).

7. Stephanie Coontz, *The Social Origins of Private Life: A History of American Families, 1600–1900* (London: Verso, 1988), 267, argues that middle-class Americans in the late nineteenth century did not envision the home as a refuge from the outside world but rather as an ideal space in which to prepare children for its demands. In this way, middle-class family values did not stand in opposition to industrial capitalism but supported the public world.

8. Fraser, "Rethinking the Public Sphere," 73.
9. Ibid., 78, n. 14.
10. "The Big Bird Orbits Words of Peace," *Life*, January 5, 1959, 10–23.
11. I thank Camille Guerin-Gonzalez for pointing this out to me.
12. "Cars, Clocks and the Four-Power 'Klatsch': Foreign Ministers Dispose of Some Routine Talk and Get Down to the Business of Hard Diplomacy," *Life*, February 8, 1954, 32–33.
13. From the broad literature on this topic, see, e.g., Barbara Laslett, "The Family as a Public and Private Institution: An Historical Perspective," *Journal of Marriage and the Family* 35, 3 (August 1973): 480–492; Joan Kelly, "Family and Society," *Women, History and Theory* (Chicago: University of Chicago Press, 1984), 110–155; Steven Mintz and Susan Kellogg, *Domestic Revolutions: A Social History of American Family Life* (New York: Free Press, 1988); Coontz, *Social Origins of Private Life*;

Mary P. Ryan, *Women in Public: Between Banners and Ballots, 1825–1880* (Baltimore: Johns Hopkins University Press, 1990); and Dorothy O. Helly and Susan M. Reverby, eds., *Gendered Domains: Rethinking Public and Private in Women's History* (Ithaca: Cornell University Press, 1992). For a historiographic essay on this topic, see Linda Kerber, "Separate Spheres, Female Worlds, Woman's Place: The Rhetoric of Women's History," *Journal of American History* 75, 1 (June 1988): 9–39.

14. This all too brief summary does not adequately address the complexities of class transformations, gender negotiations, and ideological struggles in industrializing America during the nineteenth century. For an excellent discussion of these processes, see Coontz, *Social Origins of Private Life.*

15. For discussion of the differences between this white, middle-class ideology and the public and private lives of working-class women of color, see, e.g., Patricia Hill Collins, *Black Feminist Thought: Knowledge, Consciousness, and the Politics of Empowerment* (London: HarperCollins Academic, 1990), chap. 3; and Teresa L. Amott and Julie A. Matthaei, *Race, Gender, and Work: A Multicultural Economic History of Women in the United States* (Boston: South End Press, 1991).

16. There are extensive debates on the effects of capitalism on women's lives. Edward Shorter, "Women's Work: What Difference Did Capitalism Make?" *Theory and Society* 3, 4:513–529, offers a contrasting perspective, arguing that industrial capitalism brought advantages to women through rising standards of living and political actions that, he suggests, put working women "within shouting distance of social equality with men," 513. For a discussion of these debates and an analysis of sex-segregated labor, see Harriet Bradley, *Men's Work, Women's Work: A Sociological History of the Sexual Division of Labour in Employment* (Minneapolis: University of Minnesota Press, 1989). For a his-

torical analysis of American women's labor history, see, e.g., Alice Kessler-Harris, *Out to Work: A History of Wage-Earning Women in the United States* (New York: Oxford University Press, 1982); and Julie A. Matthaei, *An Economic History of Women in America: Women's Work, the Sexual Division of Labor, and the Development of Capitalism* (New York: Schocken, 1982).

17. See Collins, *Black Feminist Thought,* chap. 4, for a discussion of the myth of the black matriarch and other negative stereotypes that continue to condemn women who do not conform to normative ideals of family and social relations.

18. For an excellent discussion of these historical changes, see Linda J. Nicholson, *Gender and History: The Limits of Social Theory in the Age of the Family* (New York: Columbia University Press, 1986), chap. 4.

19. Susan M. Hartmann, *The Home Front and Beyond: American Women in the 1940s* (Boston: Twayne, 1982), 18.

20. Kerber, "Separate Spheres, Female Worlds, Woman's Place," 21.

21. Ruth Milkman, "Women's Work and the Economic Crisis: Some Lessons from the Great Depression," in *A Heritage of Her Own: Toward a New Social History of American Women,* ed. Nancy F. Cott and Elizabeth H. Pleck (New York: Simon and Schuster, 1979), 507–541.

22. See Hartmann, *Home Front and Beyond,* chap. 4.

23. Maureen Honey, *Creating Rosie the Riveter: Class, Gender, and Propaganda during World War II* (Amherst: University of Massachusetts Press, 1984); Serafina K. Bathrick, "The True Woman and the Family-Film: The Industrial Production of Memory," Ph.D. diss., University of Wisconsin, Madison, 1981.

24. Hartmann, *Home Front and Beyond,* 24, 90–94.

25. Elaine Tyler May, *Homeward Bound: Ameri-*

can Families in the Cold War Era (New York: Basic Books, 1988), 76.

26. Rochelle Gatlin, American Women since 1945 (Jackson: University Press of Mississippi, 1987), 39.

27. Kessler-Harris, Out to Work, 300–303.

28. See Leila J. Rupp and Verta Taylor, Survival in the Doldrums: The American Women's Rights Movement, 1945 to the 1960s (New York: Oxford University Press, 1987), for a discussion of the repressive effects of anticommunism on the National Women's Party during the Cold War. However, feminist historians are now reexamining studies like Rupp and Taylor's that claim that the postwar period was one of inactivity for feminism, because they look only at a small group of elite women and ignore other women's social struggles. See, e.g., Amy Swerdlow, "Ladies Day at the Capitol: Women Strike for Peace versus HUAC," Feminist Studies 8, 3 (Fall 1982): 493–520; Nancy F. Gabin, Feminism in the Labor Movement: Women and the United Auto Workers, 1935–1975 (Ithaca: Cornell University Press, 1990); and Susan Lynn, Progressive Women in Conservative Times: Racial Justice, Peace, and Feminism, 1945 to the 1960s (New Brunswick, N.J.: Rutgers University Press, 1992).

29. "An Introduction by Mrs. Peter Marshall," Life, December 24, 1956, 2–3. For an analysis of this special issue, "The American Woman," see Chapter 5.

30. For an extensive discussion of postwar domestic ideologies, see Elaine May, Homeward Bound. See also William H. Chafe, American Woman: Her Changing Social, Economic and Political Roles, 1920–1970 (New York: Oxford University Press, 1972), 199–225; Barbara Ehrenreich, The Hearts of Men: American Dreams and the Flight from Commitment (New York: Anchor, 1983); and Mintz and Kellogg, Domestic Revolutions, chap. 9.

31. For an excellent discussion of how tele-

vision translated the marketing strategies of the consumer-products industries into suburban situation comedies, see Mary Beth Haralovich, "Sitcoms and Suburbs: Positioning the 1950s Homemaker," Quarterly Review of Film and Video 11, 1 (1989): 61–83.

32. For a discussion of the popularization of Freudian theories of gender, see Julie Weiss, "Womanhood and Psychoanalysis: A Study of Mutual Construction in Popular Culture, 1920–1963," Ph.D. diss., Brown University, 1990; see also Mary Ann Doane, The Desire to Desire: The Woman's Film of the 1940s (Bloomington: Indiana University Press, 1987), chap. 2, for an analysis of Hollywood's adaptation of psychoanalytic concepts of sexuality and gender identity.

33. Jacques Donzelot, The Policing of Families, trans. Robert Hurley (New York: Pantheon, 1979), 198.

34. As mentioned in Chapter 1, in the 1959 kitchen debates, Nixon battled Khrushchev on similar grounds that linked middle-class domesticity to American democracy. See Elaine May, Homeward Bound, 16–20.

35. Joan Kelly, "The Doubled Vision of Feminist Theory: A Postscript to the 'Woman and Power' Conference," Women, History and Theory (Chicago: University of Chicago Press, 1984), 57; see also Nicholson, Gender and History; and Susan Moller Okin, Justice, Gender, and the Family (New York: Basic Books, 1989), esp. chap. 6.

36. See Mintz and Kellogg, Domestic Revolutions, for a discussion of these historical developments.

37. Donzelot, Policing of Families, xxvi.

38. See Leonore Davidoff and Catherine Hall, Family Fortunes: Men and Women of the English Middle Class, 1780–1850 (Chicago: University of Chicago Press, 1987), for an analysis of the role domesticity played in constructing middle-class

male identity in England in the eighteenth and nineteenth centuries.

39. Nicholson, *Gender and History*, 100.

40. Almost fifty years of historical debates exist on the origins, causes and responsibilities for the Cold War. Since the collapse of the Soviet Union and the declared end of the Cold War, historians are once again scrutinizing this history. In this study, however, I do not consider the Cold War itself; rather, I am interested in how *Life* relied on the family to represent certain perspectives on it. For recent discussions of Cold War historiography and current reassessments, see, e.g., Thomas J. McCormick, *America's Half Century* (Baltimore: Johns Hopkins University Press, 1989); and Charles S. Maier, ed., *The Cold War in Europe* (New York: Markus Wiener, 1991).

41. "The 36-Hour War: Arnold Report Hints at the Catastrophe of the Next Great Conflict," *Life*, November 19, 1945, 27–35. See James L. Baughman, *Henry R. Luce and the Rise of the American News Media* (Boston: Twayne, 1987), 148–149, for a discussion of *Life*'s anti-Communist position.

42. For discussions of the repressive measures taken against homosexuals during the Cold War, see Lillian Faderman, *Odd Girls and Twilight Lovers: A History of Lesbian Life in Twentieth-Century America* (New York: Penguin, 1991), chap. 6; Elaine May, *Homeward Bound*, chap. 4; and John D'Emilio and Estelle B. Freedman, *Intimate Matters: A History of Sexuality in America* (New York: Harper and Row, 1988), 292–293. The media often represented homosexuals as dangerously corrupt or as threats to national security because they were potential blackmail victims.

43. Cf. Paul Boyer, *By the Bomb's Early Light: American Thought and Culture at the Dawn of the Atomic Age* (New York: Pantheon, 1985), 67; and Marty Jezer, *The Dark Ages: Life in the United States 1945–1960* (Boston: South End Press, 1982), 32.

44. Elaine May, *Homeward Bound*, 26–28.

45. See William Chafe and Harvard Sitkoff, eds., *History of Our Time: Readings in Postwar America*, 2d ed. (New York: Oxford University Press, 1987), for contemporary documents and historical arguments about the Cold War. For discussions of the Truman administration's exaggerated claims of Soviet insurgency, see, e.g., Jezer, *Dark Ages*, 41–45 and 56–59; and Stephen E. Ambrose, *Rise to Globalism: American Foreign Policy since 1938*, 5th ed. (New York: Penguin, 1988), 78–86.

46. *Life*, March 19, 1951, 35–39.

47. "52s Shrink a World: A Historic Show of U.S. Air Power," *Life*, January 28, 1957, 21–27.

48. "The Communist Peace Dove . . . And the Wife of a Prisoner of War," *Life*, April 13, 1953, 27–31.

49. Doane, *Desire to Desire*, 80, uses this phrase in her analysis of World War II films such as *Since You Went Away* (1944), in which photographs function as reminders of absent husbands' male authority when they are away at war.

50. Haralovich, "Sitcoms and Suburbs."

51. "Love Triumphs over Ideology: Communist Prague's Crowds Share Joy as U.S., Czech Olympians Wed," *Life*, April 8, 1957, 50–52.

52. *Life*, November 21, 1955, 33–39.

53. Jezer, *Dark Ages*, 126.

54. Ibid., 124–127.

55. See Kenneth T. Jackson, *Crabgrass Frontier: The Suburbanization of the United States* (New York: Oxford University Press, 1985), 203–218.

56. See Nancy Armstrong, *Desire and Domestic Fiction: A Political History of the Novel* (New York: Oxford University Press, 1987), who argues that the textual strategies in eighteenth- and nineteenth-century English domestic novels redefined political desires into psychological ones. This redefinition of desire was "a decisive step in producing the densely interwoven fabric of common sense and sentimen-

tality that even today ensures the ubiquity of middle class power," 9.

57. Davidoff and Hall, *Family Fortunes*, 29–30.

58. Ad for Equitable Life Insurance, *Life*, November 21, 1955, 4–5.

59. For discussions of the domestic components of postwar anticommunism, see, e.g., Jezer, *Dark Ages*, chap. 4; and Lary May, ed., *Recasting America: Culture and Politics in the Age of Cold War* (Chicago: University of Chicago Press, 1989). For a discussion of the effects of anti-Communist purges on labor activism, see George Lipsitz, *Class and Culture in Cold War America: "A Rainbow at Midnight"* (South Hadley, Mass.: Bergin and Garvey, 1982), chaps. 7 and 8.

60. Juan Ramon Garcia, *Operation Wetback: The Mass Deportation of Mexican Undocumented Workers in 1954* (Westport, Conn.: Greenwood Press, 1980), 122.

61. Elaine May, *Homeward Bound*, chap. 4.

62. Dana Polan, *Power and Paranoia: History, Narrative, and the American Cinema, 1940–1950* (New York: Columbia University Press, 1986).

63. Jackie Byars, *All That Hollywood Allows: Re-reading Gender in 1950s Melodrama* (Chapel Hill: University of North Carolina Press, 1991), 114.

64. An ad for Betty Crocker, *Life*, April 13, 1953, 24.

65. Nina C. Leibman, "Leave Mother Out: The Fifties Family in American Film and Television," *Wide Angle* 10, 4 (1988): 24–41, argues that in response to momism, film and television often deemphasized the mother's importance, "decisively reconfiguring the father as the crucial molder of his children's psyches," 31. Hence, even though mothers on television domestic sitcoms like "Leave It to Beaver," and "Father Knows Best" are not evil or destructive, they become "implicitly superfluous, unnecessary or subordinate," 26.

66. "House of Horrors Stuns the Nation," *Life*, December 2, 1957, 24–31.

67. Michael Paul Rogin, *Ronald Reagan, the Movie and Other Episodes in Political Demonology* (Berkeley: University of California Press, 1987), 242.

68. James Gilbert, *A Cycle of Outrage: America's Reaction to the Juvenile Delinquent in the 1950s* (New York: Oxford University Press, 1986). See Lynn Spigel, *Make Room for TV: Television and the Family Ideal in Postwar America* (Chicago: University of Chicago Press, 1992), 52–55, for a discussion of social critics who blamed television for the presumed high incidence of juvenile delinquency.

69. Elaine May, *Homeward Bound*, chap. 4.

70. Rogin, *Reagan, the Movie*, 255.

71. *Life*, March 24, 1947, 36.

72. Cited in Jezer, *Dark Ages*, 201.

73. Rogin, *Reagan, the Movie*, 245.

74. "Letters to the Editor," *Life*, April 14, 1947, 20.

75. David Riesman, *The Lonely Crowd* (New Haven: Yale University Press, 1950).

76. Ehrenreich, *Hearts of Men*, 34.

77. Jezer, *Dark Ages*, 221–223; Mintz and Kellogg, *Domestic Revolutions*, 199–201.

78. Fred Pfeil, "Postmodernism as a 'Structure of Feeling,'" in *Marxism and the Interpretation of Culture*, ed. Cary Nelson and Lawrence Grossberg (Urbana: University of Illinois Press, 1988), 381–403, argues that postwar changes in family life also affected psychological developments that resulted in an incomplete or weakened Oedipal break for middle-class Americans. He explains this as de-oedipalization, which results when the boundaries between the subject and object of desire remain indeterminate. Opening up possibilities for the emergence of desires different from Oedipal forms of control, this dialectical relationship between self and other nonetheless does not ensure unambiguous

pleasure because it is accompanied by a fear of dissolution. The de-oedipalized subject, moreover, is susceptible to a needy narcissism that consumption promises to fulfill.

79. "The U.A.W.'s Fight for an Annual Wage: A Family Shows Why Union Wanted It from Ford," *Life*, June 13, 1955, 34–35.

80. "Letters to the Editor," *Life*, July 4, 1955, 6.

81. Ad for The Travelers Insurance, *Life*, March 11, 1957, 12.

82. Ad for John Hancock Insurance, *Life*, March 11, 1957, 29.

83. "The Poignant Figures of a Modern Exodus," *Life*, January 6, 1958, 8–13.

84. *Life*, October 13, 1952, 26–33.

85. There is a great deal of debate over American political objectives in the Marshall Plan and its degree of effectiveness. For a recent examination, see Maier, *Cold War in Europe*, including Alan S. Milward, "The Reconstruction of Western Europe," 241–269, who remains skeptical about the extent to which the plan aided European recovery.

86. "The Murderers of Her Father . . . Or What Stands between France and Germany," *Life*, February 23, 1953, 21–25.

87. See Erica Carter, "Intimate Outscapes: Problem-Page Letters and the Remaking of the 1950s West German Family," in *Becoming Feminine: The Politics of Popular Culture*, ed. Leslie G. Roman and Linda K. Christian-Smith with Elizabeth Ellsworth (New York: Falmer Press, 1988), 60–75, who examines similar discursive strategies in German magazines in the postwar period that attempted to reconstruct the fractures in social identity by promoting nuclear family ideals.

88. "Letters to the Editor," *Life*, November 3, 1952, 2.

89. The son's name, Ivan, indicates that Pavla Pirečnik was of either Slovenian or Croatian ethnicity. I thank Sibelan Forrester for this information.

90. Byars, *All That Hollywood Allows*, similarly points out that in many postwar maternal melodramas, like *The Imitation of Life* (1959), the "narrative contortions necessary for the production of these deus-ex-machina endings expose the improbability of actually achieving the 'happiness' the endings depict," 252.

91. *Life*, January 21, 1946, 25–29.

92. One notable exception is "The Weekend Woe of a Father Named Joe: He Gives the Wife Time Off and Bravely Takes Charge," *Life*, July 16, 1956, 85–89. In this feature photo-essay by Joe Scherschel, the father cares for his children for a weekend while his wife goes on a vacation. The narrative, however, reproduces stereotypical assumptions about women's unique competence in the home, for the husband becomes frantic and harassed by domestic chores and responsibilities. The story's (exceptional) existence underscores how rarely *Life* represented alternative domestic roles.

93. Judith Williamson, *Consuming Passions: The Dynamics of Popular Culture* (London: Marion Boyars, 1986), 118.

94. See Spigel, *Make Room for TV*, 147–148, for a discussion of the erasure of ethnic identities in postwar television.

95. "The Showdown," 38.

96. See Armstrong, *Desire and Domestic Fiction*, 255.

97. For a discussion of this point, see Michael Denning, "The End of Mass Culture," *International Labor and Working-Class History* 37 (Spring 1990): 4–18.

CHAPTER 5: Resisting the Domestic

1. "Puerto Rican Migrants Jam New York," *Life*, August 25, 1947, 25–29.

2. For an overview of U.S. colonial policies in

Puerto Rico, economic conditions, and immigration practices, especially as these factors affect women, see Teresa L. Amott and Julie A. Matthaei, *Race, Gender, and Work: A Multicultural Economic History of Women in the United States* (Boston: South End Press, 1991), 257–287, esp. 274–275. See Chandra Talpade Mohanty, Ann Russo, and Lourdes Torres, eds., *Third World Women and the Politics of Feminism* (Bloomington: Indiana University Press, 1991), for analyses of the effects of postwar capitalism on third world women.

3. Laura Mulvey's landmark "Visual Pleasure and Narrative Cinema," *Screen* 16, 3 (Autumn 1975): 6–18, uses feminist, semiotic, and psychoanalytic theories to investigate spectatorship and voyeurism in film. More recent work on spectatorship in film includes Teresa de Lauretis, *Alice Doesn't: Feminism, Semiotics, Cinema* (Bloomington: Indiana University Press, 1984); E. Deidre Pribram, ed., *Female Spectators: Looking at Film and Television* (London: Verso, 1988); and bell hooks, "The Oppositional Gaze: Black Female Spectators," *Black Looks: Race and Representation* (Boston: South End Press, 1992), 115–131. See Malek Alloula, *The Colonial Harem*, trans. Myrna Godzich and Wlad Godzich (Minneapolis: University of Minnesota Press, 1986); and Sarah Graham-Brown, *Images of Women: The Portrayal of Women in Photography of the Middle East 1860–1950* (London: Quartet, 1988), who use theories of spectatorship to analyze gender, race, and imperialism in studies of European photographs of the Middle East.

4. See Horace M. Newcomb, "On the Dialogic Aspects of Mass Communication," *Critical Studies in Mass Communications* 1 (1984): 34–50; and John Fiske, "Television: Polysemy and Popularity," *Critical Studies in Mass Communication* 3, 4 (December 1986): 391–408, for analyses of the dialogic nature of mass media.

5. Stuart Hall, "Culture, Media and the 'Ideological Effect,'" in *Mass Communications and Society*, ed. James Curran, Michael Gurevitch, and Janet Woollacott (Beverly Hills: Sage, 1976), 333.

6. "Night Watch: It Guards Negroes in a Chicago Housing Project against Violence," *Life*, November 9, 1953, 57–60.

7. M. M. Bakhtin, *The Dialogic Imagination*, trans. Michael Holquist and Caryl Emerson (Austin: University of Texas Press, 1981), 276.

8. The third photograph is similar in composition to the photograph of Fireman Olesiak seated on a couch with his wife while the boys play with toy missiles in the foreground, published in "The Big Bird Orbits Words of Peace," *Life*, January 5, 1959, 10–23. See Chapter 4 for a discussion of this image.

9. "Integration Troubles Beset Northern Town: Its First Negroes Meet Protests, Then Order, New Friends Prevail," *Life*, September 2, 1957, 43–46.

10. Ad for Federal Savings and Loan Insurance Corporation, *Life*, September 2, 1957, 42.

11. Marty Jezer, *The Dark Ages: Life in the United States 1945–1960* (Boston: South End Press, 1982), 185; Kenneth T. Jackson, *Crabgrass Frontier: The Suburbanization of the United States* (New York: Oxford University Press, 1985), 209–215.

12. "Letters to the Editor," *Life*, November 30, 1953, 4.

13. Ibid.

14. Ibid., September 15, 1947, 24.

15. "'Integration' in the South," *Life*, November 28, 1960, 38.

16. Fiske, "Television: Polysemy and Popularity," 394.

17. Newcomb, "On the Dialogic Aspects of Mass Communication," 48.

18. For analyses of the emergence of the civil rights movement, see Harvard Sitkoff, *The Struggle for Black Equality, 1954–1980* (New York: Hill and Wang, 1981); and Aldon D. Morris, *The Ori-*

gins of the Civil Rights Movement: Black Communities Organizing for Change (New York: Free Press, 1984).

19. John H. Mollenkopf, The Contested City (Princeton, N.J.: Princeton University Press, 1983), 28.

20. See Sitkoff, Struggle for Black Equality, esp. chaps. 1 and 2. For a discussion of the federal government's response to the civil rights movement during the 1950s, see Robert Fredrick Burk, The Eisenhower Administration and Black Civil Rights (Knoxville: University of Tennessee Press, 1984).

21. See, e.g., "Bulge of Braceros at the Border: Mexican Workers Create Pandemonium Trying to Get U.S. Farm Jobs," Life, February 15, 1954, 26–29.

22. "Go Slow, Now," Life, March 12, 1956, 37. This editorial was written in response to attempts to integrate the University of Alabama. The editors criticized the African American student Autherine Lucy for creating antagonisms "by being driven to school ostentatiously in a Cadillac, by being registered ahead of others waiting in line and by suing for immediate admission to dormitory and mess as well as classes (although most whites as old as she is board outside. . . . Such carping can't alter Miss Lucy's claim to justice . . . but need to avoid needless scraping of Southern sensitivities and emotions." Three weeks later, when Roger Wilkins of the NAACP refuted these charges, Life defended its position in the letters section by insisting on the accuracy of its statements and again accusing African Americans of moving too fast.

23. Sitkoff, Struggle For Black Equality, 22–28; Morris, Origins of the Civil Rights Movement, 27–29.

24. John Taylor, War Photography: Realism in the British Press (London: Routledge, 1991), argues that the purposes of the media and the state are not fundamentally different; rather both express an "offi-cial perspective, an orthodoxy that has a resilient philosophic and historic respectability," 12.

25. Hall, "Culture, Media and the 'Ideological Effect,'" 340–346; see also John Hartley, Understanding News (London: Methuen, 1982), esp. chap. 4.

26. Life, August 1, 1949, 22–23.

27. Morris, Origins of the Civil Rights Movement, 32–35.

28. Ibid., 40–63.

29. "Emmett Till's Day in Court: Mississippians Refuse to Convict White Men of Killing a Negro Boy," Life, October 3, 1955, 36–38. For historical accounts of the trial, see Juan Williams, Eyes on the Prize: America's Civil Rights Years, 1954–1965 (New York: Penguin, 1987), 38–46; and Stephen J. Whitfield, A Death in the Delta: The Story of Emmett Till (New York: Free Press, 1988).

30. Sitkoff, Struggle for Black Equality, 16.

31. "Klan Is in Trouble: An Interstate Abduction Sets FBI on Floggers," Life, March 31, 1952, 44–49.

32. Hall, "Culture, Media and the 'Ideological Effect,'" 342–343.

33. Stuart Hall, "The Toad in the Garden: Thatcherism among the Theorists," in Marxism and the Interpretation of Culture, ed. Cary Nelson and Lawrence Grossberg (Urbana: University of Illinois Press, 1988), 44.

34. Polan, Power and Paranoia, 11–12.

35. "'You Have Cried Enough Tears for Me,'" A Look at the World's Week, Life, October 10, 1955, 33.

36. Susan M. Hartmann, The Home Front and Beyond: American Women in the 1940s (Boston: Twayne, 1982), 149–150; see also Eugenia Kaledin, Mothers and More: American Women in the 1950s (Boston: Twayne, 1984), chap. 5, for a discussion of women's political activities in the 1950s; see Lynn, Progressive Women in Conservative Times, for an

analysis of women's experiences in the YWCA and AFS.

37. "Petticoat Rule Scores Again: Washington, Va. Gets Pretty Mayor," *Life*, September 18, 1950, 48–49.

38. For a discussion of anchorage, see Roland Barthes, *Image—Music—Text*, trans. Stephen Heath (New York: Hill and Wang, 1977), 37–41.

39. "The American Woman: Since She Is Clever and Beautiful, Why Can't She Also Be Politically Effective?" *Life*, October 21, 1946, 36.

40. Quoted in Kaledin, *Mothers and More*, 87.

41. See Linda Kerber, *Women of the Republic: Intellect and Ideology in Revolutionary America* (Chapel Hill: University of North Carolina Press, 1980), for a discussion of republican motherhood; and Sara M. Evans, *Born for Liberty: A History of Women in America* (New York: Free Press, 1989), chap. 6, for an analysis of the ideological framework within which reformers attempted to build a maternal commonwealth.

42. "Earned Place in Politics: After 36 Years of Suffrage, U.S. Women Are a Force from Grass Roots to Senate," *Life*, December 24, 1956, 49–55.

43. Jackie Kennedy appeared on the covers of the April 21, 1958, August 24, 1959, November 21 and December 19, 1960, issues.

44. "The Lady from Minnesota: She Brings Charm, Savvy, to National Committee Jobs," *Life*, July 4, 1960, 74–77.

45. For a contemporary account of these gender conflicts, see Betty Friedan, *The Feminine Mystique* (New York: W. W. Norton, 1963).

46. Quoted in Steven Mintz and Susan Kellogg, *Domestic Revolutions: A Social History of American Family Life* (New York: Free Press, 1988), 181.

47. Kaledin, *Mothers and More*, 65.

48. "Letters to the Editor," *Life*, January 14, 1957, 21.

49. "Busy Wife's Achievements: Marjorie Sut-ton Is Home Manager, Mother, Hostess and Useful Civic Worker," *Life*, December 24, 1956, 41–46.

50. "The First Baby: Georgette Mapes and a Million Others Share a Rich Experience," *Life*, December 24, 1956, 57–63.

51. "A Teen-Age Fledgling Starts to Grow Up: 13-Year-Old Finds Tomboy Antics Giving Way to Adult Graces," *Life*, December 24, 1956, 97–101.

52. Fiske, "Television: Polysemy and Popularity," 403.

53. Sitkoff, *Struggle for Black Equality*, 13.

54. "Women Hold Third of Jobs: They Have Moved en Masse into Business World," *Life*, December 24, 1956, 30–35.

55. Ibid.

56. "The Great Housing Shortage," *Life*, December 17, 1945, 27–35; see Chapter 3 for a discussion of this photo-essay.

57. " 'My Wife Works and I Like It': Jim Magill Argues that Jennie's Full-Time Job Is Good for Her, Good for Him, Good for Their Children—and Good for the Budget," *Life*, December 24, 1956, 140–141.

58. Alice Kessler-Harris, *Out to Work: A History of Wage-Earning Women in the United States* (New York: Oxford University Press, 1982), 302.

59. Coughlan, "Changing Roles in Modern Marriage," *Life*, November 30, 1953, 25–29; see Chapter 3 for a discussion of this article.

60. "A New American Comes 'Home,'" *Life*, November 30, 1953, 25–29.

61. Kaja Silverman, *The Subject of Semiotics* (New York: Oxford University Press, 1983), 241.

62. Michael Denning explains Voloshinov's concept in *Mechanic Accents: Dime Novels and Working-Class Culture in America* (London: Verso, 1987), esp. 82–84; see also Hartley, *Understanding News*, 21–24, for an application of this concept to news discourses.

63. Denning, *Mechanic Accents*, 83.

64. *Life*, September 18, 1950, 41–47. See

Chapter 4 for a discussion of a later photo-essay, "Marines Come Home from the Front," *Life*, March 19, 1951, 35–39, which reuses one of Duncan's photographs from this photo-essay.

65. For an insightful analysis of the construction of masculinity and the exclusion of women in Vietnam War narratives, see Susan Jeffords, *The Remasculinization of America: Gender and the Vietnam War* (Bloomington: Indiana University Press, 1989).

66. "International Row over a GI: Angry Words Fly in U.S. and Japan over Jurisdiction in Shooting Case," *Life*, June 17, 1957, 92–93.

67. Fredric Jameson, "Reification and Utopia in Mass Culture," *Social Text* 1 (Winter 1979): 130–148.

68. Fiske, "Television: Polysemy and Popularity," 391–392.

69. Linda Williams, " 'Something Else Besides a Mother': *Stella Dallas* and the Maternal Melodrama," *Cinema Journal* 24, 1 (Fall 1984).

70. Stephen E. Ambrose, *Rise to Globalism: American Foreign Policy since 1938* 5th ed. (New York: Penguin, 1988), 97–110.

71. Ibid., 116–131; Jezer, *Dark Ages*, 56–61.

72. See Elaine Tyler May, *Homeward Bound: American Families in the Cold War Era* (New York: Basic Books, 1988), 193–199, for a discussion of middle-class men's discontents in marriage.

73. Sloan Wilson, *The Man in the Gray Flannel Suit* (New York: Simon and Schuster, 1955). For an analysis of this novel, see Elizabeth Long, *The American Dream and the Popular Novel* (Boston: Routledge and Kegan Paul, 1985), 82–89.

74. Jackie Byars, *All That Hollywood Allows: Re-reading Gender in 1950s Melodrama* (Chapel Hill: University of North Carolina Press, 1991), 217–219; and James Gilbert, *Another Chance: Postwar America, 1945–1968* (New York: Alfred A. Knopf, 1981), chap. 3.

75. Allan Bérubé, *Coming out under Fire: The History of Gay Men and Women in World War II* (New York: Plume, 1990); John D'Emilio and Estelle B. Freedman, *Intimate Matters: A History of Sexuality in America* (New York: Harper and Row, 1988), 288–295.

76. Jeffords, *Remasculinization of America*, defines the masculine point of view as the "disembodied voice of masculinity, that which no individual man or woman can realize yet which influences each individually. In this way, it is possible to identify the voice through which dominance is enacted in a narrative representation, though it may not consistently be spoken by any one character. Such a construct is especially important when dealing with relations among men in groups, as is the case in representations of warfare," xiii.

77. "Exultant Birthday for Israel: Nation Celebrates Its 10th Anniversary with a Proud Show of Power," *Life*, May 5, 1958, 32–34.

78. Laura Mulvey, "Changes: Thoughts on Myth, Narrative and Historical Experience," *History Workshop* 23 (Spring 1987): 1–19, 18.

79. Newcomb, "On the Dialogic Aspects of Mass Communication," 48.

80. Hartley, *Understanding News*, 81–86; see also Daniel C. Hallin, "Where? Cartography, Community, and the Cold War," in *Reading the News*, ed. Robert Karl Manoff and Michael Schudson (New York: Pantheon, 1986), 109–145, who identifies a "cold war view" in the news that divides the world into a global struggle between democracy and communism.

81. See Fiske, *Television Culture*, 399–404, on polysemy and closure.

CHAPTER 6: Conclusion

1. Richard M. Fried, *Nightmare in Red: The McCarthy Era in Perspective* (New York: Oxford Uni-

versity Press, 1990), 115, 179–180; Marty Jezer, *Dark Ages: Life in the United States 1945–1960* (Boston: South End Press, 1982), chap. 4.

2. "A-Bomb vs. House," *Life*, March 30, 1953, 21–25.

3. See John H. Mollenkopf, *The Contested City* (Princeton: Princeton University Press, 1983); and Jezer, *Dark Ages*, 138–146.

4. See Gaye Tuchman, *Making News: A Study in the Construction of Reality* (New York: Free Press, 1978), for an excellent visual analysis of television news. Other sources influencing television news include the news reels of the 1930s and 1940s and documentary films that also promoted film's status as evidence; see Erik Barnouw, *Documentary: A History of the Non-Fiction Film*, rev. ed. (New York: Oxford University Press, 1983).

5. Lynn Spigel, *Make Room for TV: Television and the Family Ideal in Postwar America* (Chicago: University of Chicago Press, 1992), 1.

6. Erik Barnouw, *Tube of Plenty: The Evolution of American Television*, rev. ed. (New York: Oxford University Press, 1982), 168–172, 401.

7. See Curtis Prendergast, *The World of Time Inc.: The Intimate History of a Changing Enterprise*, vol. 3: 1960–1980 (New York: Atheneum, 1986), chap. 3.

8. Elaine Tyler May, *Homeward Bound: American Families in the Cold War Era* (New York: Basic Books, 1988), 220, argues that 1960 was a "demographic watershed" because the age at marriage began to rise and the birthrate to decline. By the end of the 1960s, the birth rate was at a record low, and the marriage rate had also significantly dropped.

9. George Bush, "State of the Union 1990," delivered to a Joint Session of Congress, January 31, 1990; reprinted in *Vital Speeches of the Day* 56, 9 (February 15, 1990): 261.

INDEX